working to learn

transforming learning in the workplace

EDITED BY
KAREN EVANS
PHIL HODKINSON
LORNA UNWIN

KOGAN
PAGE

First published in 2002

Kogan Page Limited
120 Pentonville Road
London N1 9JN
UK

Stylus Publishing Inc.
22883 Quicksilver Drive
Sterling VA 20166-2012
USA

© Individual contributors, 2002

British Library Cataloguing in Publication Data

A CIP record for this book is available from the British Library.

ISBN 0 7494 3685 9

Typeset by JS Typesetting, Wellingborough, Northants
Printed and bound in Great Britain by Biddles Ltd, Guildford and King's Lynn
www.biddles.co.uk

Contents

List of figures

List of tables

List of contributors

David Ashton is founder of the Centre for Labour Market Studies, University of Leicester. He has researched and published extensively on labour market topics, concentrating in recent years on the area of skill formation. His current interests are in the comparative analysis of skill formation and workplace learning. Recent publications include *Education and Training for Development in East Asia,* Routledge, with F Green, D James and J Sung. He has just completed (with J Sung) *Supporting Workplace Learning for High Performance Working,* for the International Labour Office, Geneva.

Martin Bloomer is Professor of Education and Social Theory and Director of the Centre for Educational Development and Cooperation at the University of Exeter. A 1960s engineering apprentice, he became a mathematics teacher in the 1970s. His interests in sociology and research developed through the 1980s when he gained his PhD. He has a wide experience of teaching in the FE sector and his research, much of it carried out with Phil Hodkinson, has centred on the learning and lives of young people in their post-school years.

Michael Eraut is Professor of Education at the University of Sussex. His research is focused on practical knowledge and its acquisition in the workplace. He has pursued this theme in the contexts of professional and vocational qualifications, during early post-qualification employment and in mid-career. Areas of special attention include use of scientific knowledge in practice contexts, tacit knowledge, informal learning, and concepts/representations of competence and expertise.

Karen Evans is Professor and Head of the School of Lifelong Education and International Development at the University of London Institute of Education. She was previously Professor of Post-Compulsory Education at the University of Surrey, and has directed international and comparative studies of learning and work in Europe, North America and the Commonwealth. She is currently Co-Director of the ESRC Research Network,

'Improving Incentives to Learning in the Workplace'. Her recent publications include the book *Learning and Work in the Risk Society,* Palgrave, 2000.

Alan Felstead is Reader in Employment Studies at the Centre for Labour Market Studies, University of Leicester. His research is focused on non-standard forms of employment, training and skills formation in Britain and overseas. His books include *In Work, At Home: Towards an understanding of homeworking,* Routledge, 2000, and *Global Trends in Flexible Labour,* Macmillan, 1999. He was a leading member of the team that carried out the ESRC-sponsored 1997 Skills Survey and is similarly involved in the DfES-sponsored 2001 Skills Survey. He also holds two ESRC grants under the Future of Work Programme.

Alison Fuller is a Senior Research Fellow at the Centre for Labour Market Studies at the University of Leicester. She has published widely on vocational education and training. In 1998 she co-edited (with Lorna Unwin) a special issue of the *Journal of Vocational Education and Training* on the theme of contemporary apprenticeship. Alison has recently completed projects on Key Skills and on Modern Apprenticeship. She is currently working on an ESRC-funded project on 'learning at work'. This project is part of the Teaching and Learning Research Programme Network, 'Improving Incentives to Learning in the Workplace'. Alison is also interested in the changing patterns of participation of mature students in higher education.

Phil Hodkinson is Professor of Lifelong Learning at the University of Leeds. He is a founder member of the Working to Learn group of researchers working on vocational education and training in the UK. He has published widely on transitions from education to work, and is currently researching the ways in which schoolteachers learn as part of their normal working practices. With Martin Bloomer and others, he is also researching the transformation of learning cultures in further education.

Ewart Keep has a BA in modern history and politics (London University) and a PhD in industrial relations (Warwick University). Between first degree and doctorate, he worked for the Confederation of British Industry's Education, Training and Technology Directorate. Since 1985 he has been employed at the University of Warwick, first in the Industrial Relations Research Unit (IRRU) and, since 1998, as deputy-director of a new ESRC centre on Skills, Knowledge and Organisational Performance (SKOPE). He has published extensively on UK vocational education and training policy, work-based learning for the young, the links between skills and competitive strategy, and the learning society and learning organization.

Jonathan Payne is a qualified teacher with five years' teaching experience in secondary schools. Since 1998 he has worked as a research fellow for the ESRC's centre for Skills, Knowledge and Organisational Performance (SKOPE) based jointly at the universities of Oxford and Warwick. His research interests include the political economy of skill, UK vocational education and training (VET) policy, social partnership and the Norwegian VET system.

Helen Rainbird is Professor of Industrial Relations at University College Northampton and an Associate Fellow at the Industrial Relations Research Unit, University of Warwick. Her research interests lie in the intersection between industrial relations and training, and in particular the role of trade unions in negotiating and representing employee interests in relation to workplace learning. She is the author of *Training Matters: Trade Union perspectives on industrial restructuring and training,* Blackwell, 1990, and editor of *Training in the Workplace: Critical perspectives on learning at work,* Macmillan, 2000.

Peter Senker: After working at the Science Policy Research Unit (SPRU), University of Sussex, Peter Senker has been Chairman of IPRA Limited and Visiting Professor at the Department of Innovation Studies, University of East London, since 1995. His research involves studying relationships between technological change, innovation, learning, skills, and training, with the aim of contributing to the improvement of public policy. As a director or trustee of five small organizations he has both practical and research-based insights into policies for the small and medium-sized enterprise sector.

Jim Sutherland was, until recently, Director of Education and Training for UNISON, the UK's largest trade union, when he was responsible for creating the Unison Open College with its groundbreaking approach to partnership with employers in creating new opportunities for employee development. He has undertaken a range of projects for Public Services International advising both trade unions and employers in various countries on learning and training strategies. He was chair of the workplace learning task group established by the Secretary of State's national advisory group for continuing education and lifelong learning.

Lorna Unwin is Professor of Vocational Education at the Centre for Labour Market Studies, University of Leicester. She is currently researching the changing nature of apprenticeship in contemporary workplaces and the 'teaching and learning' relationship between older and younger workers. She is the co-author of *Young People's Perspectives on Education, Training and Employment*, Kogan Page, 2001.

Michael Young is Emeritus Professor of Education at the Institute of Education, University of London, where he was Professor of Education and Head of the Post-16 Education Centre. Among the books he has written or edited are *Knowledge and Control: New Directions for the Sociology of Education*, and most recently *The Curriculum of the Future*, Falmer Press, 1998. He is currently an international member of the team reviewing the South African qualifications system and co-director of a project supported by the City and Guilds on the role of knowledge in vocational education.

Editors' introduction

Karen Evans, Phil Hodkinson and Lorna Unwin

> Management gurus, academics and policy advisers across the developed world
> have insisted that higher levels of skill within the workforce are basic building
> blocks. . . for the adoption of a new model which moves economic activity
> out of the old Fordist and Taylorist paradigms into a new high skills, high
> performance mode of working. (European Commission COST Review, Brown
> and Keep, 1999)

The overall aim of this book is to develop an evidence-based and theoretically
informed understanding of the transformations in the nature of work that
affect the learning and skills requirements of jobs and individuals, and the
ways in which these requirements can be met. It challenges many of the
presuppositions and generalizations about the changing nature of work, skills
and learning which have come to permeate thinking about the options 'on
the table' for modern societies. Our starting point is that the workplace is a
crucially important site for learning and for access to learning. The editors
have worked together with contributing authors to develop an analytical
perspective on workplace learning that takes the social context of the
workplace and the wider systems for management and regulation of employment fully into account.

The need for deeper research-based insights into learning at, for and
through the workplace was a conclusion from the recent national Economic
and Social Research Council (ESRC) Learning Society Programme: 'much
more needs to be known about the key processes of learning as embedded
in particular workplaces, in organizational structures and in specific social
practices' (Professor Frank Coffield). This position is restated in the 1999
EC review of the state of research into vocational education and training
(VET), which points to the need not only to 'audit' the learning opportunities
available, but also to evaluate the particular combinations of education,
training, employment and community contexts which can produce 'excep-
tionally rewarding learning environments' on the one hand, or 'sterility, where

challenges and a series of mundane experiences lead to little learning' (Brown and Keep, 1999: 47).

This edited book focuses on the need to transform workplace learning. It brings together the latest thinking in the field, and considers what needs to be done to move from scattered 'islands of excellence' in practice to policies and systems that support excellence and equity in workplace learning consistently and comprehensively. The core contributors are founder members of the Working to Learn Group, a well-recognized group that is engaged in high profile national and international research in VET and lifelong learning. The group collectively produced the influential IPD report, *Working to Learn* (Evans *et al*, 1997). Since then, the group has secured funding for an ESRC seminar series on workplace learning (1999–2001) and has recently been awarded one of the four Research Networks in the ESRC's National Teaching and Learning Research Initiative. This has enabled the group to extend its research activities in this field for a further three years with a series of studies designed to increase understanding of workplace learning in its social context under the heading, 'Improving Incentives to Learning at Work'.

The chapters have been developed from papers presented to mixed audiences of policy makers, researchers and practitioners in the 'Working to Learn' seminar series. They cross the boundaries of several disciplines, bring together writers from business schools and labour market specialists, educationalists and specialists in VET policy and practice. The contributions have been informed by debate and discussion with members of the policy and practice communities who participated in the seminars. They focus on questions of the likely impact of public policy and the ways in which the improvement of policy and practice can be informed by the available evidence and 'cutting edge' thinking in the field.

This inter-disciplinary perspective is significant. Much of the existing literature about learning in the workplace is fragmented into different academic locations. There is an ongoing tradition of work in what might be broadly termed the 'industrial relations field', focusing on the contested nature of human relations at work. Other research is found within industrial sociology, where much has been written about, for example, occupational socialization (Coffey and Atkinson, 1994). However, in recent times, arguably the dominant literature has been that in a broadly Vygotskyan tradition, be it situated cognition (Lave and Wenger, 1991) or activity theory (Engestrom, 2001). Though this sort of research clearly acknowledges power differentials in the workplace, they are seldom addressed as a central concern. Furthermore, there is a tendency in this literature to see the context of workplace learning as rather narrowly drawn – focusing on the workplace, community of practice or activity system, rather than wider social, economic and political factors. By drawing on work from a range of writers, from different academic traditions, this book enables readers to make connections between some of these bodies of literature.

In crossing the boundaries of previous work in the field, the collection of contributions aims to provide a unique resource and stimulus to debate for the policy and research communities, for students of business studies, vocational education and training and industrial relations; and for practitioners, employer organizations and trade unions who are seeking to improve workplace learning. While many of the contributions focus on British experience, this is offered as the basis of an understanding of the wider factors that are important in policy success and failure. Contributions bring in international comparisons where this challenges us to think more deeply about the assumptions that are often brought to policy formulation, and the other scenarios and strategic options that could be available. In this way, the volume also aims to inform an international readership, particularly where readers have been seeking to draw lessons from the ongoing experimentation that has characterized VET policy in Europe.

The opening chapters focus on workplace learning, lifelong learning and qualifications. Chapter 1 (Evans and Rainbird) discusses the significance of workplace learning for a learning society, making connections between the types of programme which incorporate work-based learning and the non-formal aspects of learning which run through everyday workplace practices and between the workplace and wider life/work relationships. It also connects frameworks that can contribute to a better understanding of the social nature of workplace learning and the economic and political frameworks which shape, regulate and drive policy.

In Chapter 2, Phil Hodkinson and Martin Bloomer explore the significance of individual learning careers as part of our understanding of work-based learning. They draw upon recent research evidence to argue that effective policy and practice in this area should take more seriously the need for a longitudinal dimension to workers' learning. What is more, this dimension should be understood in terms of the broader biographies of the people concerned.

Michael Young's chapter discusses the role of qualifications in lifelong learning. He focuses on the growing interest of countries around the world in developing national qualifications frameworks. Some countries are adopting the UK outcomes-based model, whereas others prefer a process-based or institution-based model. Young argues that these approaches reflect significant differences in national histories and cultures, roles of the state, and employer and social class cultures. He argues that national frameworks will have to be based on the shared values and practices of new 'communities of trust'.

Michael Eraut's chapter explores how the interaction between qualifications and work-based learning differs according to the purpose and nature of the qualifications, their role in a person's 'learning career', the type of work involved and the nature of the working context. Such interactions may have a positive, negative or neutral effect on learning in the workplace. Eraut argues that there is a great deal of innovation in qualifications concerned with continuing learning in the workplace, but that this needs to be supported by appropriate infrastructures, including, for example, an adequate supply of experienced teachers and trainers.

The set of four chapters that follows (Evans, Fuller and Unwin, Sutherland, Senker) explores the policy-practice interface. Karen Evans considers the place of key competences and tacit skills in VET programmes and workplace practice and discusses how moves to codify and 'make these visible' may have the unintended consequence of increasing inequalities in the workplace. In focusing on adults with interrupted occupational and learning careers, this contribution considers the position of people on different sides of the 'learning divide' (Sargant et al, 1997) and their attempts to return to learning and work.

Fuller and Unwin's chapter explores the ways in which episodes of 'formal' teaching occur regularly in the workplace as employees share their skills and knowledge, crossing boundaries of age, status and work domain to do so. In particular, their chapter challenges the traditional apprenticeship concepts of 'novice' and 'expert' by presenting research data that show how apprentices are often to be found 'teaching' older workers in the contemporary workplace.

Sutherland's chapter describes how one of the UK's largest trade unions, Unison, which represents public sector workers, has developed 'Return to Learn' for its members. The programme operates in partnership with education and training providers and employers. Unison's early work in these areas was reviewed by Kennedy (1995) as pointing to new ways forward. Sutherland considers the role of unions in promoting learning opportunities for employees and presents examples of how one union's approach is operating in practice.

Unionized workplaces generally have higher take-up of workplace learning opportunities. It is well recognized that some of the greatest challenges for workplace learning come in the small and medium-sized enterprise (SME) sector, much of which is non-unionized, and Senker's chapter considers the various ways in which firms can learn. It considers why SMEs need to innovate. The vast majority of SMEs operate in traditional sectors and find it extremely difficult to access the knowledge they need. One UK government supported initiative, the Teaching Company Scheme, provides a powerful mechanism for enabling SMEs to acquire and use the knowledge they need. The contributions of this and other types of training intervention to the SMEs' performance are considered. These examples raise a host of pedagogical questions.

Any analysis of work-based learning has to be situated in an understanding of the macro frameworks, the politics and economics behind the policy frameworks. The final set of chapters presents research-based evidence and critique. Ashton considers the links between learning and work organization, drawing on international case studies to illustrate how the transformation of the broader relationships within work is responsible for bringing about radical changes in the demands work makes on the skills of workers. In the cases selected it was the use of high performance techniques, involving a way of organizing the process of production that is different from the conventional Fordist and Taylorist techniques, which transformed the learning process. The implication is that as long as conventional techniques are used, the opportunities for workers to learn at work will be at best restricted and at worst reduced.

Alan Felstead's chapter illustrates the importance of a better understanding of the demand for skills in framing VET policies. With reference to regional variations in the demand for skills in the UK over time, he shows how misconceptions about and variations in the demand for skills can fundamentally influence the operation of VET policies. Other missing links in policy formulation are homed in on in the closing chapters. In a contribution which uncovers the deep origins and explanations for long-term VET policy failure, Keep and Payne argue for a much more connected and holistic appraisal of the policy options, while Rainbird illuminates the growing gap between rights and responsibilities in UK VET policies by contrasting them with developments in France, which are underpinned by different concepts and approaches.

We conclude with six challenges for the future, if credible and sustainable approaches to workplace learning are to be realized. Workplace learning has never had as high a profile as it has now. Those who do not remember the past policy failures are condemned to repeat them. The time has come to grasp the nettle, to give workplace learning a better future.

References

Brown, A and Keep, E (1999) *Review of Vocational Education and Training Research in the United Kingdom*, European Commission, Brussels

Coffey, A and Atkinson, P (1994) (eds) *Occupational Socialization and Working Lives*, Cardiff Papers in Qualitative Research, Avebury, Aldershot

Engestrom, Y (2001) Expansive learning at work: towards an activity-theoretical reconceptualisation, *Journal of Education and Work*, **14** (1), pp 133–56

Evans, K, Hodkinson, P, Keep, E, Maguire, M, Raffe, D, Rainbird, H, Senker, P and Unwin, L (1997) *Working to Learn: A work-based route to learning for young people*, Chartered Institute of Personnel and Development, London

Kennedy, H (1995) *Return to Learn: Unison's fresh approach to trade union education*, Unison, London

Lave, J and Wenger, E (1991) *Situated Learning*, Cambridge University Press, Cambridge

Sargant, N, Field, J, Francis, H, Schuller, T and Tuckett, A (1997) *The Learning Divide. A study of participation in adult learning in the United Kingdom*, NIACE, Leicester

Chapter 1

The significance of workplace learning for a 'learning society'

Karen Evans and Helen Rainbird

For most people the workplace is the site of tertiary socialization, after the family and the education system. It is here that workers learn to modify their performance and to understand their roles, including their gender roles, in the structures and interactions of the organization. In this respect, job roles, position within a hierarchy and inclusion or exclusion from career ladders contribute to people's expectations of their own and others' potential to learn. Workplace learning is of central importance and a crucially important site for learning, whatever vision is held of a learning society. At the same time, workplace learning is poorly understood and under-researched, but has moved to centre stage in discourses about the so-called 'knowledge-based economy' and in policies based on that concept.

There are different versions and different understandings of what a 'learning society' is and could be. For the purposes of this chapter, we adopt that of the ESRC's programme of research on the learning society, as the most generous and inclusive we know. In this version, all citizens would:

> acquire a high quality general education, appropriate vocational training and a job (or series of jobs) worthy of a human being while continuing to participate in education and training throughout their lives. A learning society would combine excellence with equity and would equip all its citizens with the knowledge, understanding and skills to ensure national economic prosperity and much more besides. The attraction of the term 'the learning society' lies in the implicit promise not only of economic development but of regeneration of our whole public sphere. Citizens of a learning society would, by means of their continuing education and training, be able to engage in critical dialogue and action to improve the quality of life for the whole community and to ensure social integration as well as economic success. (Coffield, 1997: 450)

This chapter addresses two sets of issues that run throughout and underpin the contributions to this volume and are themselves interconnected. The first is the need to rethink what counts as learning and knowledge in relation to the workplace as a site of learning. This will allow us to arrive at a better understanding of them in the knowledge-based economy, and to do this in a way that moves beyond the dualisms which divide and fragment the field. The second set of issues concerns the balance of responsibilities and rights, in the employment relationship and in the wider society. The fact that we are talking about a learning 'society' means that we are talking about something more than aggregated individuals. Most of the new policies in the advanced economies such as the UK, the USA and parts of Europe have become increasingly focused on individual responsibilities with little attention paid to reciprocal rights or the social and collective dimensions of society as it relates to the workplace and the role of work in people's lives (see, for example, DfEE, 1998). Other European partners have taken different perspectives, and the French experience (discussed in Chapter 12) illustrates how these are carried through in policy and practice. Both clusters of issues require us to make new kinds of connections while recognizing the barriers and incentives that operate.

Mapping the field of workplace learning

Our focus is on the workplace as a site of access to learning or, as the Workplace Learning Task Group defined it, 'that learning which derives its purpose from the context of employment' (Sutherland, 1998: 5). This does not mean *training*, which is narrowly focused on the immediate task and restricted to business needs, but *learning*, which addresses the needs of a variety of stakeholders: employees, potential employees, employers and government. The distinction between training and learning is significant. The Task Group's definition included 'learning in, for and through the workplace' (1998). It therefore includes a range of formal and informal learning; learning which is directed to organizational as well as employees' needs; and learning which is accessed through the workplace. This definition is important because, in the UK at least, the workplace has become a site for 'initiatives', which means it becomes embroiled in acronyms and it is easy to lose sight of the heart of the central issue in the various 'schemes' that are either being hatched or re-branded.

Four broad but overlapping forms of learning involve workplace learning as a central feature:

A. Initial work-based learning, in traineeships and apprenticeships.
B. Work-based degrees and 'foundation' degrees.
C. Non-formal work-based learning.
D. Access to continuing non-formal learning opportunities *through* the workplace.

Group A encompasses various types of apprenticeships and traineeships undertaken by young people end-on to compulsory education. In the UK the various schemes and programmes that have evolved over the past two decades are involved in an ongoing process of re-branding.

Figure 1.1 shows that the numbers of young people involved in work-based programmes levelled out overall as foundation modern apprenticeships took over from previous 'traineeships' and the higher level programmes became re-branded as 'advanced modern apprenticeships'.

Work-based training for young people in England and Wales

Numbers starting training programme (thousands)

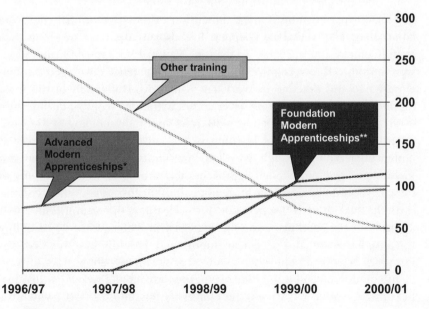

*Formerly known as Modern Apprenticeships.
**Formerly known as National Traineeships.

Figure 1.1   *Trends in numbers following traineeships and apprenticeships in Britain*

These programmes have their parallels in most advanced economies, the differences being in how central they are to the wider systems of education and training. Apprenticeship is central to the German system, and sets the 'rules of the game' for all other forms of work-related education and training. In the USA, by contrast, apprenticeship is peripheral to full-time college-based routes into the labour market.

Programmes in the second group (B) are on the increase in higher education, particularly in the USA, Australia and the UK (Boud and Solomon, 2001). In these programmes, the work experiences and achievements of 'clients' are given credits towards the award of degree, according to the system of assessment and regulation of the degree awarding body. Corporate clients are important users of these programmes. In the USA, the two-year associate degree achieved a high take-up among people already in employment. Its recent counterpart in the UK, the Foundation Degree initiative, has had a slow start although work-based versions of the degree are seen as having particular potential for expansion. Developments in Group A and Group B in the UK are being seen by government as instruments for meeting the official target of a 50 per cent participation rate of younger adults in higher education by 2010. It has become clear that the target is not likely to be achievable through the full-time education route.

Non-formal learning (C) is a dimension of initial vocational education and training and work-based degrees. It is also an important area in its own right (Coffield, 2000a; 2000b). In the UK, National Vocational Qualifications were introduced to recognize and accredit competence developed through experience and practice in work environments. But much of the most significant workplace learning never comes within the scope of qualification – it is part of mastery of the job, work roles and understanding of the work environment. Non-formal learning is defined for our purposes here as embracing learning through work and community experience, but may also include planned and explicit approaches to learning carried out in any of these environments, where these are not part of the formal education systems.

In the final group (D), where non-formal learning opportunities are made available in the workplace through external providers, the role of online learning has assumed a particular importance. The UK has provided two examples of government schemes aimed at specifically supporting lifelong learning undertaken on the initiative of the individual. These are Individual Learning Accounts (ILAs) and the University for Industry (UfI), which has been translated into 'LearnDirect'. These are discussed further in Chapter 12. Although there is less support for collective initiative, trade unions have become advocates of lifelong learning in the workplace as part of the 'new bargaining agenda' (Storey et al, 1993). An exception has been the DfEE/

DfES Union Learning Fund, which has supported a range of trade union initiatives on learning (see Cutter, 2000, for an evaluation).

Tensions in workplace learning

The workplace has enormous potential as a site of learning, though this is rarely fully realized. The Fryer Report (1997) argues that 'for many (people) the workplace is the only place where they will engage in formal learning'. It is also affords many informal learning opportunities which result from interactions in workgroups and from the structure of the work environment. The discourses of Human Resource Management (HRM), the 'learning organization' and 'knowledge management' would seem to suggest that learning is a central concern in the workplace. Yet the harsh reality of the operating environments of many public and private sector organizations means that the rhetoric is not even an aspiration, let alone a reflection of practice. Indeed, research evidence suggests that there are significant organizational and cultural barriers to the promotion of individual and organizational learning, which are all too prevalent in the UK. These include:

- cost-based competition;
- standardized products and services;
- a heavy reliance on economy-of-scale advantages, low trust relationships and hierarchical management structures;
- people management systems that emphasize command, control and surveillance, and an underlying belief that (whatever the rhetoric) people are a cost or a disposable factor of production;
- little slack or space for creativity, and a culture of blame for where mistakes (particularly those of lower-status workers) are punished. (Keep and Rainbird, 2000: 190)

The relatively low levels of investment of British employers in workforce development compared to their economic competitors are well known and many factors contribute towards this. The nature of financial markets, competitive strategy, organizational structures and labour market deregulation have all been identified as contributing to an environment in which there are disincentives to employers to invest in workforce development.

Company structure may itself affect the usefulness of having a central training function. In any large organization, tensions are inevitable between the professional entrepreneurs within business units and specialist corporate functions, and this affects the advantages, if any, of a central training function and organization-wide training activities. Carey (2000) identifies three types of structure found in large companies. These are strategic planning companies, with a small number of related businesses; strategic control companies, with diversified businesses with common strategic characteristics; and financial control companies, which are owned rather than managed centrally. She argues that strategic planning companies have characteristics that contribute to the integration of training within an HRM model. In contrast, strategic control structures inhibit central coordination and the development of training standards, while financial control structures positively discourage lateral integration (p 23).

Even where organizations are fully committed at corporate level to investing in the training and development of their employees, structural factors may undermine their capacity to put these policies into practice.

Within organizations, investment is hampered by:

- the weak role of training and development within corporate structures;
- the absence of a 'champion' at board level;
- the tendency for training and development to be seen as an operational rather than a strategic issue;
- conflicts between corporate Human Resource strategy and operational management contribute to the difficulties of operationalizing workforce learning strategies. (Rainbird, 2000)

At the level of the workplace, this is compounded by issues relating to the management, socialization and control of the workforce. Performance management systems provide organizations with a tool for aligning individual performance with organizational objectives. Managers' performance is assessed (and rewarded) on the basis of a short timescale and this is at odds with the longer-term nature of training and development strategies (Hansen, 2000). Product market strategies focused on price competition rather than producing quality goods for niche markets are unlikely to result in a concern for the long-term development and adaptability of the workforce. Rather, jobs are likely to be designed to involve a limited range of tasks and discretion. Consequently, the focus of intervention (or non-intervention) is more likely to reduce employees' expectations of training and development.

Individuals are located within occupational hierarchies that provide differential access to formal learning opportunities and in jobs that provide differential access to informal learning opportunities and career progression. There is a substantial body of survey evidence which suggests that well-educated workers in professional roles are more likely to receive employer-provided training than those in routine and manual jobs on the lowest salary grades (see Ashton *et al,* 1999; Cully *et al,* 1999). As a result, some workers enter employment with expectations of access to learning and career progression and will find opportunities to learn informally in the work environment. Others will enter jobs with few opportunities for learning and progression, and low aspirations for themselves, which are reinforced by the low expectations of their managers. Their jobs may be narrowly constructed, and the pace of work, staffing levels and physical isolation may restrict opportunities for informal learning. Decisions made about training and development are not neutral: the context of workplace politics is significant to workers' and managers' perceptions of it. It may be regarded as a reward, giving status where there was previously little; it may serve as recognition for effort and a signal of value to the organization; and it may indicate suitability for promotion. Equally, it may be perceived as a threat, an indicator of poor performance or a signal that work is about to be intensified (Rainbird *et al,* 1999).

Therefore any attempt to enhance incentives (and minimize disincentives) to workplace learning has to recognize that it is not sufficient to identify forms of effective learning. They must be located in the structures and contexts that support them. Forms of learning which work effectively in one context may not be transferable to others where they are undermined by other aspects of the employment relationship, for example, job insecurity, work intensification and absence of employee voice.

The search for ways of raising workers' skill levels through workplace learning interventions has first to grapple with the problem of identifying the complexity of learning in work settings, particularly the sources of informal learning. Ways of talking about and conceptualizing workplace learning need to be found. A second step is to investigate what counts as effective learning in workplaces, from the perspectives of the learners themselves, their employers and other interested parties such as trade unions, training organizations and government agencies. In addition to the range of learning activities within and around the job, it is important to establish how learning is perceived and experienced. This is affected, in particular, by the questions, 'Who initiates?' and 'Who benefits?' from learning opportunities. This is because similar developments, such as job enlargement, can be experienced in very different ways according to whether they were initiated by the worker, by management, by the worker and the manager, or by the union and management (Rainbird *et al,* 1999). A lack of interest among employees in a particular training course or NVQ certification should not necessarily be interpreted as a lack of willingness to learn about the job, nor a lack of commitment to learning per se. Given the routine nature of many jobs, the absence of career progression, and the ways in which paid work is articulated with caring responsibilities within the family, learning motivations may be linked to educational and career development strategies external to the job.

Any assessment of what constitutes effective learning must recognize that workplace learning needs to be defined broadly rather than focusing on conventional definitions of job-related instruction. Given the complexities of analysing workplace learning outlined above, the difficulties of evaluating learning outcomes or 'measuring attainment', especially in relation to informal learning, will be appreciated. Clearly, there are mechanisms for evaluating formal training interventions, but these operate best with simple processes. For example, statistical process control can identify faults and so it may be relatively easy to attribute reductions in faults to training under-taken. Interventions that are aimed at cultural change or improving customer service may be much harder to isolate from other developments in the work environment and thus harder to assess (Holly and Rainbird, 2000). Technically, it might be possible to consider the extent to which tools such as appraisal contribute to the measurement of learning attainment. However, caution is needed in assessing the significance of formal tools that have the difficult task of reconciling the identification of organizational and individual needs, usually to the benefit of the former (Antonacopoulou, 2000). Where there is potential for job progression and associated learning opportunities, it may be a useful tool. Where there are few opportunities for job progression, development opportunities are unlikely to be justified. Therefore measures identified through appraisal might improve work performance, but might not contribute to the motivation to learn. Managers' adoption of a formal role in the appraisal process does not necessarily imply that they see themselves as teachers and mentors with an active role in creating learning opportunities for their staff.

Need for theoretical integration and enhancement

Our argument is that the realities of workplace learning are best investigated by juxtaposing two conceptual/theoretical frameworks that are seldom connected: on the one hand, the family of theories known as 'social learning theories', embracing what is sometimes called 'activity theory', notions of situated learning, learning through peripheral participation and cognitive apprenticeship; and on the other hand, a perspective on the workplace that focuses on broader issues concerning the regulation of the employment relationship and developments in work organization and the extent to which they create incentives to learning for employees and employers.

There are theoretical and practical challenges with both of these approaches (Eraut, 1999; Popkewitz, 1998) and we aim both to problematize them and to transform them through our current research. This is because they show considerable potential for first understanding and then improving learning. They recognize that the majority of workplace learning is informal and is best understood through examining the relationship with practical work activities, the cultural and social relations of the workplace, and the experience and social world of the participants. In order to use research to effect improvements in learning, such conceptualization needs to be closely linked to the realities of contrasting and diverse workplaces. Current research in the Economic and Social Research Council's (ESRC) Network on Improving Incentives to Learning at Work (directed by Rainbird, Evans, Hodkinson and Unwin) is using these frameworks and exploring how they may intersect to produce better understandings of workplace learning processes and to uncover the extent to which strategies to increase incentives to learn are themselves situation-specific or generalizable. The range of situations make it possible to relate learning to wider social, economic and political contexts than are normally accommodated in the literature.

Situated learning and communities of practice

The concept of 'socially situated learning' emerged strongly in the 1980s. It was, in part, a reaction against the dominant views of learning derived from psychological traditions which emphasized learning as:

- *individual,* in the sense that the locus of intelligence is taken to be the single person;
- *rational,* in that deliberative, conceptual thought is viewed as the primary example of cognition;
- *abstract,* in the sense that implementation and the nature of the physical environment are treated as of secondary importance (if relevant at all);
- *detached,* in the sense that thinking is treated separately from perception and action;
- *general,* in the sense that cognitive science is taken to be a search for universal principles, true of all individuals and applicable in all circumstances.

Situated approaches question all of these assumptions, arguing instead that cognition (indeed all human activity) is:

- *social,* in the sense of being located in humanly constructed settings among human communities;
- *embodied,* in the sense that physical constraints of realization and circumstance are viewed as of the utmost importance;
- *located,* implying that context dependence is a central and enabling feature of all human endeavour;
- *specific,* with dependency on particular circumstances;
- *engaging,* in that ongoing interaction with the surrounding environment is recognized as of primary importance.

Learning, as it normally occurs, is a function of the activity, context and culture in which it occurs. In that sense it is situated. It sits at the heart of the model of learning-in-context and learning-in-action (see Figure 1.2). This model has particular value in enabling us to examine, at a deeper level, the potential and the tensions within workplace learning, occupational and professional development.

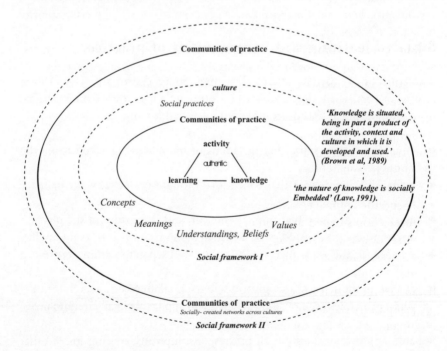

Source: Evans and Hoffmann, 2000

Figure 1.2   *Situated learning*

In this model, conceptual knowledge is built up and understood through use and activity in social settings. This contrasts with those learning activities that involve knowledge which is abstract and learnt 'out of context'.

Social interaction is a critical component of situated learning. Extending that idea, learners become involved in a 'community of practice', which embodies certain beliefs and behaviours to be acquired. Situated work-based and professional learning can best be defined by approaches, methods and processes that are consistent with the ideas of community. As the beginners or newcomers move from the periphery of the community into the centre, they become more active and engaged within the culture and eventually assume the role of expert or old-timer. As they do so they become able to influence that community in different ways. This feature is neither linear nor simple, in that expert status also has to be continuously renewed and newcomers can challenge existing practices with fresh ways of thinking.

Communities of practice form themselves or are set up within *social frameworks* – explained broadly as the environment which all communities of practice share. *Outer social frameworks* are created by the outer world and are hard to influence (but not impossible – eg, legislation, geographical/cultural conditions). *Inner social frameworks* are generated through the communities of practice themselves.

The conflicts inherent in the wage relationship, the tensions in the accountability of employees and professionals and the debate between self-regulation and external regulation can all be analysed with reference to their inner and outer social frameworks. Continuing vocational and professional development involves learning situated in the work context and within the community of social practice. It involves ongoing continuous development that has both individual and mutual learning components. *Situated learning* as used here, entails:

- A specific approach to learning, viewing learning as a social process of interaction situated in a community of social practice.
- A set of methods situating learning in authentic contexts.
- A process aiming for full participation.

It can be argued that situated approaches strengthen learning processes and the prospects of enhancing learning success through 'engagement' (Evans and Hoffmann, 2000). The following principles apply:

- *Engagement* is essential for learning to take place.
- Learning may be *situated* in three ways:
  - *practically;*

- – in the *culture* of the profession or workplace;
- – in the *social world* of the participants.
- Learning which is *well situated* in each of these three ways will promote worker development.
- Learning which is *poorly situated* in any of these three respects may impede development.

The following scenarios illustrate how learning may be well or poorly situated.

Situated learning in *practical tasks* has been a method used in educational programmes ranging from woodwork classes in school to the experiment in the science laboratory or the workshop activity in the continuing professional development (CPD) programme. In professional development, learning which is *well situated* in practical terms is based on reflection on practical experience, in reflection on action and in action, to use Schon's terms. Learning which is well situated in a practical sense occurs when the task has meaning and has the status of being somehow 'necessary'. Similarly, experimentation that arises in response to a problem identified 'naturally' by the learner is more likely to lead to significant learning. Mentors can aid this process.

In the workplace, activities that are performed as part of the daily work process are linked into the culture of the workplace and the occupational group or profession. Here, the power of authentic work settings can be harnessed as resources for learning. The culture of the workplace embodies the social practices that are crucial to engagement and learning. Experience that is poorly situated in relation to the culture of the workplace or occupational group is unlikely to enhance learning. This is not to say that learning programmes should not engage in critical dialogue with the cultural norms and expectations of workplaces. Indeed, engagement of businesses and professional bodies with higher education providers has particular potential for improvement through critical analysis and challenge. But, in modern workplaces, how can conflicts between the authenticity of the experience and the time/resources needed for reflective learning be resolved?

Learning has also, we argue, to be well situated in *the social world of the participants* in the sense of taking the social and biographical position of the learner fully into account. This applies to adjustments that must be made within the shared communities and working groups of workplaces. It also recognizes that people have their own occupational and career trajectories which may involve changes of direction in the future, and continuing vocational development (CVT/CPD) increasingly recognizes the possibility of mobility. The management of situated learning processes within workplace learning or CPD involves developing the support structures and creating the learning environments and activities needed. It has to recognize the strengths of individuals and teams, building positively on previous experience and overcoming blocks or impediments to learning.

It has been argued in a previous analysis (Evans and Hoffmann, 2000) that learning will be fostered, and new knowledge created, in learning environments which have the features shown in Figure 1.3. This model aims to:

- provide an authentic context that reflects the way knowledge will be used in real life;
- provide insight in multiple perspectives and changing roles for the members of the community;
- support collaborative construction of knowledge;
- provide support and aid/help, mentoring;
- promote reflection to enable abstractions;
- promote articulation to enable tacit competencies to be built up;
- provide clarification for the learner's own position.

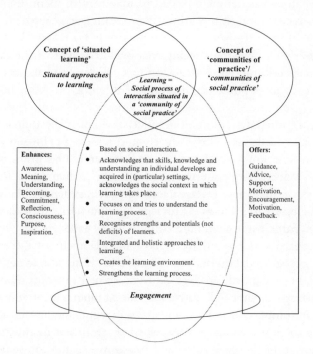

Source: Evans and Hoffmann (2000)

Figure 1.3   *A supportive framework for workplace learning*

The 'situated learning' perspective also draws upon the learner's previous experiences, links concepts and practices, encourages reflection and the transfer of knowledge from one situation to another. These features can be elaborated with reference to workplace learning as shown in Figure 1.3.

This figure presents an ideal model. But how often is that model found in practice? It may be found in specially funded 'model programmes' and it may be found in programmes for certain types of high level 'knowledge workers', but in everyday learning environments, the realities for most workers and employees often involve:

- limited access to formal learning opportunities and career progression;
- narrowly defined jobs with little opportunity to develop skills through informal learning, work placements and 'acting up';
- managers' prerogative in decisions relating to training and development with little scope for the expression of employee 'voice';
- developments in work organization and job design which actively de-skill and intensify work;
- where job expansion takes place this may involve work intensification and no recognition or reward for increased responsibility;
- absence of cover for paid release from work or for informal job rotation;
- managers and supervisors seeing well qualified workers as a threat;
- managers and supervisors believing specific groups of workers have no learning or job aspirations. (Rainbird *et al*, 1999.)

These are also manifestations of conflicts and contradictions within and between the social frameworks. A situated learning environment is not restricted to the world, work, or life environment, but also to 'situations', beliefs and values. The 'community of practice', when operating ideally, embraces the context and sets free a learning environment. At the same time 'space' is being created and thus provides an opportunity for active engagement of the participants within the 'community of practice'. Within the inner social framework self-regulation may take place in ways that may be outwardly recognized. External assessments and checks can achieve a degree of control, but safeguards are best achieved through worker commitment, ethics, self-responsibility and motivation. Strong inner social frameworks will maintain and improve standards, involve self-regulation and challenge any tendencies to closed enclaves that seek to protect their members over the public interest. In the professions and in many occupations, standards and the employment relationship need to be secured by regulatory frameworks in which the external world can have confidence. A key issue for many professional associations, for example, is the extent to which self-regulation can provide the controls necessary to ensure maintenance of standards, and can provide the evidence which testifies to the competence and professionalism of its members. The conflicts inherent in this were highlighted by Friedman's research, which found that:

> Again and again throughout the research, such tensions were in evidence. For example, a set of guidelines will intersperse its promotion of CPD as a dynamic and empowering process with looming 'extracts', which function essentially as faceless warnings, about the need to take control of one's career given the insecurities and precariousness of the modern workplace. These positive and negative aspects sit uneasily together, the veiled threat and the happy vision of an empowered, enlightened future. . . Sanctions and accreditation, the two sides of the motivational coin, are used selectively, and at times in an apparently *ad hoc* way. For all the vaunted dynamism of the CPD process, it also contains a great potential for instability and internal conflict. (Friedman *et al,* 2001: 205)

Burgeoning applications of the concepts of 'communities of practice' and their potential for learning do not, at present, sufficiently recognize (or include in the analysis) the power relationships that define the real scope for learning and employee development.

Tacit skills and hidden abilities

The part played by tacit skills and knowledge in work performance is well recognized but not well understood. These implicit or hidden dimensions of knowledge and skill are key elements of 'mastery', which experienced workers draw upon in everyday activities and continuously expand in tackling new or unexpected situations. This chapter argues that it is important to understand better how individuals harness and use tacit forms of key competences as they move between roles and settings. What part does the recognition of tacit forms of key competences play in the development of occupational and learning biographies? Does the recognition of tacit forms of key competences increase or decrease inequalities? What are the implications when considered in the contexts of 'technocratic' and 'democratic' versions of the learning society?

Within the ESRC network, the significance of tacit forms of learning, knowing and engaging in practice is being manifested in different ways in and across the linked studies. For example, research into key skills in steel industries is finding the significance of the tacit dimensions of key skills, which raises particular questions when it comes to measurement. The official articulation of key skills which has codified them into six categories

(Communication, Application of Number, Information Technology, Problem Solving, Working with Others and Improving Own Performance) simplifies their complex nature and decontextualizes them. Fuller and Unwin's research is finding that the workplace context both shapes and transforms these skills (see Chapter 6) and that the boundary with tacit skills and knowledge is regularly crossed. In Evans and Sakamoto's study of adults with interrupted occupational and learning careers, early evidence is suggesting that the extent to which learners themselves recognize their underlying abilities and draw assurance from them is linked to prior experience in education and the labour market. Learning environments that can capture hidden abilities can result in large learning and achievement gains for those with interrupted occupational and learning biographies (discussed further in Chapter 5). Later on, in looking at learners moving into workplaces from institutional learning environments, the research is asking under what conditions these gains are consolidated, expanded or undermined. Teachers and trainers are also engaged in work-based learning in their own environments and career development. For example, from Hodkinson's study there is early evidence in schools of teachers' learning which is not intentional and which is not recognized either by them or by those who assess their development as teachers or who seek to manage their performance.

All of the studies in this network are finding gaps apparent between skills and knowledge officially required to do jobs, and those that are actually used in the workplace. The gap contains the tacit dimensions, which are poorly understood, which are very important for learning and achievement, but which are largely ignored in the development of learning programmes. All projects are also exploring where skills and knowledge are 'stored' in terms of individuals and teams in the workplace. For example, the traditional view that younger workers learnt from their older colleagues (as in the apprentice-ship model) is being challenged by the research which is finding that young people are bringing a range of skills to the workplace, some of which they are imparting to experienced workers. There are important pedagogical implications here related to the nature of how teaching and learning are organized in the workplace. This and other evidence is highlighting the importance of understanding and enhancing learning environments, and this is where consideration of incentives and barriers in the workplace is so vital. There are many definitions and theoretical perspectives for tacit skills and learning. The latest work is aiming to come up with new understandings that can better be applied to the improvement of learning and teaching processes in a range of contrasting work-sites. But the call for wider recognition of skills gained through non-formal learning is only one facet of a debate centred on the nature of the so-called 'knowledge-based economy' and the way in which the 'knowledge' concerned is codified and used.

The knowledge-based economy?

This debate has been newly fuelled by economists and labour market specialists, creating new possibilities for interdisciplinary endeavour, in trying to understand better what it is that actually constitutes the 'knowledge base' of the economy and the place of non-formal learning in this scenario. Cowan *et al* (2000) recently identified the distinction between codified and tacit knowledge as being in need of redefinition in the knowledge-based economy. They argue that it is a mistake to view any knowledge or skill as inherently tacit – nearly all knowledge, they say, is codifiable. From their economists' point of view the only real issue is whether the benefits of doing so outweigh the costs. Furthermore, they have pointed out that any acceptance of the view that knowledge can be both inherently tacit and important undermines the basis for standard micro-economic theory and any attempts to model human behaviour. Johnson and Lundvall (2001) take issue with them as fellow economists, showing how the concept of the knowledge-based economy is poorly understood and raising fundamental issues which lie behind the drive to codify previously uncodified knowledge and skill for 'systematic use'. How does 'codification' actually take place in relation to different types of knowledge? What are the driving forces that lie behind efforts to codify? What are the consequences of codification of different kinds of knowledge for economic development and for the distribution of wealth?

These questions are centrally important in considering questions of inequalities in skill recognition and access to learning at, for and through the workplace. This is not an 'academic' discussion. The European proposals for Personal Skills Cards place this debate close to the heart of the political and economic agenda in the expanding European Union, and the proposals merit critical examination.

There are four types of knowledge, as shown in Table 1.1. Knowledge is taken in its widest definition as incorporating, at an individual level, knowing that, knowing why, knowing how and knowing who. At the organizational level, these four types of knowledge are found in shared information, shared views of the world, shared practices and shared networks. At the societal level

Table 1.1   *Four types of knowledge*

Know that	Shared information	Institutions
Know why	Shared interpretations	Culture
Know how	Shared practices	Communities
Know who	Networks	Networks

we may talk about knowledge that is stored as personal knowledge, knowledge embedded in culture, knowledge stored in institutions and in networks. Know-how is of particular significance for this discussion, referring to flexibility in abilities, know-how to go about things and *to do* things. It involves complex linkages between skill formation and personal knowledge developed through experience.

The idea of individuals being able to transfer skills and competences between jobs in the interests of 'flexibility' fitted the 'modernization' and deregulation agendas of the 1980s and 1990s in the UK, and key competences came to the fore as an instrument of 'lifelong learning' policy. Treating these as completely codifiable leads to claims that workers whose skills have previously been unrecognized or taken for granted can, through their codification, gain formal recognition for them irrespective of when and how they were learnt, and demand re-grading of their jobs and pay structures (Bjørnåvold, 2000; CEDEFOP, 2001). If we can codify and compare key competences against 'objective' criteria, some of the assumptions commonly held about skill levels of different occupations might be challenged.

But there are two fundamental problems with Bjørnåvold's claim. First, skill tends to represent a combination of factors including bargaining power and status in society. Second, job evaluation tends to reproduce gendered assumptions about the value of different types of work. Furthermore, research on 'work process knowledge' such as Boreham's (2000) finds that these skills derive much of their meaning from the context in which they are used. Chapter 5 argues that it may be more helpful to regard these skills as partly structural and partly embedded contextually, recognizing that people do take things with them into new jobs and occupations, but not in simple ways. This is one of the gaps in our knowledge. Much of the work on key competences has focused on extracting these from tasks rather than understanding the dynamics of the ways in which people carry knowledge and learning into new environments. The importance of this is now being recognized in the economic domain as well as in VET research and practice, as reflected in Johnson and Lundvall's paper, which calls for 'a major interdisciplinary effort' (2001). We know that the idea of simple skill transfer from one setting to another is very problematic – the fact that we can use common language to describe a skill group does not mean it is transferable intact.

What we need to understand better are the *processes* by which skills are 'transformed' from one setting into another. Naïve mappings of key skills from one environment into another are not a basis for occupational mobility. Even 'near' transfer into related activities is far from simple, leading to the recognition by activity theorists such as Engestrom (2000) that it is whole activity systems that count. The knowledge-based economy raises fundamental questions about what counts as knowledge, and who owns, manages and controls it. As Johnson and Lundvall (2000) argue, a much more satisfactory mapping of the knowledge base is needed, and such a mapping has to capture the competencies and competence building of individuals, organizations and regions, 'in order to understand what is learnt, how and by whom, in different contexts and to construct better indicators of different kinds of knowledge' (p 18). As well as constructing improved indicators of types of knowledge, we need to understand better how these constructions contribute to the conceptions of a 'learning society' introduced earlier. We also need to know how they fit with concepts and policies of social inclusion, citizenship and the reduction of inequalities.

Wider questions of relationships between work, life and citizenship

Any analysis of how citizenship culture can be advanced has to take account of the changing nature of work and the effects on people's lives of the changing social landscape. What are the conditions under which learning for adult life takes place? Which versions of citizenship are required? How can they best be achieved?

In all European countries, young adults are experiencing uncertain status and are dependent upon state and parental support for longer periods than would have been the case a generation ago. Faced with changing opportunity structures, people have to find their own ways of reconciling personal aspirations with available opportunities and values in the domains of education, consumption, politics, work and family life. In the work arena, transitions to worker status are defined by institutionalized rules concerning recognized qualifications and credentials. These credentials are used by the holder to negotiate institutional and selection systems (Ainley, 1994; Raffe, 1991). This in turn is heavily influenced by cultural and social 'capital', the resources that come from family background and social networks and are important in access to information, advice, social, financial and career support. Adults bring different behaviours to life situations, and success in negotiating these structures and networks can bring stability or instability to the life course. For those who are unsuccessful in gaining entry to jobs, long-term unemployment cuts them off from the opportunities of the market, from access to work-based credentialing systems and from the exercise of citizenship in any significant sense (as discussed in Evans, 1998, and Evans and Heinz, 1994).

Successful entry to the labour market can bring another set of limitations. Entering work too early can create premature foreclosure of options and stereotyped work identities, and for those in the increasing ranks of casualized labour, training in narrowly based competences is unlikely to be of any use over time. Members of casualized pools of labour kept in ongoing insecurity are also unlikely to be able to fully participate in society in the sense implied in the maximal definitions of citizenship discussed earlier.

In public policy debates about preparing people for the demands of 'adult and working life' the exercise of citizenship has tended to be treated as though it were an adjunct to the main business of working for a living. The rather lukewarm reception given to proposals to strengthen citizenship education in schools turns cold when the proposals start to extend beyond 16. Preparation for the 'real world' of employment starts to dominate. Yet, as Crick (1999, para 5.5.3: 27) has argued:

> preparation for citizenship clearly cannot end at age sixteen just as young people begin to have more access to the opportunities, rights and responsibilities of adult citizenship and the world of work. The need for an exploration of the ideas and practices of citizenship is evident whether young people are in education or in work-based training.

We argue that this extends into and through adult life. These ideas are impeded by the concept of citizenship as a status acquired at a fixed point. They are facilitated when we approach citizenship as a lifelong process of engagement with the ideas and practices of democracy, in a developmental way. How citizenship is thought about plays an important role in shaping perceptions and beliefs about the 'right' domains for the exercise of social responsibility and collective action. Citizenship, when viewed as a process, overarches work and economic contributions to society and encourages us to see the workplace as being as important an environment for the exercise of social responsibility as the community and neighbourhood are.

Summary

This chapter has set out to map issues in the field of workplace learning. We have argued that many of the currently dominant discourses of learning organizations are ideologically constructed and fail to acknowledge adequately the effect of power relations in the workplace and the wider society. Explorations of the intersections of approaches which focus on regulation of the employment relationship with theories of socially situated learning have been proposed as ways forward in improving understanding, policy and practice in the field of workplace learning. The 'voice' of the individual learner or employee also needs to be found and listened to. (The issues and questions raised are returned to in greater detail and depth in the following chapters.) Finally, some connections between the 'agendas' of workplace learning, social inclusion and citizenship have been sketched.

Policies and practices of workplace learning cannot be understood or developed in sustainable ways without critical insights into the wider social frameworks in which they sit and from which they derive their meaning and purpose.

References

Ainley, P (1994) *Class and Skill*, Cassell, London

Antonacopoulou, E (2000) Reconciling individual and organizational development: issues in the retail banking sector, in *Training in the Workplace: Critical perspectives on learning at work*, ed H Rainbird, Macmillan, Basingstoke

Ashton, D, Davies, B, Felstead, A and Green, F (1999) *Work Skills in Britain*, ESRC Centre for Skills, Knowledge and Organisational Performance, Universities of Oxford and Warwick

Bjørnåvold, J (2000) *Making Learning Visible*, CEDEFOP, Thessalonica

Boreham, N (2000) *Final Report of TSER Project on Work Process Knowledge,* European Commission, Brussels

Boud, D and Solomon, N (2001) *Work-based Learning – A new higher education*, SRHE/ Open University Press, Buckingham

Brown, J S, Collins, A and Duguid, P (1989) Situated cognition and the culture of learning, *American Educator*, **18** (1) p 32

Carey, S (2000) The organisation of the training function in larger firms, in *Training in the Workplace: Critical perspectives on learning at work*, ed H Rainbird, Macmillan, Basingstoke

CEDEFOP (2001) Press Release based on the work of Bjornavold, J (2000), CEDEFOP, Thessalonica

Coffield, F (1997) Introduction and overview: attempts to reclaim the concept of the learning society, *Journal of Education Policy*, **12** (6), pp 449–55

Coffield, F (2000a) *Visions of a Learning Society*, Policy Press, Bristol

Coffield, F (2000b) *The Necessity of Informal Learning*, Policy Press, Bristol

Cowan, W M, David, P A and Foray, D (2000) The explicit economics of knowledge codification and tacitness. Paper originally presented at the DRUID International Conference on National Systems of Innovation, Rebild 1999, and subsequently published in *Industrial and Corporate Change*

Crick, B (1999) *Preparing Young People for Adult Life*, DfEE, London

Cully, M, O'Reilly, A, Millward, N, Forth, J, Woodland, S and Bryson, A (1998) *The 1998 Workplace Employee Relations Survey. First findings*, The Stationery Office, Norwich

Cully, M, Woodland, S, O'Reilly, A and Dix, G (1999) *Britain at Work. As depicted by the 1998 workplace employee relations survey*, Routledge, London

Cutter, J (2000) *A Second Evaluation of the Union Learning Fund*, DfEE Research Report RR208, DfEE, Nottingham

Department for Education and Employment (DfEE) (1998) *The Learning Age: A new renaissance for a new Britain,* HMSO, Norwich

Engestrom, Y (2000) *Training for Change,* ILO, London

Eraut, M (1999) Non-formal learning in the workplace – the hidden dimension of lifelong learning: a framework for analysis and the problems it poses for the researcher. Paper presented to the 'Researching Work and Learning' conference, University of Leeds, 10–13 September

Evans, K (1998) *Shaping Futures: Learning for competence and citizenship,* Ashgate, Aldershot

Evans, K and Heinz, W R (1994) *Becoming Adults in England and Germany,* Anglo-German Foundation, London

Evans, K and Hoffmann, B (2000) Engaging to learn, in *Combating Social Exclusion through Education,* Garant, Netherlands

Friedman, A *et al* (2001) *Continuing Professional Development in the UK,* PARN, London

Fryer, R (1997) *Learning for the Twenty-First Century. First REPORT of the National Advisory Group for Continuing Education and Lifelong Learning,* Northern College, Barnsley

Hansen, B (2000) Performance management and training, in *Training in the Workplace: Critical perspectives on learning at work,* ed H Rainbird, Macmillan, Basingstoke

Holly, L and Rainbird, H (2000) Workplace learning and the limits to evaluation, in *Training in the Workplace: Critical perspectives on learning at work,* ed H Rainbird, Macmillan, Basingstoke

Johnson, B and Lundvall, B-A (2001) Why all this fuss about codified and tacit knowledge? Paper presented at the DRUID International Conference, Aalborg

Keep, E and Rainbird, H (2000) Towards the learning organization?, in *Personnel Management: A comprehensive guide to theory and practice,* eds S Bach and K Sisson, Blackwell, Oxford

Lave, J (1991) Situated learning in communities of practice, in Resnick, L, Levine, J and Behrend, S (eds) *Perspectives on Socially Shared Cognition,* American Psychological Association, Washington DC

Popkewitz, T S (1998) Dewey, Vygotsky and the social administration of the individual: constructivist pedagogy as systems of ideas in historical spaces, *American Education Research Journal,* **35**

Raffe, D (1991) Beyond the mixed model, in *Social Research and Social Reform,* eds C Crouch and A Heath, pp 287–314, Oxford University Press, Oxford

Rainbird, H (2000) Training in the workplace and workplace learning. Introduction, in *Training in the Workplace: Critical perspectives on learning at work,* ed H Rainbird, Macmillan, Basingstoke

Rainbird, H, Munro, A, Holly, L and Leisten, R (1999) *The Future of Work in the Public Sector: Learning and workplace inequality,* Future of Work Programme Working Paper No. 2, University of Leeds

Storey, J *et al* (1993) The 'new agenda' and human resource management: a round table discussion with John Edmonds, *Human Resource Management Journal,* **4**, pp 63–70

Sutherland, J (1998) *Workplace Learning for the Twenty-First Century. Report of the Workplace Learning Task Group,* Unison, London

Chapter 2

Learning careers: conceptualizing lifelong work-based learning

Phil Hodkinson and Martin Bloomer

Introduction

In the current UK policy context, work-based learning and lifelong learning are seen as closely related. Despite the rather broader rhetoric of the introduction to the *Learning Age* White Paper (DfEE, 1998), both are primarily seen as necessary parts of the government's strategy to increase employability and economic competitiveness. They are central to the concerns of the new Learning and Skills Council. More generally, increasing awareness of the significance of informal learning (Coffield, 2000) as part of lifelong learning has resulted in more attention being paid to learning in work.

Yet there is very little research or theorizing about what *lifelong* work-based learning might look like in what some describe as late-modernity. Yet simple, linear, job for life trajectories, that are often assumed to have been the norm in earlier times, are credible only in a minority of cases (Arthur *et al*, 1999; Collin and Young, 2000). This chapter draws on a longitudinal study of 16- to 19-year-olds, and examines the concept of 'learning career' as one possible way to advance our thinking.

The traditional view: learning at the start of an occupational career

Policy and practice approaches to work-based learning in the UK have been dominated by a single, often implicit, model in which learning opportunities are concentrated in the early stages of a job or career. Thus, apprenticeships prepared and initiated workers into skilled jobs; doctors or lawyers served their time in junior posts before entering the profession; and initial teacher education/training and teaching practice preceded employment in teaching. The implicit assumptions were that a job or career would last for a substantial part of a person's life and that the nature of the work entailed would remain essentially unchanged. Thus, induction into practice was a one-off event/period, which often had a primarily ritualistic function. One of the reasons why apprenticeship models of training went out of fashion in the UK during the 1980s was the perceived need to replace what were considered outmoded time-serving rituals with training which led to measurable outcomes (Jessup, 1991). Apprenticeships are now back in fashion, but still with a front-loaded view of work-based learning at least implicit.

Also, many in-service work-based schemes are still based on the related assumption that retraining should take place before occupational advancement or redirection. Thus, police and civil servants complete qualifying courses and examinations prior to promotion. These practices have not significantly altered following the introduction of National Vocational Qualifications (NVQs) despite the fact that NVQs were intended to enable workers to demonstrate competence in, rather than prior to, work. Even within the NVQ system, once competence has been established, learning in that field is effectively deemed to be complete. New learning is only accredited where responsibilities change as, for example, in the advancement of a career from level 2 to level 3. This practice, whereby stages of learning are equated with rungs on an occupational promotion ladder, created particular problems for Youth Training (YT) schemes in the early 1990s, partly because the funding system linked to YT rewarded rapid accreditation at the higher levels, thus pressuring rapid progression from level 2 to 3 (Hodkinson et al, 1996). Outside these and other career and qualification structures, informal learning, commonly conceptualized in terms of growth in experience, is often deemed essential for progress in careers with an assumed, ladder-like structure.

The one-off, pre-service education and training model is evident elsewhere in current UK social, economic and educational policy. In the structure of the New Deal, for example, the unemployed are presumed to need an injection of up-front training in order to be able to take their active places in the labour market. Government-funded training largely ceases after that initial stage. Within lifelong learning policy, much emphasis has been placed upon increasing the take-up of initial education. For example, the aims of the Connexions Service are that all young people should be engaged in education and training up to the age of 19, while Foundation Degrees were originally aimed primarily at those under the age of 30.

But there are fundamental problems with traditional, front-loaded work-based learning. First, it is incongruous in the context of the rhetoric and reality of the rapidly changing nature of work and labour markets. Thus, people are exhorted to become lifelong learners, to improve their skills and abilities to meet the continually changing demands of the workplace, or to contribute to learning organizations that are supposedly increasing their corporate intelligence and their performances. Alternatively, or at the same time, people are encouraged to become portfolio workers: to continually acquire new skills and attributes of employability in order to be able to move seamlessly to a new job when the need arises. Of course, reality for many falls far short of this largely rhetorical ideal. Secondly, the traditional view of work-based learning also breaks down in the face of current labour market conditions. It may work well for that shrinking minority of the workforce, the 'core workers', who have some form of stable, rewarding employment. However, even for core workers, the nature of work is rapidly changing, while the 'half life' of knowledge and skills they might have developed at the onset of a career is arguably becoming progressively shorter. Where front-loaded work-based learning works even less well is for those in peripheral, unstable and temporary jobs who commonly endure low wages and progressive marginalization. Peripheral workers, from a learning perspective, include those suddenly made redundant or forced to accept changes in their terms of employment; those working in many small (and sometimes larger) firms where planned in-service training is largely non-existent; and those large numbers working in low-skill jobs, where little front-loaded learning is provided.

Both the traditional view of work-based learning and the criticisms of it raise issues of substance at a theoretical level. For example, most contemporary learning theories lack a well-developed life-course dimension. Constructivist writings often assume an implicitly beginning perspective (Driver et al, 1994), while situated cognition theory tends to take a largely timeless slice through the complexity of learning (Brown et al, 1989). Although timeserving is an integral part of cognitive apprenticeship, or of becoming a full member of a community of practice, even the currently influential anthropologies of work-based and everyday learning (eg Lave and Wenger, 1991) lack an explicitly developed, longitudinal, lifelong dimension. Contemporary neo-Vygotskyan psychologies, in the form of cultural psychology (Cole, 1996), activity theory (Engeström, 1987; 2001) and sociocultural theory (Wertsch, 1991) have argued the importance of cultural and historical continuities in the under-standing of learning. However, these perspectives have generated very little work that has centred on the individual life-course. Furthermore, though the traditional model of work-based learning highlights the need to link understanding about learning with a clear notion of career development, the career development field is itself in a theoretical hiatus (Arthur *et al*, 1999; Chen, 1998; Collin and Young, 2000; Hodkinson, 1999).

The research project

In a recent study, funded by the Further Education Development Agency (FEDA) and reported more fully elsewhere (Bloomer and Hodkinson, 1997; 1999; 2000), we followed 50 young people from their final year of compulsory schooling for a period of four years, interviewing them at 6- or 12-monthly intervals. The cohort included equal numbers of male and female students, contained representatives of the Asian ethnic community and roughly equal representation of students intending to proceed to A-level or International Baccalaureate courses, Advanced GNVQ courses (or equivalent), and other full-time post-16 courses. Over the course of the project 289 interviews were carried out. Because of illnesses, injuries and other unplanned events, the nominal sample of 50 fluctuated over successive interviews, although 49 still participated in the fourth interview sweep and 42 in the fifth sweep. Seven students were also interviewed in a pilot study, while five additional interviews were carried out towards the end of Year 12 with young people who were nearing the end of one-year courses. The interviews, which were semi-structured, tape-recorded and transcribed, focused on young people's contemporaneous and prior experiences of learning, aspirations they may have held, and any further experiences or events that they considered had some bearing on their learning.

Though the research did not address work-based learning directly, it provided some pointers to the theorizing needed in order to relate lifelong and work-based learning, for it allowed us to explore in detail young people's perceptions of, and dispositions towards, learning in further education (FE) in relation to their anticipated occupational careers. In this chapter, we examine the cases of Luke and Fazarna, both of whom initially saw their post-16 education as the means of progression to the jobs they wanted, despite having gained poorer examination grades at 16-plus than they had expected. Their subsequently contrasting careers illustrate ways in which lifelong learning might be usefully considered.

Luke's story

On leaving school, Luke planned to take an Intermediate General National Vocational Qualification (GNVQ) in business studies at his local tertiary college. However, his General Certificate of Secondary Education (GCSE) results (two Ds, two Es and five Fs) fell short of his expectations and he enrolled on the lower level GNVQ Foundation course. Luke admitted to being very disappointed with his GCSE results: 'they depressed me a bit actually. I mean, I wished I'd done better in them'. When asked about his vocational plans, he said:

> I thought it would be better if I had more experience as well. Like, if I was to do four years here, then I'd have more knowledge about the course. . . One year of foundation, one year of intermediate, and two years for the rest (presumably Advanced GNVQ).

Luke's main purpose in embarking on the four-year marathon was to get a job, probably in an office:

> I think that's probably why I am here, to get the qualification to get the job. I'd rather have four years to learn about the subject. Then, if I go out and get a job, maybe I can stay with it for quite a long time.

This was an unknowingly ironic remark given what was to follow. When we interviewed him towards the end of what would have been his first year in FE, Luke told us that he had dropped out of his course at about Easter time and had applied for a warehouse job with training, as part of the YT scheme. He had been bored by the Foundation course, and found it to be:

> much too basic, really. Too easy for my liking. . . As soon as we looked at the sheets, when we first started in this lesson, we just laughed at it. Basically, we just thought, that's so easy. . . They were already trying to teach us something that we already knew. I didn't finish the course completely because I decided to get a job when I started to get tiresome of it, and so I dropped out, thinking I was gonna come back (next) year. . . But at the moment, I'm just going down the careers office every week, seeing if they're getting any jobs in. . . And if I get on all right with this (warehouse job). . . then I'll probably might go back to college next year.

Luke took advice before deciding what to do. He claimed that college tutors suggested that he either changed to a different course or left to get a job. He had found the advice to be helpful. Significantly, perhaps, he reported that many other people had also left the Foundation course: 'When we started there was about 20 people in the class. By the end of the first six months there was only about eight left.' Of course, we have no way of knowing whether Luke would have succeeded had he been able to take the Intermediate course he had hoped for, but embarking on the Foundation course was the precursor to a turning point in his (educational) career.

When we interviewed him about eight months after he had left college, Luke told us that he had joined a YT programme in a camping shop, linked to an NVQ level 2 in retailing. He resented the fact that he was doing the same work as other shop assistants but was only receiving the training allowance of £45 per week. He subsequently dropped out of the training programme and sought employment with improved pay.

> I found that I was enjoying it. . . because there was plenty to do. . . but it just came to a point where. . . I needed the money. So at the moment I'm getting crewed up by (a) recruitment agency, so they're going to find me some jobs like driver's mate and that, because it's good money there as well so I can just build up some money at first so I can move out to Portugal.

This last comment refers to Luke's plan to move to Portugal to live with his godparents, who had persuaded him that he would be able to get a job there. By the following summer, Luke had still not made it to Portugal.

> I'm still hoping to go out to Portugal with my friend and look for some job out there, staying with my godfather, but I've sort of put that back a bit for the time being and (I'm) working at County Hall full-time now. I'm sort of building up the money to sort of go out there. . . I've been working at County Hall for about two months now.

He was doing seasonal relief work in the print room of a local authority headquarters. This had been arranged through his mother's best friend. However, other print workers told him that they had been relief workers before being taken on as full-time employees and Luke had hopes of doing the same. 'I'm getting on with a lot of the people there and the work's quite good as well. . . If they did ask me to stay on full-time then I probably would.'

Our sixth interview was about six months after this. The temporary job with the local authority had come to an end and, as there were some full-time staff redundancies, there had been no prospect of Luke being taken on permanently. Since then, he had been doing agency work in a variety of unskilled jobs: 'anything from warehouse work to stuff like driver's mate. . . bit of labouring stuff as well'. Portugal was still an intention, 'once Christmas is out of the way, and I've saved up a bit of money'. Two years further on, little had changed:

> Basically I carried on through agencies for a little while. I got a job selling double-glazing, telesales – that lasted for about two and a half months – then went back to a few agencies and then after that I'm now working at (a furniture

project on a local trading estate). It's just like furniture removals but it's like coping with warehouse duties anyway. It's like stashing goods, stuff like that, plus I get a good reference as well so it's all right. . . at the moment, it's about three and a half to four days a week, so it's part time, about 30 hours, something like that. . . I'm still looking for jobs in other areas as well because I want to go more into work areas, possibly getting a forklift licence and stuff like that.

By this time, Portugal was no longer in his plans since his godparents were returning to the UK. The prospect of further education or training was coming more into focus, however, as he repeatedly failed to land the type of job that he really wanted:

It makes you think about going back to college doing another training course, something like that. Maybe day release.
Have you any idea what type of qualification you'd like to do?
IT (information technology) because that would give me more experience with computer work which I might need for warehousing, for checking goods, stuff like that. . . Well, as you get older you realize more about what you've got to do and what sort of area you've got to go into work, and what sort of skills you want to get and maybe, one day, settling down for a family and that as well.

Fazarna's story

Fazarna is a young Hindu woman of South Asian ethnic origin. When we spoke to her before she took her GCSEs, she planned to proceed to an A-level course.

At the beginning I wanted to do something that's not examination-like, so I chose GNVQ. Then people said, 'If you want to go to university, you'd better do A-levels', and my mind's been going from one to the other. My grades always go down at exams.

She had clear ambitions to go to university but was vague about career intentions beyond that. She was also confused about subject choices, having considered several seriously, including sociology and graphic design. At the time of our first interview in her final year of schooling, she was opting for both of these subjects with IT as her third choice. She said, 'I didn't know anything about IT until I went to the open evening (at the college). They're just starting an A-level. I think it will combine with it (graphic design).'

By the time she arrived at college, Fazarna had changed her A-level subject choices, with law replacing graphic design. She had also decided that she wanted to study law at university. However, her GCSE results (three grade

Cs, five grade Ds and one grade E) meant that she had failed, by just one grade, to achieve the minimum requirements for entry to the A-level programme at the sixth-form college. Fazarna described her feelings when she arrived at the college at the start of term:

> Well I had a problem when I first came here because I didn't get the grades I wanted. So they said, 'Try (the) FE college because they will put you onto A-levels there with the grades you got.' So I went there and they put me on an A-level course, but I didn't like it there. It's not as good as this college. . . It wasn't the. . . sort of working environment I wanted to be in. The teachers were ok, but I just walked out. The only course I could do here (the sixth form college) was this one (the Intermediate GNVQ in IT). I asked if I could do GCSE retake, but it was full. The only one (I could choose). . . is what I am doing now. It's not what I expected, but it's all right.

When we asked for more detail, Fazarna described what happened when she found out about her GCSE results:

> They were nothing like I had expected. (In) my mock results I got nine passes (grade C or better), nearly, but the GCSEs were nowhere near it. I was surprised and disappointed because I don't know where I went wrong. In Spanish I was hoping for an A, because I'd got a B in my mock, and it came out as a D, which was really disappointing. So I appealed because there was something wrong, and I got a C.

Had her original results included the grade C for Spanish, which she was eventually awarded through the appeal, Fazarna could have started the A-level courses she had originally wanted to follow. But by the time her re-marked result came it was too late. She had started the Intermediate GNVQ course and had missed too much work to transfer to the A-level programme. This situation left her disappointed and confused.

> I don't fancy staying on (at college). It's a one-year course and I'm thinking of doing part-time evening classes next year in A-levels. . . I'm wasting a year. . . I'm not sure what I want to do anymore. . . I don't want to do A-level IT. I think it's totally out of the question unless I really enjoy it when I get further. . . I'm totally confused. . . At that time I wanted to go to university to study law and now all I can do is some degree in IT or software management or something like that, which I don't want to do.

Despite these setbacks, Fazarna was determined to work hard and succeed on her GNVQ course. She said:

I want to get some training on the computer even if I find the subject boring. There are some areas that I find interesting but I really want to know about computers at the same time, which will be good if I get a Distinction or Merit (grade) or whatever. It will count to something and that's why I'm keeping to it.

Our third interview with Fazarna took place towards the end of her one-year GNVQ course. She had apparently gained more from the course than she had expected. Despite her initial resentment she had enjoyed it and felt that she had done well. Despite her negative views about IT, she was now intending to enrol for A-levels in IT, law and philosophy the following term. She gained a Merit grade in her Intermediate GNVQ and a grade C in GCSE mathematics and this, together with her revised Spanish GCSE result, restored some of her confidence and she was looking forward to her A-levels. But she did not see her GNVQ year as wasted. She went on to study A-levels in law and IT, and an AS (half an A-level) in the philosophy of religion. She described how these choices had been made:

I. . . talked to my tutor and talked to people on the A-level courses that I wanted to do. I talked about the three I'm doing. . . but I talked about psychology as well and I was actually put down for that plus law and information technology, but at the last minute I thought I wouldn't be able to cope so I changed one of my A-levels. And I wanted to do psychology AS level but there was no room left and I was interested in the philosophy of religion and so I rung in during the holidays and said, 'Can I change one of my As to an AS?' And so they put me down to do philosophy of religion at AS, as there was no room in psychology AS.

During the early stages of her A-level career, Fazarna found the work difficult. However, her characteristic perseverance and hard work once more worked in her favour and she eventually achieved an A grade in law, a D in IT, a D in philosophy of religion and an N (no grade–effectively a fail) in general studies. She progressed to a local university to read for a BSc in Information Technology and Management with the intention of finding employment in IT, the subject she had so despised three years earlier.

Learning careers

Despite the differences in detail, both stories illustrate similar facets of what we have termed 'learning careers'.

Learning career refers to the development of a student's dispositions towards learning over time (Bloomer and Hodkinson, 1997). Just as it is possible to speak of political, spiritual and even motoring careers, so it is possible to think in terms of a learning career in which all other relevant human experiences, and ways of experiencing them, are described in terms of their relationships with the pivotal concept, learning. (Bloomer and Hodkinson, 2000: 590–91)

Thus, learners' interests in learning and the actions they take as learners are located within the contexts of their material and cultural surroundings and, most importantly, their perceptions, evaluations and appraisals of those surroundings. The development or evolution of a learning career is to be understood principally in terms of changes in the relationships between a learner's personal identity, his or her material and cultural surroundings and dispositions to learning. While the young people from our study provided numerous examples of changes in identity and disposition, it was apparent that none had completely abandoned former identities. New phases of learning career evolved from previous phases; learning careers were marked by both continuity and change. For this reason, 'transformation' is better suited to describing the development of learning careers than alternatives such as 'change' or 'transition' (Bloomer and Hodkinson, 2000). However, transformations in learning career are often gradual and partial, and the term should not be read as implying that dramatic changes are the norm.

Learning career transformations take many forms. They are not predetermined although they are oriented by the existing habitus (Bourdieu, 1977) of the individual: that is, by largely tacit or intuitive dispositions and by the material and cultural contexts within which the habitus has developed and is located. They are strongly affected by an individual's sense of identity, itself bound up in existing dispositions and the habitus. However, transformations are also inextricably linked to the ever-changing social, cultural and economic contexts in which people live their lives, including, of course, those of employment and education.

Luke and Fazarna initially saw their learning as being closely linked to their occupational career ambitions. Luke hoped that his intended Intermediate GNVQ course would eventually lead to a job in business, while Fazarna saw her chosen A-levels as leading to university and an eventual, unspecified professional career. We have chosen these two cases because both had their career plans disrupted by relatively poor examination results. Despite this, both initially aimed to stay broadly on track, intending to return to their original career route after one year of forced extra study. At that time, Luke seemed to us to be less troubled by this than Fazarna, who was very upset. However, whereas a combination of determination and what she regarded as a positive learning experience helped Fazarna to succeed, Luke, as we have seen, dropped out following what he described as unsatisfactory experiences of learning.

The career aspirations and dispositions to learning of both of these young people changed in ways that suggested that their aspirations, dispositions and experiences were inter-related. For Fazarna, changes were relatively minor as she abandoned thoughts of a law career and became more attached to her IT work. For Luke, however, it seemed that any sense of planned career was gradually eroding as he responded to a patchwork of opportunities that opened up and closed down around him. It was almost as if he lived two lives: a real one of pragmatic shifts from low-skilled job to low-skilled job, paralleled by a dream one of moving to Portugal. In these respects, his story resembles those related by Alheit (1994) of unemployed young men in Germany who did little about their situation because they believed it was only temporary and that the good job they craved was just around the corner.

One way to make sense of these and many other stories from our study is to examine relationships between young people's experiences of, and dispositions towards, learning and employment on the one hand, and a variety of factors, including individual agency, the actions of others and serendipitous events, which appeared to have some bearing upon them, on the other. Both Luke and Fazarna had become partly transformed as learners by the end of our research period, although many characteristics of the original learners persisted and can be identified in the transcripts. While few of those we studied faced the serious challenges that Fazarna and Luke did, many experienced significant transformations in their learning careers. This is not unexpected given that late adolescence is a period of uncertainty and change. The learning careers of these young people might well look different from those found, say, in middle age, although Elliott (1999) reports similar findings to ours in the careers of mature access students preparing for possible late entry into HE.

The implications of learning careers for thinking about work-based learning

Both Luke and Fazarna implicitly subscribed to the traditional model of front-loaded work-related learning. Their stories parallel current rhetorics about post-Fordist portfolio working, core-periphery employment and life in late modernity and the risk society, where changes are frequent and unexpected. However, they illustrate two very different responses to such a situation in that, on the periphery, Luke lost the ability to plan effectively for the future while, in the educational part of the core, Fazarna managed to do just that. The stories illuminate transforming learning careers, where change and continuity were simultaneously present, complementing, contradicting and/or disarticulating with each other. The concept of learning career provides a way of describing the contingent transformation of deeply rooted habitus, and of theorizing a longitudinal dimension to learning, without simplistic recourse into teleological personal growth, unchanging psychological traits, determining social structures or, alternatively, complete unpredictability in a post-modern flux. As regards occupational careers, it is one of several possible ways of steering a course between implicitly deterministic trajectory models on the one hand, and naive policy declarations about individual responsibility and agency on the other. For Luke and Fazarna, both such views of career development hold limited truth, but neither does justice to the complexity of their stories. From the trajectory point of view, Luke fits that common category of a working-class young person who lacks the cultural capital (Bourdieu and Passeron, 1990) to succeed in education, or achieve a secure job. However, it is dangerous to over-simplify this, for he sits uncomfortably across two different categories of lifelong learner in the Gorard et al (1997) model. He appears to have most in common with what they term 'disaffected learners', but by staying on in FE for a few months, also counts as a transitional learner. Fazarna's story can also be located in their trajectory model. She possessed greater cultural capital than Luke. Not only had her elder sister studied A-levels before her but she possessed the common desire in parts of the British Asian community for a high status professional career as well as the determination and willingness to work hard to achieve such a goal. In Gorard et al's (1997) terms, she was either a transitional or a lifetime learner, depending upon when her learning eventually stops.

Both young people exercised agency on several occasions and in different ways, often in conjunction with, or in opposition to, other people. In ways reminiscent of the theorizing of Giddens (1991) and Bourdieu (eg, Bourdieu and Wacquant, 1992) they were reflexively constructing their developing lifestyles and identities and contributing, in small ways, to the rules of the fields of education and employment where they were located. The complex detail of their stories is not fully captured by either individual choice or discrete trajectory models.

The concept of learning career opens a number of opportunities for researching and thinking about work-based learning. It allows for the examination of the longitudinal dimensions of work-based learning in ways that are not constrained by restricted models of either linear progression or extreme uncertainty. It also makes it possible to explore the uniqueness of individual careers, without losing sight of broader social, cultural and economic conditions. Furthermore, it easily incorporates both formal and informal learning, thus avoiding what can be an unhelpful dualism. However, the research reported here rather neglected the latter. The concept of learning career also highlights the importance of relationships between the multi-faceted and ever-changing contexts of learning and transformations in learners' dispositions. This is significant given current policy dilemmas such as the paradox of work-based learning defined largely in terms of employers' needs and interests, set against a political rhetoric of individual responsibility for learning. In addition, it points up an area of weakness in much current writing about learning in the workplace: the need to consider the perspective of the individual learner as well as that of the organization/activity system/community of practice that an individual belongs to. Much of the learning literature tends to focus on one or the other.

Finally, the concept of learning career provides a number of opportunities for thinking through some old problems and gaining new insights into how work-based learning and learners might be supported. First, a learning career integrates both formal and informal learning from a wide range of learning situations and contexts. It offers insight into how learners continually select, adapt, create and utilize learning opportunities under hugely diverse conditions, in response to their needs as they experience them. Indications from our study (Bloomer and Hodkinson, 1997; 1999; 2000) are that young people partially impose themselves upon the opportunities made available to them, often making significant contributions to the shaping of their own learning, sometimes to the point of challenging existing structures and overcoming the restrictions embedded within them. This, we maintain, has to be seen in the context of identity formation, one key dynamic of the learning career. Engagement in communities of practice is a major source of identity formation. 'We cannot become human by ourselves (but only through) negotiating the meanings of our experiences of membership in social communities' (Wenger, 1998: 145 and 146). This process becomes visible as individuals seek to impose themselves upon, contribute/belong to, or challenge the structures of existing communities. The individual and the community constitute each other, each continually shaping and re-shaping the other: 'The purpose is not to learn *from* talk as a substitute for participating in the practice itself, but to learn *to* talk as a key to participation. Thus, engaging in a practice is a condition for any kind of learning' (Soden and Halliday, 2000: 174, emphasis in the original).

If work-based learning were to be developed with these considerations in mind, it would become possible, at least in principle, to encourage and support learners in the creation, development and exploitation of learning opportunities suited to their needs, which are not always the same as those prescribed and/or advocated by policy makers or employers. Furthermore, the thrust of learning career theory points to the wisdom of replacing detailed universal work-based learning patterns and structures with supporting systems and frameworks that maximize the chances for locally developed approaches to flourish, which are more focused to individual needs and circumstances (see also Evans *et al,* 1997). However, even the best of such localized approaches will face major problems while deep inequalities in employment and education persist. Significant improvement of learning and learning opportunities, for people like Luke, depends on ameliorating some of the major social, cultural and economic difficulties/disadvantages that they face.

Above all, it is our belief that using the learning career as a conceptual tool is a realistic way to reconsider longitudinal patterns of work-based learning and to step away from the traditional, front-loaded model that is still heavily implicit in thinking and planning around this topic. Of course, pursuing this opportunity may give rise to new problems and new issues. For example, if employers are mainly concerned with those workers who are employed by them, and educators are primarily concerned with students on vocationally- or occupationally-focused pre-service courses, there will be difficulties in establishing who or what holds responsibility for supporting lifelong learners who change employers, change career directions, and move in to and out of formal learning structures. The old, increasingly discredited market approach, where the individual learner has to take responsibility for his or her own career, looks threadbare at best when set against the trials and tribulations of Luke, Fazarna and many others like them.

References

Alheit, P (1994) *Taking the Knocks: Youth unemployment and biography – a qualitative analysis,* Cassell, London

Arthur, M B, Inkson, K and Pringle, J K (1999) *The New Careers: Individual action and economic change,* Sage, London

Bloomer, M and Hodkinson, P (1997) *Moving into FE: The voice of the learner,* FEDA, London

Bloomer, M and Hodkinson, P (1999) *College Life: The voice of the learner,* FEDA, London

Bloomer, M and Hodkinson, P (2000) Learning careers: continuity and change in young people's dispositions to learning, *British Journal of Educational Studies,* 26 (5), pp 583–98

Bourdieu, P (1977) *Outline of a Theory of Practice,* Cambridge University Press, Cambridge

Bourdieu, P and Passeron, J-C (1990) *Reproduction in Education, Society and Culture,* 2nd edn, Sage, London

Bourdieu, P and Wacquant, L J D (1992) *An Invitation to Reflexive Sociology*, Polity Press, Cambridge

Brown, J S, Collins, A and Duguid, P (1989) Situated cognition and the culture of learning, *Educational Researcher,* **18** (1), pp 32–42

Chen, C P (1998) Understanding career development: A convergence of perspectives, *Journal of Vocational Education and Training*, **50** (3), pp 437–61

Coffield, F (ed) (2000) *The Necessity of Informal Learning*, Policy Press, Bristol

Cole, M (1996) *Cultural Psychology*, Harvard University Press, Cambridge MA

Collin, A and Young, R A (eds) (2000) *The Future of Career*, Cambridge University Press, Cambridge

DfEE (1998) *The Learning Age: A renaissance for a new Britain*, The Stationery Office, Norwich

Driver, R, Asoko, H, Leach, J, Mortimer, E and Scott, P (1994) Constructing scientific knowledge in the classroom, *Educational Researcher*, **23** (7), pp 4–12

Elliott, G (1999) *Lifelong Learning: The politics of the new learning environment*, Jessica Kingsley, London

Engeström, Y (1987) *Learning by Expanding: An activity-theoretical approach to developmental research*, Orienta-Konsultit, Helsinki

Engeström, Y (2001) Expansive learning at work: Towards an activity-theoretical reconceptualisation, *Journal of Education and Work*, **14** (1), pp 133–56

Evans, K, Hodkinson, P, Keep, E, Maguire, M, Raffe, D, Rainbird, H, Senker, P and Unwin, L (1997) *Working to Learn: A work-based route to learning for young people*, Issues in People Management, IPD, London, no 18

Giddens, A (1991) *Modernity and Self-identity: Self and society in the late modern age*, Polity Press, Cambridge

Gorard, S, Rees, G, Fevre, R and Furlong, J (1997) Lifetime learning trajectories: close encounters of five kinds, *Patterns of Participation in Adult Education and Training*, Working Paper 7, School of Education, University of Wales, Cardiff

Hodkinson, P (1999) Personal career development. Paper presented to Enterprise plc, February

Hodkinson, P, Sparkes, A C and Hodkinson, H (1996) *Triumphs and Tears: Young people, markets and the transition from school to work*, David Fulton, London

Jessup, G (1991) *Outcomes: NVQs and the emerging model of education and training*, Falmer Press, London

Lave, J and Wenger, E (1991) *Situated Learning*, Cambridge University Press, Cambridge

Soden, R and Halliday, J (2000) Rethinking vocational education: a case study in care, *International Journal of Lifelong Education*, **19** (2), pp 172–82

Wenger, E (1998) *Communities of Practice: Learning, meaning, and identity*, Cambridge University Press, Cambridge

Wertsch, J V (1991) *Voices of the Mind: A sociocultural approach to mediated action*, Harvester Wheatsheaf, London

Chapter 3

Contrasting approaches to the role of qualifications in the promotion of lifelong learning[1]

Michael Young

Emerging trends and issues in qualification reform

The issues discussed in this chapter arise from three recent developments with implications that most countries are or will soon be facing. The first is the growing interest of governments in the idea of a national qualification *framework* based on outcomes defined according to a common set of criteria and including all types of qualification whether they are school or work based, general, vocational or professional in purpose. Furthermore, frameworks such as those proposed in New Zealand, Scotland and South Africa are designed to include *all* levels of qualification, from those certifying basic skills to postgraduate degrees. The origin of the idea of a qualification framework based on outcomes can be traced back to the NVQ framework introduced by the National Council for Vocational Qualifications (NCVQ) in the UK in 1987.[2]

As far as I am aware, this was the first attempt to establish a national qualifications framework that was based on outcomes and was independent of any specific learning programmes provided by educational institutions. Although the NVQ framework was restricted to including only vocational qualifications, Gilbert Jessup (Jessup, 1991), one of those involved in its design from the early days, saw the idea of an outcomes-based framework having a much wider potential. He envisaged that learning outcomes could be the basis for a comprehensive framework for *all* qualifications.

What was not recognized at the time of the launch of NVQs but has become much clearer since is that the concept of qualification-based learning outcomes is not as neutral as it appears. In other words, like the closely related idea of competence, outcomes imply specific ideas about learning. A qualification described in terms of a set of learning outcomes implies that any kind of learning can be included. However, if there is to be formal comparability between different qualifications within a framework, the criteria for learning must be precisely specifiable in advance of any assessment. It follows that qualifications defined within an outcomes-based framework neglect learning that might be important and valued but is not specifiable in advance or indeed may not be specifiable at all except in very general terms.[3] Some kind of pre-specification of outcomes is of course a feature of any qualification in so far as one of its functions is to communicate something about a person's capability to a user, whether an employer involved in recruitment or a tutor considering whether to accept someone on a course. However, with the launch of NVQs, not only did the pre-specification of outcomes became much more detailed, but other features of a qualification such as a requirement to attend a course of study were explicitly excluded. The definition of outcomes that is a feature of any qualification changed from being a guide to those devising assessments and curricula and an indication of a person's capabilities, to claiming to be a precise definition of a person's competence or what he or she could do. In other words the precise specification of outcomes was designed to replace the kind of normative criteria which, in more traditional qualifications, were used to compare an individual with others. There was also an assumption in the NVQ approach that precisely defined outcomes would not only remove the need to relate a qualification to how and where it was achieved but would at least minimize the human judgement required for assessing learning.

The advantages of an approach to qualifications based on outcomes apply most readily to vocational qualifications where in many cases it is important to know that someone is capable of competently carrying out specific tasks. Furthermore, a common definition of outcomes is crucial to the feasibility of a *single* national framework for all qualifications. However, the implications of an outcomes-based framework are far more problematic in relation to the goals of general education, such as personal intellectual development, which can never be expressed in terms of precisely specified outcomes. At best, pre-specified outcomes are congruent with the some of the purposes of low level qualifications where the skills and knowledge needed are relatively unambiguous and where there is less likelihood of a learner needing to demonstrate new (in the sense of unexpected) knowledge. Furthermore, for beginning and low level learners, pre-specification of outcomes may actually be an advantage in helping them to establish achievable goals and develop a confidence in their own capacities. Detailed pre-specification of outcomes of the kind attempted by NCVQ downgrades the role of the professional judgement of teachers and trainers as assessors of student or trainee learning.[4] It also under-emphasizes the forms of learning that cannot be expressed in terms of outcomes but which learners, especially low level learners, will need if they are to progress.

The interest in outcomes-based frameworks has been paralleled by approaches to funding that are linked to the achievement of qualifications[5] and can be understood in relation to attempts to make schools, colleges and other training providers more accountable. The educational implications of a single outcomes-based qualifications framework explain the strong opposition to such a framework on the part of those universities that see their mission as promoting excellence and encouraging their students, where possible, to go beyond what is known by their teachers.

The second significant development is the growing body of research and experience that suggests that the qualification framework strategy being adopted by Anglophone[6] countries is not working out as its proponents hoped (Young, 2001). At least as conceived up to now, the approach appears to have some unfortunate consequences. The question that I will return to is whether these consequences are best seen as 'teething problems' likely to be associated with any radical innovation or whether they are an indication that relying on outcomes is based on some fundamentally flawed assumptions about the role of qualifications.

The third issue that I want to consider in this chapter is that a number of other countries, most notably those associated with the Germanic and Nordic traditions of education and training, have remained largely immune from the pressures to develop outcome-based qualification frameworks of the kind found in the UK and other Anglophone countries (Young, 2001). The question is whether the former group of countries is right to be sceptical of outcomes-based approaches or whether it is a trend that no country seeking to be competitive in the global economy will be able to avoid. There is no doubt that both groups of countries are having to reform their education systems and rethink the role of qualifications in light of global economic changes and the related changes in skill and knowledge demands (Lasonen, 1996; Lasonen and Young, 1998; Young, 2001). In this chapter, I will contrast the approach that sees a *qualification framework* as the best way of responding to these changes with one that focuses on improving a country's *institutional framework*. In the latter case I will refer primarily to the links between different levels of educational institution and their links with private and public employers in different sectors.

Outline of the chapter

The remaining sections of this chapter explore the three trends already introduced by considering the increasingly significant role given to qualifications by governments and the growing interest in what I have referred to as a qualification framework approach. It then proposes a typology for comparing the approaches of different countries towards qualification reform. The major distinction that I make is between countries adopting a primarily 'outcome-based' approach to qualifications and those using what I shall refer to as a 'process-based' or 'institutional' approach. I will then discuss some of the benefits and problems of each approach. Finally, in considering whether an approach can be developed that draws on the benefits of each, I will draw on a distinction introduced by Raffe (1992) between the 'intrinsic' and 'institutional' logics of any educational policy. I will take Raffe's conceptualization a step further by distinguishing between the 'macro' and 'micro' aspects of each type of logic.

Intrinsic logics refer to the claims made for a reform such as a single qualifications framework that are independent of the actual context in which the reform might be implemented. It is the intrinsic logic of a reform that represents its political rationale and tends to set the terms on which it is justified or attacked by its critics. Intrinsic logics are important because they are designed to express people's aspirations and goals and are linked to the political purposes of governments. *Institutional logics,* on the other hand, refer to the social, political and institutional contexts, the divisions, power relations and interests that constitute them and the role that they will play in how (and whether) any reform is implemented. The institutional logic of any educational reform can be separated into its 'macro' and 'micro' aspects. Whereas 'macro' aspects refer to forms of stratification, power relations and institutional hierarchies, 'micro' aspects include the specific practices, patterns of interaction and shared values that are the basis for the credibility and acceptance of a qualification by users. It is the macro aspects that act as the most visible constraints on educational reform. A well-known example is how the selective role of secondary education based on social class divisions persisted despite the claims for parity of esteem between different types of secondary schools in the 1944 Education Act (Banks, 1954).[7] It is the less visible micro aspects of institutional logic that are the condition for a process like qualification, assessment or even learning to take place at all.

The experience of those countries that have developed (or are developing) outcomes-based approaches suggests that while they tend to share a common notion of their 'intrinsic' logic – what they hope a qualification framework will achieve – they have given very little attention to either aspect of their 'institutional' logic. However, it does not follow that we should dismiss the goals of an outcomes-based qualifications framework that are expressed in its intrinsic logic, for they highlight a number of problems with approaches they are designed to replace. The contrast between the two approaches can shed light on a) the limitations of outcomes-based approaches; b) the enduring strengths (as well as the weaknesses) of the more traditional models; and c) the dangers of assuming that qualification reforms on their own, and in particular the introduction of an outcomes-based qualification framework, can play more than a modest role in improving education and training.

Qualification reforms: the context

The main official goals of recent qualification reforms in the UK and other EU and OECD countries have been to improve the flexibility of education and training systems, to widen participation and to enhance the mobility of learners and potential learners. In furthering these goals, most reforms have emphasized:

- encouraging people to see qualifying as a process that starts in initial education and training and continues throughout their adult lives;
- improving opportunities for people to move between different types of qualifications (especially general and vocational) and between vocational qualifications for different occupational sectors;
- promoting informal learning and the links between informal and formal learning, and improving opportunities for people to use their informal learning to gain recognized qualifications.

These are relatively uncontroversial aims, if difficult to realize in practice. However, a number of questions about the link between such aims and the kind of qualification reforms that have emerged, especially in Anglophone countries, need to be asked. First, why have governments focused on qualifications as their main instrument to reform their systems of education and training? Second, given that as yet there is only limited experience of implementing outcomes-based qualification frameworks, why has the idea proved so attractive to governments, even in countries that have up to now relied on quite different approaches to the organization of education and training and to the role of qualifications? Third, given the enormous diversity of learning demands in a modern society, is it realistic to envisage common criteria that could be the basis of a single framework for the whole range of qualifications – vocational, professional and general? Fourth, given that some of the most effective education and training systems up to now (for example those in East Asia and continental Europe) have relied on developing learning pathways located in specific, institutional, occupational and academic communities and not on the detailed specification of outcomes, why is an outcomes-based framework that is independent of such communities seen as providing the best basis for qualification systems of the future in Anglophone countries?

Finally, although it is widely seen as a solution to the problems of globalization, the concept of lifelong learning is itself a highly confusing term used more rhetorically than analytically (Coffield, 1997; Young, 2001). In government policy statements, lifelong learning tends to refer to the importance of individuals taking more responsibility for their own learning (Keep, 1997). However, a growing body of research suggests that not only is learning a social rather than an individual process (Lave and Wenger, 1994) but that an individual's motivation to learn is largely shaped by whether learning is valued in the workplaces or communities in which they find themselves. It follows that policies to promote lifelong learning need to be as much about creating a demand for learning as about the structure of qualifications through which it may be accredited. Furthermore, lifelong learning embraces a number of different policies with very different implications for qualification reform. They include encouraging those leaving school to continue learning, supporting those in work to develop their skills and knowledge, and supporting those without work or in unskilled jobs to get qualifications and improve their prospects for progression.

Why qualifications?

It seems likely that one reason why governments have become so interested in qualifications in recent decades is that not only do they motivate learners, they can serve quite other roles that are just as important but frequently less explicit aspects of government policy. For example, a greater emphasis on qualifications enables central governments to:

- increase their control of education in areas where it is relatively weak;
- provide simple measurable criteria for allocating funds to institutions;
- make local and regional education and training organizations more accountable;
- provide quantitative measures of the success of government policies.

Two historical parallels in the development of policy are worth noting. The first is the congruence between the growing interest in qualifications by

Conservative governments in the UK from the 1980s and their support for neo-liberal, market-oriented approaches both to the economy and the public sector. The second is that qualification reform from the 1980s was given most support in those countries which a) had weaker traditions of central government involvement in education and training (for example. the UK) and b) most readily endorsed the Reagan-Thatcher neo-liberal policies (the UK, Australia and New Zealand). In the UK case, the Labour government that followed the general election in 1997 continued to use qualifications as an instrument to regulate institutions such as schools, colleges and Training and Enterprise Councils (TECs), which are supported by public funds. This emphasis on qualifications as measures of performance was linked to the freeing of schools and colleges from local government control and forcing them to compete in quasi-markets for students, and therefore for funds. There are parallels with the role of regulatory bodies controlling the new private monopolies such as water, gas and electricity. Qualifications offer an ideal regulatory instrument to a reforming government as they appear to serve a dual purpose. They provide incentives for individual learners[8] *and* can be used as mechanisms for making educational institutions accountable. The educational problem however is that these purposes can be in conflict with each other. More emphasis on accountability leads to tighter specification of outcomes – a trend in all qualification-led reforms. Promoting learning, however, especially among those with previous experience of school failure, requires teachers and learners to feel the confidence to take risks and learn from them. In other words it requires qualifications that rely more on professional judgement and are *less* specified in advance. Furthermore, a greater emphasis on qualifications as outcomes puts pressure on institutions and workplaces to give more time to assessment and less to the teaching and learning activities that might in the longer term lead to more appropriate types of learning and more people gaining qualifications.

Why qualification frameworks?

Qualification arrangements in England and Wales have in the past had a number of features in common with those found in other European countries which it has long been argued are in need of reform. For example:

- General and vocational qualifications have developed separately with quite distinct systems of assessment and with limited possibilities of progression between them.

- Vocational and professional qualifications are often organized by sectors or occupations independently from each other and there are few opportunities for movement or transfer of credit across sectors.
- Most qualifications are closely linked to specific programmes and periods of study in educational institutions. Access is difficult for those with skills but who cannot attend specific institution-based programmes.
- Qualifications have traditionally been underpinned by 'specialist communities' with shared practices such as trades, crafts and professional organizations in the case of vocational and professional qualifications, and by subject and disciplinary associations in the case of general qualifications. These communities inevitably set the terms for decisions about who should and should not qualify. Historically these 'specialist communities' have been (and in some cases continue to be) exclusive, both generally and in relation to specific disadvantaged groups distinguished by race, class and gender.
- Traditional qualifications have offered limited forms of access to adult learners who have been expected to retrace the steps of young learners rather than build on their adult experience and knowledge.
- Many occupations and even sectors have been characterized by very few of those employed having any qualifications at all. This has been especially the case in the UK, where a statutory requirement to be qualified has only applied in the case of a small number of occupations. Qualifications have, until recently, been developed in a largely ad hoc manner by a whole variety of commercial, professional, educational and charitable bodies and with minimum state intervention.

In the 1980s all these features were seen by reformers associated with the Employment Department and NCVQ as barriers and rigidities to maximizing opportunities to expand learning and at odds with the blurring of occupational boundaries, and the flexible and fast changing skill and knowledge demands of the global economy. A single framework in which all qualifications were located according to a clear set of levels and progression criteria appeared in principle to be a logical way of overcoming these rigidities. The shift that was argued for, albeit not always explicitly and still largely in relation to vocational qualifications, was from a qualification system based on 'shared practices' to one based on formally explicit 'criteria' that were capable of being defined independently of any specific experience or practice.

Support for a change from a qualification system based on 'shared practice' to one based on 'criteria' was rooted in political as much as educational factors. The old 'provider culture' of FE colleges, local employers and the Awarding

Bodies was widely discredited among civil servants and national employer organizations. This view fitted in with the marketizing zeal of the Thatcher government, which had a general scepticism towards professional interests and wanted a more 'user-led' and market-driven education and training system. In the case of vocational qualifications, support for reform was closely tied to the government's determination to break the power of trade unions that they saw as using trade and craft qualifications to perpetuate restrictive practices (Raggatt and Williams, 1999). The attempt to 'break with the past' has been a familiar feature of qualification reform and not necessarily associated with the political Right. The frameworks being introduced in Wales and Scotland are strongly supported by the new Assembly and Parliamentary Executives and the symbolic role of a national framework has played an important part in support for the National Qualification Framework being introduced by the post-apartheid government in South Africa.

Lastly, it has been claimed (Jessup, 1991) that a qualification framework is a mechanism for freeing qualifications from their traditional link with educational institutions and formal learning and that it can provide access to groups who have in the past been excluded by schools and colleges. In principle, at least, a qualifications framework defined in terms of a clear set of outcomes allows anyone who thinks they have acquired the necessary skills and knowledge to become qualified without further study. It is not surprising therefore that the idea of a qualification framework has been closely linked to promoting informal learning and the broader lifelong learning agenda (DfEE, 1998). It is, however, difficult to find evidence of the existence of a significant body of people with skills and knowledge that they have acquired informally and therefore have not led to qualifications. Furthermore, it seems likely that in most cases[9] the assessment procedures for converting informally acquired knowledge and skills into the formal requirements of qualifications may be perceived as being as much of a barrier as the existing learning programmes to those denied opportunities for formal learning as the existing learning programmes themselves.

The typology: outcomes-based and institution-based approaches

Arising from the previous discussion of different national approaches to the reform of qualifications, a typology is proposed that distinguishes between *outcomes-based* and *institution-based* approaches. Before discussing the two models it is important to recognize that qualification reforms should not be seen in isolation. There are other dimensions on which national approaches to the reform of education and training can vary and which will shape the way in which qualifications operate. These are not the focus of this chapter but can be seen as elements of the context that shapes the role of qualifications in a society. Examples are:

- the extent to which funding of education and training is based primarily on individuals or the performance of organizations;
- the extent to which government of education and training is devolved (for example the role of the 'Lande' in Germany might be contrasted with the more centralized systems found in France, Scotland and England);
- the extent to which the state or the private sector is the main provider and funder of vocational education and training;
- the location of responsibility for assessment (this can be educational institutions, governments, public agencies, private bodies and employer organizations).

Let us consider the main characteristics of the two models (treating them as 'ideal types' and not descriptions of the approaches of particular countries) and some of the problems each gives rise to.

Outcomes-based approaches

Qualifications are:

- used as an independent instrument of reform;
- defined in terms of common criteria (or outcomes) and levels and do not involve reference to specific inputs or programmes;
- defined independently of the route that learners take to become qualified;
- designed to maximize flexibility, user choice, portability and ease of access to assessment.

There are some problems:

- Outcomes-based frameworks assume that: a) a single definition of a qualification can be applied to the wide diversity of levels and types of learning that takes place in a society; and b) level equivalencies can be agreed for extremely diverse types of learning, for example plumbing and business administration (and history and other academic subjects if the framework is to apply to both vocational and general qualifications). Furthermore, in using precise specification of outcomes as the main guarantee of quality, outcome-based qualifications can lead to jargon, assessment bureaucracy and the trivializing of learning as an activity (Wolf, 1995).

- There is evidence that, in prescribing learning outcomes in advance, such frameworks encourage resistance rather than support from high status institutions which have traditionally had responsibility for devising learning programmes and awarding qualifications (eg universities and professional bodies).

- In giving priority to creating flexible pathways and making boundaries permeable, outcomes-based frameworks can neglect that distinct types of qualification (eg vocational and academic) and clear boundaries between different occupational sectors can have a positive role in promoting learning (especially higher level learning).

- In emphasizing that there are generic criteria for all qualifications, single frameworks tend to neglect the importance of specific content in both vocational and general subject areas and can lead to a mismatch between qualifications defined within a framework and the learning and qualification needs of specific employers (and learners).

- As a consequence of their specific national character, qualification frameworks can appear to replace the need for national leadership of education and training policy. They can therefore over-emphasize the role that qualifications can have in promoting learning rather than seeing them as one element in a much broader process.

- In claiming that qualifications can be achieved in a wide variety of sites, an outcomes-based framework can underplay the inescapable 'institutionality' of education and training as well as its dependence on the availability of widely distributed assessor expertise.

- Lastly, there is as yet very little evidence as to how far the quality and amount of learning has been enhanced in countries that have introduced national frameworks. In the case of NVQs in the UK, the gross numbers achieving vocational qualifications have not changed significantly since they were introduced. What has changed is the proportion gaining NVQs as opposed to other types of vocational qualification (Bellamy, 2001). In a voluntarist system such as that found in the UK, which lacks a broad employer community with a major interest in the provision and use of qualifications, the take-up of qualifications is almost entirely determined by what is funded.

Institutional approaches

These approaches are less easy to characterize, partly because in many countries they are very much taken for granted and have a long history.

Qualifications are more embedded in other institutional processes as accepted features of education and training systems. In a case such as Germany, vocational qualifications are an integral part of an education and training system that includes institutional links, syllabuses, assessment methods and learning programmes, and partnerships between employers, trade unions and providers. Qualifications 'on their own' are not used by governments adopting institutional approaches as an independent lever for change. They rely on broad rather than specific criteria, clear input definitions based on syllabuses and learning programmes, and progression depends on peer and partnership trust, primarily through institutional links.

However, in the context of global economic changes, institutional approaches are not without their weaknesses. For example:

- they are based strongly on consensus and exhibit inertia and resistance to change;
- they make it difficult to change anything as any change involves the whole system;
- they are slow to adapt to the learning needs of new occupations;
- progression between different sectors and general and vocational qualifications is difficult;
- traditional divisions such as those between opportunities for men and women are difficult to change.

Conclusions

Most industrial countries, such as those that are members of the OECD, still have largely institution-based systems of qualifications, though some are exploring the scope of outcomes-based approaches. The exceptions appear to be the Anglophone countries, a number of which followed England and went down the outcomes-based route. England is now hesitantly stepping back from the extreme outcomes position initially adopted by the NCVQ (Raggatt and Williams, 1999). Furthermore, there has been little progress, even in countries where an outcomes-based approach has been longer established, towards a single national framework for all qualifications including those awarded by universities. This uncertainty suggests that we need to explore a middle way that is not, like most compromises, the worst of both worlds. Drawing on the earlier distinction between intrinsic and institutional logics, this concluding section will attempt to chart such a possibility for the future by considering a number of key questions that arise from an analysis of framework approaches in different countries.

The rationale for a framework

The rationale for introducing a single qualifications framework can be summarized as follows. First, by doing away with distinct types of qualifications it fits in with the increased flexibility of qualifications that are needed in modern economies. Second, a single framework provides learners, throughout their working lives, with the confidence that they can transfer qualifications between sectors and move between jobs and places of study and at the same time accumulate 'credit' towards further qualifications. Third, the clear specification of levels means that, in principle, no one is excluded from obtaining higher level qualifications, even if they do not have access to a university – nurses can become doctors and craftsmen can become engineers. This is the intrinsic logic of an outcomes-based qualification framework. However, this rationale comes up against a number of features of what I referred to earlier as the 'macro' and 'micro' aspects of the institutional logic of modern societies. Let us begin by considering the 'macro' aspects.

'Macro' aspects

First, the global changes towards more flexible economies have not turned out to be as progressive and evenly distributed as predicted by political economists such as Piore and Sabel (1984) and Reich (1991). The majority of people in work still stay in the same field if not the same company or organization for most of their working lives. The new industries of the e-economy with their new learning demands have had much publicity but quantitatively they create remarkably few jobs. As is increasingly apparent from the recent cutbacks in the IT sector, the transformative capacity of the new technologies, at least in the short term, has been vastly exaggerated. Furthermore, some of the most characteristic jobs of the new economy are those in call centres and the fast food and security industries, none of which requires many 'knowledge workers'. In other words, the increasingly mobile and qualified society on which the claims for qualification frameworks are based bears little relationship to the realities of modern economies.

Second, a seamless framework of qualification levels does not of itself guarantee progression or provide a basis for overcoming deep-seated divisions between different types of qualifications. In England there is a five-level vocational qualifications framework. However, a) the majority of vocational qualifications are awarded at levels 1 and 2, b) there are extremely few qualifications at level 5 and few of the established professions have shown any interest in including their qualifications within the framework, and c) many of those who obtain vocational qualifications at levels 4 and 5 have not progressed from lower levels but have entered the framework as graduates, having progressed through the institutional route of school and university. These are examples of the inability of a national qualifications framework to fulfil its aims and reflect the influence of what I referred to as the institutional logic of qualifications – in particular, the continued significance of academic/vocational and professional/vocational divisions that can be found to varying extents in every country.

The solution to overcoming these divisions is not primarily to be found through a qualification framework. It will depend on expanding the range of higher-level professional occupations and strengthening the opportunities for people to progress from lower level occupations that are linked to vocational qualifications. The old links between National and Higher National Certificates and the access they provided to membership of professional bodies is one model. However, its weakness was that it only applied to a very limited range of occupations and sectors. A recent successful example is the links that have been established between vocational qualifications for Accountancy Technicians and access to professional accountancy qualifications. The key factor is not the qualifications themselves but the role of the professional body, which controls both professional and vocational qualifications.

The future tasks are not just to create new qualification levels within a single framework. They are: a) to create genuine *occupational* progression pathways in sectors that have had few qualified people in the past such as care, retailing and hospitality and the emerging range of service occupations, and b) to create new routes for people without initial qualifications to gain access to occupations such as engineering and banking.

'Micro' aspects

The micro aspects of the institutional logic of qualifications are less visible but no less fundamental in the problems they pose for reformers. They reflect what appears to be almost a sociological law. This law states that the credibility, quality and currency of a qualification are only partly based on what it says the person who is qualified can do or knows; far more important is the trust that society in general and specific users in particular (those whom select, recruit or promote) have in the qualification. This trust, as mentioned earlier, has in the past been embedded in various forms of community – trade and craft associations, occupational and professional organizations and, in relation to general education, academic subject and disciplinary associations often linked to organizations with high status such as elite schools and universities. These 'communities of trust' have taken time to establish and developed their own forms of exclusiveness. Not surprisingly they have been seen as barriers to increased access and participation. However, the implications of the micro institutional logic argument is if these traditional communities of trust are destroyed, either as a result of explicit policies (as in the case of NVQs) or as the unintended consequences of economic change, they cannot be replaced by an outcomes-based framework alone, however well specified. If new 'communities of trust' or some equivalent do not underpin any new qualification, it will have a problem of credibility among users. This problem may in part account for the phenomenon of academic drift. Most academic qualifications still rely on traditional 'communities of trust' such as those linking specialist subject teachers with colleagues in universities and have therefore retained their 'currency value' beyond their communities of origin.

Relying on qualifications based on old 'communities of trust' is not a solution. As has already been noted, not only have they been exclusive and elitist, but they have rarely been the basis for envisaging new skill and knowledge demands. It was partly these features that led to professions and trade unions being criticized in the 1980s as sources of vested interest and for alternative and superficially more democratic proposals to be developed based on clearly specified and 'transparent' criteria. However, the new qualifications neglected what I have referred to as the 'micro' aspects of the institutional logic that underpins qualifications. The traditional 'communities of trust' disappeared and were replaced not by a strategy for building new ones but by sets of outcomes defined within a national framework (NVQs). The failure to establish new 'communities of trust' is apparent in the lack of credibility of many NVQs among employers.

In the UK the recent priority has been to establish National Training Organizations (NTOs) with the responsibility for developing National Occupational Standards and (with the Awarding Bodies) to design new qualifications and systems of assessment. In the areas with a long tradition of apprenticeship such as engineering, this approach can work because the old 'communities of trust' can be built on. In fast growing sectors such as the retail trade, which have traditionally recruited largely unskilled labour and where either no 'community of trust' existed or where those that do exist are based exclusively on particular companies, the problem is more complex. NTOs in these areas fail partly because they do not represent their employers and partly because companies continue to make profits by selling low quality services or low quality products produced by unqualified labour (Keep, 1997). Similarly, academic subject groups develop subject specifications within a framework laid down by regulatory authorities (in England the QCA). In traditional academic subjects such as physics or history, the process continues to work.[10] In the 'new' subjects such as media studies and design technology, where the links are weak or do not exist, the qualifications lack credibility whether for employment or as a basis for progressing to university.

The implication of this analysis is not to oppose the establishment of a framework that includes all qualifications (a long-term objective of a regulatory authority such as the QCA). It is rather that such a framework will serve little purpose unless the much harder task of establishing the new 'communities of trust' that will be needed to underpin any new qualifications is tackled. With the demise of old occupational communities, what will be the basis of new 'communities of trust'? An adequate answer is beyond the scope of this chapter. However, a number of pointers can be suggested. They, the new 'communities of trust', will be cross-sectoral (in terms of occupations), trans-institutional (bridging public/private, service/manufacturing, provider/users (of education and training), regional and multi-level (specifically vocational/professional) and combine virtual with real (or face-to-face) communications. Establishing these new 'communities of trust' cannot be the responsibility of a government department, a regulatory authority or even the Awarding Bodies or NTOs. It requires a much more concerted strategy involving all the partners in the education and training system. It is in the experience of this more integrated approach that England has most to learn from other EU countries. At the same time, they are learning that their old forms of integration and partnership themselves are in need of reform.

A final note

The two approaches to qualification reform that I have discussed reflect the very different national histories of the countries where they originated as well as the different roles of the state and different employer and social class cultures. A model for the future does not involve a choice between qualifications based on 'shared practices' or 'institutions' on the one hand and those based on criteria and outcomes on the other. In the past the 'shared practices' model appeared to work because skill and knowledge demands of different occupations changed only incrementally and the division of labour was such that it did not matter that the vast majority of the population never gained any qualifications at all. Neither of these conditions holds today: learning demands are constantly changing and fewer jobs are available for the unqualified. Every country has to be more proactive in updating the qualifications of its young people and its adult labour force and extending them to as large a section of each cohort as possible. This means that outcomes-based frameworks and national occupational standards that are not located in current practice do have a role in guiding future practice, albeit a more modest one than their most enthusiastic proponents imagined: they can provide a framework for questioning existing practice, developing alternatives and for exploring strategies to promote links between different 'communities of trust'. No qualification framework that is not supported by 'communities of trust' that link levels, institutions and sectors will achieve its aims.

There are two major lessons for policy makers from this analysis. The first is that although the reform of qualifications does have a role in improving any education and training system, outcomes, standards or criteria are no short cut. Real learning is always going to be a difficult process that depends on creating new opportunities, developing the expertise of teachers and trainers and finding new ways of motivating learners whether they are in school, college or at work. Qualifications are a guide to and a currency for learning just as money is a currency for buying and selling goods and services; as in the case of money, expanding qualifications without parallel expansion in learning and the demand for it is a recipe for credential inflation. Policies designed to promote learning, not qualifications, have to lead reform. Qualifications have to grow out of a need to go beyond existing 'communities of trust'.

The second lesson is that a single national qualification framework (linked increasingly to regional and other international frameworks) is an important long-term goal for any country. However, the links between different levels and types of qualification cannot be based primarily on sets of criteria or outcomes. Such links can only be formalized within an outcomes-based framework. They will have to be based on the shared values and practices of what I have referred to as 'communities of trust'. The challenge for qualifica-tion reformers is to identify new bases for these 'communities of trust' in the emerging economy. For reasons that I have discussed, they cannot be the old occupational communities, nor can they be virtual communities of Internet users. I have suggested that it is likely that they will depend increasingly on a combination of institutional networks between companies, colleges, universities and professional bodies, regional networks linking different institutions, users and providers in a region, and virtual networks enabling links between those who are too far away for face-to-face contact. New kinds of networks have always emerged with new patterns of work. The difference is that in the past, at least in the UK, networks were allowed to emerge in ad hoc and uneven ways. If the learning society of the future is to be a reality, these new networks will have to be created. In other words they have to become 'history in the making'.

Notes

1.   This chapter draws on ideas presented at an ESRC Research Network Seminar in November 1999 and developed in a paper (Young, 2000) presented to the SRHE Conference, Globalization and Higher Education – Views from the south, Capetown, 27–9 March 2001.
2.   NVQs drew on the earlier experience in the USA of competence-based certification and assessment and more generally on the method of functional analysis developed within occupational psychology (Wolf, 1995).
3.   For example, an apprentice or a student might acquire integrity or develop his or her sense of responsibility.
4.   The requirement, which was exemplified in the Training and Development Lead Body (TDLB) standards and insisted on by the NCVQ, was that teachers and trainers could be trained to interpret the criteria in the 'correct' way. It was not surprising that teachers dismissed the standards as de-skillling. The fact that the NCVQ was able to force teachers to engage in what was little more than what turned out to be ritual 'box ticking' merely compounded the problem.
5.   A kind of modern equivalent to 'payment by results'.
6.   I am thinking of the four 'home' countries in the UK that have adopted somewhat different approaches to qualifications reform, and New Zealand, Australia and South Africa, though somewhat similar reforms based on NVQs are being introduced in Mexico and some Eastern European countries.
7.   A similar point was made by later researchers concerning the continuing role of selection based on social classes in comprehensive schools.
8.   However, as I have heard a number of FE lecturers remark, although more students may have learnt that it is a good thing to get a qualification, they do not always associate this with sustained and disciplined study!
9.   An exception is those 'access' courses developed in the 1980s that were designed not to lead to qualification but to higher level programmes in further or higher education.
10.   Though even in such cases, there are questions to be raised about the old 'communities of trust' as the numbers taking scientific and linguistic subjects decline.

References

Banks, O (1954) *Parity and Prestige in British Secondary Education*, Routledge and Kegan Paul, London

Bellamy, A (2001) Paper presented to a City and Guilds Research Seminar, March 2001

Coffield, F (1997) Attempts to reclaim the concept of a learning society, *Journal of Education Policy*, **12** (6)

Department for Education and Employment (DfEE) (1998) *The Learning Age: A renaissance for a new Britain*, HMSO, Norwich

Jessup, G (1991) *Outcomes: NVQs and the emerging model of Vocational Education and Training*, Falmer Press, London

Keep, E (1997) 'There is no such thing as society. . .'. Some problems with an individual approach to creating a learning society, *Journal of Education Policy*, **12** (6)

Lasonen, J (ed) (1996) *Surveys and Strategies for Post-16 Education*, University of Jyvaskyla, Institute of Educational Research, Jyvaskyla, Finland

Lasonen, J and Young, M (1998) *Strategies for Achieving Parity of Esteem in European Secondary Education*, University of Jyvaskyla, Institute of Educational Research, Jyvaskyla, Finland

Lave, J and Wenger, E (1994) *Situated Learning: Legitimate peripheral participation*, Cambridge University Press, Cambridge

Piore, M J and Sabel, C (1984) *The Second Industrial Divide*, Basic Books, New York

Raffe, D (1992) *Modular Strategies for Overcoming Academic/Vocational Divisions*, University of Jyvaskyla, Finland

Raggatt, P and Williams, S (1999) *Government, Markets and Vocational Qualifications; an anatomy of policy.* Falmer Press, London

Reich, R (1991) *The Work of Nations*, Simon and Schuster, London

Wolf, A (1995) *Competence-based Assessment*, Open University Press, Buckingham

Young, M (2000) Bringing knowledge back in: policies and practices for lifelong learning, in *Policies, Politics and the Future of Lifelong Learning*, Kogan Page, London

Young, M (2001) The role of national qualification systems in promoting lifelong learning. Issues paper for the Meeting of National Representatives and Experts, OECD, Paris, 5–6 March

Chapter 4

The interaction between qualifications and work-based learning

Michael Eraut

Qualifications take many forms and are used in a wide range of contexts for several, often conflicting, purposes. Hence interactions between qualifications and work-based learning differ according to the purpose and nature of the qualifications, their role in a person's 'learning career', the type of work involved and the nature of the working context. Such interactions may have a positive, negative or neutral effect on learning in the workplace. This chapter starts with a broad overview of types of qualification, their intended relationship to work, and what they mean to individuals and employers; then proceeds to a more detailed analysis of interactions between qualifications and work-based learning, and the influence on those interactions of various characteristics of the qualifications themselves.

Types of qualification and their relationship to work

The commonest groups of qualifications, and those which receive by far the greatest attention, are those taken either immediately before entering full-time employment, linked to employment as apprentices or trainees or forming part of an uninterrupted sequence (except for gap-years) of qualification-based learning from the age of 15. These sequences are described as Initial Qualification Pathways, and their components as Initial Qualifications (IQs). A small proportion of these IQs (nice to give this abbreviation a different meaning!) incorporate work-based learning. IQ pathways may influence, sometimes only by omission, or almost determine occupational choice. Even when their direct influence is weak, the status of the last IQ will largely determine the level at which a learner enters the labour market.

A high proportion of learners follow IQ pathways comprising only general qualifications[1] (those not normally described as professional or vocational). Others follow pathways that incorporate varying proportions of work-related learning (as in GNVQs and LLBs) and/or work-based learning (as in NVQs, PGCEs and Diplomas in Nursing). In all cases some further learning is expected on entry to employment. The differences lie a) in how much work-based learning has already occurred during the IQ pathway, and b) in what aspects of their first job the new employees are deemed to be already competent. One major issue is the extent to which potentially transferable knowledge and skills acquired from academic learning, work-related learning or work-based learning in other contexts are considered to provide a good foundation for learning the new job; and the amount of work-based learning anticipated as necessary for acquiring job competence. Another issue is the perceived role of IQs in providing a knowledge/skill resource for work beyond the first three years. Beliefs about the breadth, depth and transferability of knowledge and skills play an important role in this debate, but the evidence to back them up is often scant, anecdotal and locally situated.

Post-initial or Mid-career Qualifications (MCQs) can be usefully divided between those with a specific upgrading function and those concerned with continuing work-related or work-based learning, though the distinction between them is not always clear. Upgrading qualifications include:

- those specifically required for employment at a higher level, eg in order to become a headteacher, a teacher of nurses or a research-active university lecturer;
- those commonly regarded as conferring a competitive advantage, eg a mature student getting a first degree; or
- those for whom a qualification is regarded as important for consolidating or developing competence in the job to which people have just been promoted, eg an accredited course for senior managers.

Qualifications associated with continuing learning are likely to involve:

- maintaining one's expertise through updating;
- expanding one's capability in one's current job role;
- extending one's competence through multi-skilling; or
- taking up a more specialist role which does not involve upgrading.

In so far as these qualifications may also lead to promotion, this is more likely to be as a result of improved job performance or general capability, ie an outcome of the qualification rather than its purpose.

The same qualification could be an IQ for one learner and an MCQ for another, though not necessarily taught to mixed groups. Even when taught to mixed groups, the participants may not learn the same things from it; and if it is work-related, we can be quite sure that the relationship between the qualification and work-related learning will be very different for initial and mid-career learners.

What do qualifications mean to individuals and employers?

Qualifications are frequently perceived by individuals as indicators of achievement. This may be viewed in personal terms as an indication of capability, ie external evidence of one's knowledge, skills and qualities, or in employment terms as an indication of competence, ie confirmation that one's performance meets external expectations for a particular job or occupation (Eraut, 1998). However, detailed records of capability and even sometimes of occupational competence may not be available to candidates in a form that could be considered useful feedback. Often, the only available information available is a grade that indicates performance relative to other candidates without describing what forms of performance evidence have been used. The significance of the result then ceases to be the nature of one's achievement and becomes an indicator of one's competitive advantage in the job market.

Grades can also be a critical factor in accessing certain qualification pathways, particularly undergraduate and postgraduate courses that have high status or are in high demand. This competitive aspect of qualifications often has a significant impact on a person's confidence, self-esteem or self-efficacy as a learner in both education and workplace settings. If feedback from the formal assessment required for most qualifications is perceived as primarily focused on one's weaknesses, it will reduce self-confidence and self-efficacy in the workplace and lower one's disposition to take up challenging learning opportunities (Bandura, 1995). Moreover, a continuing emphasis on ranking or grading rather than on achievement affects how people perceive their own performance by increasing the chance of their attributing good and bad performances to unchangeable aptitudes, rather than to perseverance and personal skill and effort. Only in the latter case will improving one's performance be perceived as an achievable goal. Confidence in developing one's own capability is more likely to be achieved by a progression model which records changes over varying periods of time along several dimensions than by the one-off partial assessment of performance required for the award of a qualification.

Another side effect of ranking and competition is to emphasize individual learning rather than group learning and to reduce people's dispositions to cooperate or work in teams. But this may not affect other aspects of occupational socialization such as the acquisition of a group identity.

MCQs are less likely to be viewed as providing occupational socialization, but have an important role in developing social networks that provide continuing resources for learning. Sharing experience with other participants is often extremely important, and may lead to increasing appreciation of other perspectives and a greater desire to consult and cooperate. Sometimes both on-course groupwork and off-course consultations with work colleagues are required activities. Though distinctions are sometimes awarded, the competitive aspect is usually far weaker than the cooperative.

To some extent the meanings accorded to IQs by employers are similar to those for individuals. This is scarcely surprising since employers' attitudes are a major influence on those of potential employees. Thus employers may use qualifications as general indicators of personal capability and/or personal competence, often giving as much attention to where they were acquired as to their detailed content. Qualifications, and grades within qualifications, may also be treated as indicators of personal qualities, possibly a wider range than those considered by individuals including, for example, dispositions like perseverance and willingness to learn as well as abilities. Qualifications are particularly useful to employers in screening large numbers of applicants quickly and cheaply, even when they have some misgivings about their validity for selection purposes; and this often gives them priority over more relevant, but unaccredited, knowledge acquired through work-based learning. They can also be regarded as a form of quality assurance that is easily defended; and in some occupations they are required by law. There is also a perspective that sees the recruitment of staff with recent qualifications in technical areas as knowledge assets for the organization.

Of particular interest to our central theme are employers' policies and practices for identifying and responding to the learning needs of their new recruits. In particular, have they tried to assess or describe the kinds of knowledge and skill that need to be developed through on-the-job learning? Have they developed any progression models for the early period of full-time employment? Have they considered, valued and tried to facilitate the sharing of the accumulated experience of workers who have supported the learning of new recruits, informally as well as formally? Have they considered how the knowledge and skill resources recruits bring with them may be made useful and further developed by workplace learning rather than ignored, dismissed as irrelevant and left to atrophy? The evidence suggests that only a minority of employers has addressed these issues, some knowingly and some through the good sense and concern of experienced workers whose contribution remains unrecognized. What some regard simply as a mismatch between qualifications and first day competence in a new job, might often be more appropriately described as negligence, a failure to provide the workplace learning opportunities and support to make good use of entry qualifications. We will discuss differences in the qualifications themselves later but here it is important to stress the improbability of any qualifications matching a diverse range of workplaces. Even work-based qualification can only provide competence in contexts similar to those where on-the-job learning occurred during the qualification process.

With MCQs, learners usually have a greater sense of agency, and opportunities to develop and use the qualifications for the employers' benefit are likely to be both more immediate and more significant. But employer assent or even sponsorship for an employee's MCQ is no guarantee of support for learning during or after a period of qualification-related learning. The relevant parts of the organization may not be receptive to new ideas, they may not recognize that discussion and consultation may be essential for transforming such ideas into useful applications. Perhaps the most important factor of all is that local micro-politics may be disturbed by a fairly rapid increase in one worker's capability, and those feeling threatened may respond defensively. The common factor in employers' use of both IQs and MCQs is their recognition of and approach to the management of learning, both on and off the job.

The value of a qualification to learners has two distinct dimensions: whether the qualification increases their chances of getting a job/promotion, ie its selection value; and whether it contributes to the quality of their performance on the job, ie its use value.[2] These two values reinforce one another in good status MCQs which are job-related and supported by employers; and also in concurrent professional qualifications, in which work-based learning is reflected upon and theorized in education settings and theory–practice links are given priority attention. However, they come into conflict when general qualifications are accorded higher status than work-related qualifications and play a major role in selection for well-paid jobs. In Britain, general degrees get priority in the job market, many professional degrees include only small amounts of work-based learning, and admission to all degree courses is primarily by the A-level route. So students are best advised to remain on an appropriate general academic pathway until they gain university entry. Such a system tends to be self-perpetuating because employers select what they believe to be the best talents using general qualifications and personal qualities as their main criteria, and with scant regard for the use value of the courses.

The effect at sixth form level is to encourage A-levels as the first choice, with advanced vocational qualifications as a second choice for those in doubt about their motivation towards A-level work or their chances of success. Initially, at least a half of those students taking what are now called vocational A-levels are still seeking progression to higher education (Wolf, 1995). Below that level the selection value of vocational qualifications is low, with employers focusing mainly on GCSEs and basic skills. Even the use value of general vocational qualifications at sixth form level can be questioned, because there is as yet little evidence that these work-related qualifications reduce the amount of early learning in the first job, even though they make students better informed about the role and nature of the sector. With work-based qualifications, the value question is entirely different. The learning is normally perceived as useful: the issue is whether incorporating such work-based learning into a qualification creates added value for either learners or their employers.

Types of interaction between qualifications and work-based learning

Four types of interaction can be discerned between qualifications and work-based learning:

1. transfer of knowledge gained from qualifications;
2. accreditation of work-based learning;
3. mutual enhancement through integrated learning;
4. competition for attention and commitment.

The transfer relationship is based on the argument that although qualifications provide varying amounts of potentially relevant knowledge, most of it does not become usable at work without further learning in the workplace itself. The traditional conception of knowledge transfer has been to view it as an event that did or did not occur. The knowledge was or was not transferable; or the knower did or did not possess the requisite 'transfer skills'. This view was sustained by the usually tacit and often lengthy nature of the transfer process, but is contradicted by recent research evidence and greater awareness of the contextually situated nature of usable knowledge. Transfer is now conceived as a learning process which requires understanding of the new context; recognizing what prior knowledge is relevant to the current situation; transforming that prior knowledge so that it fits the situation; then integrating the new assembly of knowledge and skills to create the required new situational understanding and responsive action. Depending on the novelty of the new situation and the learner's prior awareness of what might be needed, the transfer process may be quite short or very long. The main factors prolonging or even preventing transfer are likely to be developing sufficient understanding of the context, the complexity of the knowledge transformation process, and the lack of awareness that substantial further learning may be needed to make relevant prior knowledge usable.

Failure to understand the need for further learning is extremely common, and affects both employers and the learners themselves. The prevailing assumption is that knowledge that cannot be very quickly made usable is irrelevant. There are frequent references to a theory–practice group but few serious attempts to bridge it. Even prior knowledge acquired in another work context may require transformation before it can be resituated. Learning to use prior knowledge is rarely identified as a learning need in either education or employment settings, so the learners themselves often fail to appreciate their knowledge resources or what is involved in learning to use them. The resultant deprecation of what new recruits can offer may lower their self-confidence and sense of efficacy and reduce their motivation towards more complex forms of workplace learning, particularly those requiring them to take the initiative. Thus researching these aspects of workplace learning usually uncovers a sorry story of missed opportunities.

Bennett *et al*'s (2000) analysis of the transition from higher education to employment attributes this problem to the total absence from both higher education and employment contexts of any coherent theory of learning. The only evidence-based account of how higher education can prepare students for employment through a combination of general education, work-related and work-based components designed around such a coherent theory of learning is Mentkowski *et al* (2000). This evaluation of curriculum change at Alverno College over a 25-year period also includes a five-year follow-up study of its alumnae and their performance at work.

Accreditation of work-based learning appears at first sight to be the inverse of knowledge transfer from education settings to work settings, and like transfer the process is more complex than appears at first sight. In this case the complexity is introduced by the need for some formal and externally verifiable assessment. Unlike the transfer process, however, the learning benefits of formal assessment are more contentious. So also is the value of turning already recognized workplace competence into a qualification or part of a qualification. When assessment is based on naturally occurring workplace performance and the evidence is readily available, there is little additional cost to the learner. When it entails a formal examination it has become an assessment of something other than workplace learning, which is then explicitly or implicitly deemed less valuable for not being qualification-worthy in its own right. In between come a series of work-based projects that may be useful in the workplace but might not have been undertaken in the normal course of events. Their main benefit is the triggering of further learning that is clearly work-related and has value in the workplace as well as at the Examining Board.

Another assessment mode that retains workplace authenticity is the portfolio. This can also trigger further learning when it makes workplace knowledge more explicit and hence more available for self-evaluation as well as evaluation by others. In the right context it may also introduce a valuable reflective dimension and provide formative as well as summative evaluation for the learner. The problem comes when the portfolio becomes too large, stresses quantity rather than quality, and takes a great deal of time to complete, not all of which can be offset against further learning.

Another question to be asked is whether gaining a qualification adds value to a good workplace performance record and an employer's reference. The most commonly cited position is that a qualification adds value for the employees, but does not add net value for employers, for whom any learning gain is countered by a perceived higher risk of employees seeking employment elsewhere. Hence employers seeking to retain their employees may oppose their acquisition of work-based qualifications. However, the contention that qualifications make a person more marketable than a good employment record alone may not always be true, especially when an employer has a good reputation. In some sectors, such as health care, employers may find that the greater danger lies in poor recruitment when they fail to support their employees getting further qualifications. Others believe that getting workplace learning accredited improves their workers' self-confidence and morale, and hence their performance, the workplace climate, and ultimately the retention rate. But even this will fail to happen if the accreditation process is perceived as a long, bureaucratic hassle that entails very little new learning of any value. In conclusion, we can argue that accreditation will provide an incentive to the learner when it confers a qualification with significant selection or promotion value, but that it will only add use value when the assessment process entails significant further learning and a tolerable amount of cost and effort.

It is important to distinguish between 1) the accreditation of learning which has already taken place, in order to gain status or selection value from its external recognition, and 2) further learning in the workplace stimulated by the target or, as some employers call it, the reward of a qualification. In practice, it is common to find the assessment process covering a mixture of previous and newly acquired competence. A recent evaluation of level 5 NVQs in management (Eraut and Steadman, 1998) asked qualifiers to estimate what proportion of the time spent in getting their NVQ had gone on each of four types of activity:

1. collecting documents that already existed;
2. generating new evidence of competence they already had;
3. working in new areas of their job, or at a greater depth, in order to develop new competence;
4. specific learning tasks to increase their knowledge and understanding in relevant areas.

Thirty-two per cent of these respondents reported giving only 0 to 15 per cent of their NVQ time to developing new competence, ie on activities of types 3 and 4. A further 26 per cent of respondents reported giving 16 to 25 per cent of their NVQ time to new areas of competence, leaving only 42 per cent of candidates devoting more than a quarter of their time to developing new competence, rather than confirming previous competence through activities of types 1 and 2.

We also found a strong positive correlation between the percentage of time spent developing new competence and two key outcomes: working for the qualification both *helped job performance* and *led to changes in practice*. To our surprise, the average completion time was no greater for those candidates who followed a more developmental and challenging route. The implication is that accreditation of prior learning is so time-consuming that one might just as well take on new and interesting projects to demonstrate one's competence and forget about the tedious process of collecting evidence of past achievement. Some providers were able to guide candidates along more developmental pathways towards learning outcomes that were holistic rather than fragmented, and therefore more authentic and beneficial to performance at work. Others were not. Few candidates were aware of the implications of following an accreditation rather than a developmental pathway to the same qualifications, or even that there was a choice to be made.

The ideal type of interaction is characterized by the mutual enhancement of work-based learning and other qualification-oriented learning through integration at the point of use, ie when planning, conducting, managing or evaluating work-based activities, processes and/or outcomes. It could be described as using the more formal knowledge gained in working for a qualification to enhance the quality of ongoing informal learning in the workplace, while at the same time using the experience to modify that formal knowledge or make it more usable in yet other workplace situations. This involves thinking more deeply, critically and systematically about workplace practices and experiences with guidance from concepts and ideas encountered in educational/training contexts. While pursued to some extent in initial qualifications, this ideal type is more often associated with MCQs, when learners have had significantly more work experience and are less concerned with gaining basic competence than with improving their own practice and that of their work-group.

Our own research on mid-career learning in the workplace (Eraut *et al,* 1998) showed that employment-based short courses, which were conducted off the job but on employer premises or employer-hired premises, had relatively little impact on the workplace unless they were based on learners' current needs and concerns and delivered 'just in time'. Otherwise they failed to connect with the workplace agenda. Higher education-based MCQs involving work-based projects and action research had more impact because they were more learner-focused, more flexible and less ephemeral. What is often perceived as the more expensive qualification option (in terms of learner time, not direct cost) may give better value for money, especially in the long term.

The fourth type of interaction occurs when learning associated with qualifications competes for the learner's time and attention with other learning in the workplace. This can have negative effects a) when aspects of the qualification have little or no relevance to the workplace (worse still if they also fail to improve the learner's career prospects) or b) when learners' attempts to pursue valued qualifications are thwarted by being transferred to another job, or an overdose of organizational change. Some of the effects can be less obvious. For example when a qualification relates to and makes demands on some aspects of the job but not on others, it could result in those learning needs in the qualification limelight receiving more attention than others, in unbalanced personal development or even in some clients being given higher priority than others. More subtle still, especially when qualifications claim to be performance-based, is the implicit legitimization of certain kinds of workplace knowledge through explicit specification and accreditation, while other kinds of knowledge are devalued through exclusion from counting towards an award. This exacerbates a common tendency to interpret performance in terms of explicit actions alone, thus ignoring the understandings and reasoning that led to the choice of those actions. While 'soft skills' are now being accorded similar status to 'hard skills', 'soft knowledge', which is personal and tacit, is rarely given the recognition accorded to 'hard knowledge', which is codified and publishable. Yet work-based learning involves the acquisition of a considerable amount of tacit knowledge and good performance in the workplace relies on it. Such knowledge cannot easily be made explicit (as suggested by Nonaka and Takeuchi (1995) and many other writers) but some of it can be shared through engagement in joint activities, and most of it can be brought under the critical control of the knower, at least at the level of awareness (Eraut, 2000).

Characteristics of the qualifications themselves

Hitherto our discussion of qualifications has focused on their use for selection and/or developing knowledge/skills for performance at work, and also on the need for further learning in the workplace to capitalize on the potential of the knowledge base. Let us now consider what characteristics of qualifications make them more or less useful in the workplace, being careful to distinguish rhetorical claims from evidence and to include informal learning from qualification-related activities as well as that formally assessed.

General qualifications are usually justified in terms of developing and extending the mind and developing transferable cognitive and communication skills. But how general are they, and what attention do they give to the transfer of their intellectual assets? The dominant conception of a general qualification derives from a 19th century notion of 'liberal education', which an anthropologist would describe as highly specialized, as well as being taught within educational institutions separated from other social contexts. The shape of the pre-16 curriculum has remained strongly academic since 1902. Post-16 diversity has greatly increased but the highest status is still awarded to IQ pathways leading to a largely discipline-based honours degree. These 'general' education pathways are not based on any concept of the 'general good' or the 'generally useful'. Indeed knowledge and skills that might be described as important for future roles in society as a member of a family and local community, as a citizen and as a worker are but thinly represented in most post-16 qualifications. Perhaps most important for later work-based learning is the absence from most IQ pathways of opportunities to learn in a wide range of groups and contexts rather than only in academic settings (Eraut, 1997).

Some skills claimed as key outcomes of general education pathways – critical and reflective ability, flexibility, self-management and initiative – are only significantly developed by a minority of students. Others, such as problem-solving and communication skills, are proclaimed as transferable on the basis of very little evidence. When the same words are used to describe very different phenomena, the level of transfer is likely to be low because contextual factors are always very important. Indeed, it could be argued that although people learn informally in many contexts, the privileging by most IQ pathways of knowledge acquired in formal education contexts inhibits proper reflection upon, criticism and further development of informally acquired knowledge. Not only is informal learning undervalued, but its very existence is denied.

Most work-related qualifications or components also suffer from an almost total reliance on formal education settings and the initial exclusion of non-formal learning. Even training schemes for professions that make considerable use of informal learning about their clients and problematic situations give it scant attention. The work-relatedness of some supposedly work-related components can also be very limited. The occasional example may be given but little explanation of when and why some particular aspect of knowledge is used. Both that and the question of how it is used, in what form and in conjunction with what other knowledge, is assumed to be addressed later, sometimes much later, by work-based learning. Such lack of connection often affects learners' motivation. Moreover, as described in an earlier section, the need to learn how to use such knowledge on the job is rarely addressed and often unrecognized. This problem often persists when work-related and work-based components co-exist within the same qualification but little time is given to their linkage. Learning more theoretical knowledge is preferred to learning to use what has already been taught, and linkage is always someone else's responsibility.

These issues were studied in detail by Eraut *et al*'s (1995) research on learning to use scientific knowledge in pre-registration programmes in nursing and midwifery. This project comprised two components: how scientific (and social science) knowledge was used by experienced practitioners of high reputation; and how the use of such knowledge was mediated and acquired during initial training. Both components focused on six important but contrasting topics in adult nursing, mental health nursing and midwifery. Simple application of scientific knowledge without significant transformation to fit the context was relatively rare. For experienced practitioners, scientific knowledge was most frequently found embedded in decisions primed by recognizing the nature of the situation being encountered, and in action sequences following those decisions which were already familiar to them, if not routine. However, if the situation was unfamiliar or ill-defined, or monitoring indicated deviations from familiar or expected chains of events, consultation and/or problem solving took place in which more explicit use of scientific knowledge often featured strongly. This predominance of embedded theory made its use opaque to novices, even when they had been taught the relevant theory in an educational setting, and the most overt problem solving was often too complex for novices to grasp at that stage of their development. Hence, unless special effort was made to deconstruct daily practice and reveal the embedded use of theory (or in some cases the negative consequences of failing to use theory) novices were unable to access knowledge about how to use scientific knowledge.

We also found that, with one notable exception, little time was given in educational settings to discussing the why, when and how of knowledge use. The exception was a midwifery course located in a hospital-based 'academic centre'. The features that made mediation of knowledge use possible in this particular situation were:

- a more manageable amount of scientific knowledge;
- space on the timetable for considerable discussion of students' experiences in both education and practice settings;
- an appropriate size of group for such discussions;
- the flexibility to address the emerging learning concerns of students 'just in time';
- education staff able to take groups into clinical settings when they thought it would facilitate their learning;
- education staff maintaining their registered status through continuing to practise.

Even in this case, however, there was little mediation of theory by practitioners to students on placements, even by those designated as mentors. Almost all the mediation came from education staff. No such mediation occurred in the other midwifery course we studied, which lacked most of the features listed above. However, Hall (2001) found considerable mediation by education staff on a course that included regular reflection days in education settings.

Parboteah (2001) embarked on an action research project to use the knowledge maps developed by Eraut et al (1995) as mediating devices for facilitating student nurses' learning about theory–practice links. These maps were simple two-dimensional matrices, one for each topic, in which one axis listed sub-topics from the theory syllabus while the other presented nursing activities. The use of theory from a particular sub-topic was noted for those activities in which it occurred.[3] Parboteah found that, even when two or three matrices were discussed at some length in education settings, the information was not subsequently used in practice settings. Nor did introducing the matrices to mentors result in any increased attention to theory–practice links. The lecturers then entered the practice context and mediated the use of knowledge maps by individual students through discussing knowledge use as and when it occurred, or failed to occur. This proved very effective in getting students to use the maps as starter-guides and some students also began to adopt a more reflective and critical approach to their practice in general. In effect the lecturers were modelling not just the use of particular maps but a general approach to practice, and the students were beginning to appreciate it after a relatively short intervention.

The conclusion to be drawn from this research is that for qualifications in which there is significant theoretical content, the capability of using the theory in practice situations can only be finally developed in practice settings. Either this is done by education staff sufficiently engaged in practice to be able to teach in practice settings, or it is done by workplace mentors or supervisors. In both cases those supporting the learner will need:

- to be conversant with the theoretical explanations for even the most routinized aspects of their practice – this is unlikely unless they have been involved in periodic evaluation of that practice;
- the time and opportunity to discuss relevant scientific knowledge and research evidence with novices;
- to see such discussions as part of their role and be disposed to carry it out – this may depend on their work priorities and how they themselves are managed.

In many occupations these conditions are rarely found.

There are, of course, notable exceptions to these criticisms of work-related qualifications and components: but these are likely to remain a minority practice until the culture of higher education changes and parallel, complementary changes occur in employers' understanding and valuation of work-based learning. Moreover, there is now an equal danger of important work-related knowledge being squeezed out of professional and vocational qualifications by over-restrictive specifications of competence fuelled by a political culture that increasingly looks for quick-fix solutions. Nowhere is this more evident than in the growing desire for contextually insensitive modes of external assessment that reassert the hegemony of formal workplace knowledge in the name of rigour. For authentic, work-based learning the influence of many assessment regimes might be better described as 'rigor mortis'.

In MCQs, greater attention is given to learners' prior and concurrent experience. However, its effect remains very dependent on the design and implementation of teaching and learning activities and modes of assessment.

The majority of MCQs are based in higher or further education, with work-based learning being involved in a number of ways. These include:

- reflective discussions off the job of work-based problems and situations;
- assignments that require the collection of information in the work context and/or the adoption of a critical and theoretical, as well as practical perspective;
- work-based projects including case study, design, evaluation or action research;
- visits or placements in other work contexts.

The impact on work-based learning of taking a given qualification can also vary considerably, according to the learning orientation of the candidate (Webber, 2001) and the learning climate of their workplace (Eraut *et al*, 1998). Ongoing discussion about work experience, however, does not necessarily involve any attention to how it was acquired. Some attention is given to work-based learning through reflective practice, though even this can easily become over-formalized and stereotyped. Direct attention to on-the-job learning, especially implicit learning, is still very rare.

There is a great deal of innovation in qualifications concerned with continuing learning in the workplace, possibly less when upgrading is the prime purpose of an MCQ. The main constraints on them having a positive effect on work-based learning are recruiting the right teachers and financial viability. The supply of appropriate teachers is often limited by the drop in pay suffered by experienced workers who transfer into 'education jobs', and then retaining their teaching role when career pathways give greater rewards to management or research. The financial problems derive from the need for relatively small learning groups in courses of this kind.

Notes

1. General qualifications are taken to include most science qualifications but exclude engineering.
2. I owe this distinction to Hodgson *et al* (2001), but prefer the term 'selection value' to their term 'exchange value'.
3. Additional information on the mode of use was found to be relevant to teachers but a complexity too far for students.

References

Bandura, A (1995) *Self-efficacy in Changing Societies*, Cambridge University Press, Cambridge

Bennett, N, Dunne, E and Carre, C (2000) *Skills Development in Higher Education and Employment*, SRHE and Open University Press, Buckingham

Eraut, M (1997) Curriculum frameworks and assumptions in 14–19 education, *Research in Post-Compulsory Education*, **2** (3), pp 281–97

Eraut, M (1998) Concepts of competence, *Journal of Interprofessional Care*, **12** (2), pp 127–39

Eraut, M (2000) Non-formal learning and tacit knowledge in professional work, *British Journal of Educational Psychology*, **70,** pp 113–36

Eraut, M and Steadman, S (1998) *Evaluation of Level 5 Management S/NVQs*, Research Report 7, University of Sussex Institute of Education

Eraut, M, Alderton, J, Boylan, A and Wraight, A (1995) *Learning to Use Scientific Knowledge in Education and Practice Settings,* English National Board for Nursing, Midwifery and Health Visiting, London

Eraut, M, Alderton, J, Cole, G and Senker, P (1998) *Development of Knowledge and Skills in Employment,* Research Report 5, University of Sussex Institute of Education

Hall, V (2001) 'Wise Women': students' use of experience in developing midwifery knowledge. DPhil thesis, University of Sussex

Hodgson, A, Spours, K and Savory, C (2001) *Improving the 'Use' and 'Exchange' Value of Key Skills*, Broadening the Advanced Level Curriculum, Institute of Education/ Nuffield Foundation Research Report 4, ULIE

Mentkowski, M and associates (2000) *Learning that Lasts: Integrating learning, development and performance in college and beyond*, Jossey-Bass, San Francisco, CA

Nonaka, I and Takeuchi, H (1995) *The Knowledge Creating Company,* Oxford University Press, Oxford

Parboteah, S (2001) The effect of using knowledge maps as a mediating artefact in pre-registration nurse education. DPhil thesis, University of Sussex

Webber, T E (2001) An investigation of management learning during mid-career Masters degree courses which use action strategies. DPhil thesis, University of Sussex

Wolf, A (1995) *Competence-based Assessment*, Open University Press, Buckingham

Chapter 5

The challenges of 'making learning visible': problems and issues in recognizing tacit skills and key competences

Karen Evans

The part played by tacit skills and knowledge in work performance is well recognized but not well understood. These implicit or hidden dimensions of knowledge and skill are key elements of 'mastery', which experienced workers draw upon in everyday activities and continuously expand in tackling new or unexpected situations. This chapter argues that it is important to understand better how individuals harness and use tacit forms of key competences as they move between roles and settings. What part does the recognition of tacit forms of key competences play in the development of occupational and learning biographies? Does the recognition of tacit forms of key competences increase or decrease inequalities? What are the implications when considered in the contexts of 'technocratic' and 'democratic' versions of the learning society?

A recent release on the website of the European Centre for the Development of Vocational Training (CEDEFOP) pronounced that:

> Workers soon demand pay for what they have learned, no matter where they have learned it. . . learning that takes place away from the classroom, during leisure time, in the family or at work, is increasingly seen as a resource that needs to be more systematically used. (CEDEFOP, 2001)

The call for wider recognition of skills gained through non-formal learning is only one facet of a debate centred on the nature of the so-called

'knowledge-based economy' and the ways in which the 'knowledge' concerned is codified and used. The new debate has been fuelled by economists
and labour market specialists, creating new possibilities for interdisciplinary
endeavour with learning professionals and educational/social researchers in
trying to understand better what it is that actually constitutes the 'knowledge
base' of the economy and the place of non-formal learning in this scenario.
Cowan *et al* (2000) have identified the distinction between codified and tacit
knowledge as being in need of redefinition in the knowledge-based economy.
They argue that it is a mistake to view any knowledge or skill as inherently
tacit – nearly all knowledge, they say, is codifiable. From their economists'
point of view the only real issue is whether the benefits of doing so outweigh
the costs. Furthermore, they have pointed out that any acceptance of the
view that knowledge can be inherently tacit and important undermines the
basis for standard micro-economic theory and any attempts to model human
behaviour.

Johnson and Lundvall (2001) take issue with them as fellow economists,
showing how the concept of the 'knowledge-based economy' is poorly
understood and raising fundamental issues which lie behind the drive to
codify previously uncodified knowledge and skill for 'systematic use': how
does 'codification' actually take place in relation to different types of
knowledge? What are the driving forces that lie behind efforts to codify?
What are the consequences of codification of different kinds of knowledge
for economic development and for the distribution of wealth?

In this chapter I argue that these questions are centrally important in
considering questions of inequalities in skill recognition and access to learning
at, for and through the workplace. This is not an 'academic' discussion. The
European proposals for Personal Skills Cards place this debate close to the
heart of the political and economic agenda in the expanding European
Union. For the purposes of the discussion which follows, non-formal learning
embraces unplanned learning in work situations and in domains of activity
outside the formal economy, but may also include planned and explicit
approaches to learning carried out in any of those environments which lie
outside the scope of the formal education systems. It is taken that such non-
formal learning has strong tacit dimensions. While explicit knowledge is easily
codified and conveyed to others, tacit knowledge is experiential, subjective
and personal, and substantially more difficult to convey. There are numerous
perspectives on tacit skills, knowledge and learning, summarized in Figure
5.1.

Most of these perspectives accept the invisible nature of the 'tacit'. The
increasing interest in its codification stems at least in part from a growing
recognition that the tacit dimensions of knowledge and skill are very

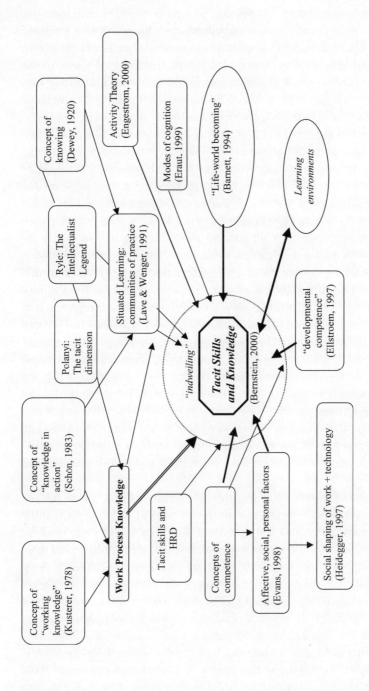

Adapted from: Tacit-Key Project UK
Director: Karen Evans; Researcher: Bettina Hoffmann

Figure 5.1 *Concepts and relationships: tacit skills, knowledge and learning*

important in the performance of individuals, organizations, networks and possibly whole communities. Knowledge is taken in its widest definition (see Chapter 1) as incorporating, at an individual level, knowing why, knowing that, knowing how and knowing who. At the organizational level, these four types of knowledge are found in shared information, shared views of the world, shared practices and shared networks. At the societal level we may talk about knowledge that is stored as personal knowledge, knowledge embedded in culture, knowledge stored in institutions and in networks.

I argue that it is more helpful to regard all knowledge as having both tacit and explicit dimensions. When we can facilitate the communication of some of the tacit dimensions, these become explicit and therefore codifiable. Why should we want to do this? This may be for the purpose of teaching someone else to do it (if we are a teacher or trainer), or communicating to others that we have skills and competences appropriate to a task, role or occupation (if we are job applicants), or identifying that a person or group has the capabilities we need for a job to be done (if we are employers or project leaders). In other words, the reasons for codification largely revolve around 'transfer'. It can be argued that, for those competences and forms of knowledge that have a high tacit dimension, transfer has to involve high levels of social interaction, demonstration and 'showing how' – manuals and written accounts are of little help. In the case of the job applicant, jobs that require a high level of skills that are not easily codified will often require a demonstration of skills and competence. In the case of a new entrant to a job and workplace, know-how will involve both skills acquired previously and the underpinning knowledge that allows these skills to be operationalized in a new environment. Beyond this a period of interaction within the social and occupational practices of the workplace will be needed for the tacit dimensions of know-how to be adjusted to the culture and environment of the new setting.

It was noted in Chapter 1 that the idea of individuals being able to transfer skills and competences between jobs in the interests of 'flexibility' fitted the 'modernization' and deregulation agendas of the 1980s and 1990s in the UK, and key competences came to the fore as an instrument of 'lifelong learning' policy. Treating these as completely codifiable leads to the claims made in the CEDEFOP statement at the beginning of this chapter. If we can codify and compare key competences against 'objective' criteria, some of the assumptions commonly held about skill levels of different occupations might be challenged. But research on 'work process knowledge' such as Boreham's (2000) finds that these skills derive much of their meaning from the context in which they are used. I argue that it may be more helpful to regard these skills as partly structural and partly embedded in context, recognizing that people do take things with them into new jobs and occupations, but not in simple ways. This is one of the gaps in our knowledge.

Much of the work on key competences has focused on extracting these from tasks and not in looking at the dynamics of the ways in which people carry knowledge and learning into new environments. The importance of this is now being recognized in the economic domain as well as in VET research and practice, with Johnson and Lundvall's latest paper calling for 'a major interdisciplinary effort' (2001). We know that the idea of simple skill transfer from one setting to another is very problematic – the fact that we can use common language to describe a skill group does not mean it is transferable intact. What we need to understand better is the *processes* by which skills are 'transformed' from one setting into another. Naïve mappings of key skills from one environment into another are not a basis for occupational mobility. Even 'near' transfer into related activities is far from simple, leading to the recognition by activity theorists such as Engestrom (2000) that it is whole activity systems that count. For people with interrupted occupational biographies, this presents particular problems, especially when they have spent extended periods away from the workplace. This fits with clear evidence that people with extended breaks from the workplace have no belief or confidence in their previous skills. Their feeling of being completely de-skilled can be seen as a lived reality, not as a lack of the personal attribute called 'confidence'.

The discussion which follows considers the origins of 'key competences' and formulations which have developed heuristically through micro-level research on the realities of how women and men recognize, use and develop their skills and the possibilities and contradictions they encounter in their occupational and learning biographies.[1] The final sections consider whether the European proposals for codification and communication of know-how via Personal Skills Cards (or other means) would decrease inequalities or increase them, and asks what the place of non-formal learning might be in the alternative scenarios for lifelong learning articulated by Coffield (2000a): the technocratic or democratic visions of a 'learning society'.

'Key competences' as carriers of tacit and explicit dimensions of knowledge and skill

Research by Billett reported in Gerber and Lankshear (2000) showed how many of the Australian 'Mayer' key competences were performed 'most of the time' by workers of different grades.

According to Billett's study, just over a half of workers graded as unskilled spent most of their time collecting, analysing and organizing information, and more than four-fifths of them spent their time working with others and in teams. While a similar proportion spent most of their time on routine tasks, one-fifth spent most of their time dealing with novel situations while two-fifths were involved in some kind of problem solving for most of their time (Billett, 2000). Dealing with novel situations and using technology were main features of the work of comparable proportions of workers in each 'official' skill banding, from unskilled to professional. Planning and problem solving discriminated most between the groups, with professional workers much more likely to be engaged in these types of activities 'most of the time'. While the nature of the skill being investigated in Billett's research is problematic, the findings are useful in highlighting the skill content of jobs cast as unskilled, a finding which is consistent with Rainbird's 'Future of work' research, which led the team to replace the term 'low-skilled' with 'low-graded' work.

Key competences have gained in importance in all EU member states over the past decade. Formulations of key competences have come from different origins and are controversial in different ways. While the ideas behind key competences in the wider European understandings contain rather broad conceptions of skills and competences, competences in the UK have to be understood comparatively in a rather narrow sense. In the European research a more holistic approach to competence was needed which would refer not only to occupational needs but also to needs of the individuals with respect to enabling them to manage their personal biography as a whole. A new learning culture also had to be envisaged which would refer to competences which are generative of future individual and group performance rather than based on reductions of present individual work activities.

While there are official formulations of key competences in most countries, these are in very different stages of development and are controversial within their respective national contexts. For example, the focus in Germany on key competences came initially from labour market perspectives on the changing nature of work, and subsequently started to permeate discourses about the development of VET systems and practices in the search for ways to meet the requirements of enterprises for new qualifications in the workforce. Key competences are controversial in Germany because of fears that they undermine the 'Beruf' principle and occupational structures that underpin the German systems. In comparing competences and qualifications within Europe, different meanings of the term 'qualification' have to be understood. This is associated with certification in UK but is more widely understood in continental Europe as the whole set of attributes required for performance of an occupation.

The key competences debate in the UK can be contrasted with that in continental Europe in general and the specific features of the German debate. The origins in the UK dated from the 1980s, where 'core skills' were explored as means of developing wider options for young people in the labour market, in response to high youth unemployment: how to prepare school leavers for jobs when the youth labour market had dried up. 'A Basis for Choice' (FEU, 1979) was an important report in the early 1980s. This was then overtaken by an attempt to redefine the entire occupational field in terms of occupational competences, with the development of new formulations of core skills based on analysis of tasks common to jobs. These formulations, evaluated by Evans et al (1986) as part of a national development programme, were also controversial in many ways. Sociologically, their social control functions were identified and contested, while in the psychological domain they were seen as representing outdated behaviourism.

In the Southern countries of Europe, key competences have entered the policy development arena more recently. In Portugal, the approach to key competences has been based on critical evaluation of European and Canadian approaches, leading to a drive for a lifelong system based on validation of formal and non-formal learning. In Greece, the traditionally weak links between education and the labour market have meant that ideas about key competences and transfer of skills have gained attention only very recently. It may be that the importance of the informal and collective networks in facilitating work entry and occupational mobility in the Southern countries means that the instrumental individual formulations of key competences of the Northern European countries will never be as important for changing employment opportunities in the Southern countries, but the ideas of key competences are nevertheless developing more strongly now in these societies.

The UK formulations and use of key skills as a policy instrument have the longest history and some important 'lessons can be learnt from the problems encountered. There has been much resistance to 'official' versions of competence enshrined in VET policy in the UK, but competence is a value-laden word – in the worlds of policy and practice development it is difficult to say you are 'against' competence. The concept is also socially constructed, taking on different meanings in different contexts and is used to support particular ideological positions.

Norris (1991) distinguished between behaviourist, generic and cognitive constructs of competence. Behavioural interpretations of competence are performance related. That is, they equate competence with the ability to perform a range of tasks to predetermined standards. Such approaches to competence are criticized for their narrowness, for confusing competence with performance and for ignoring the underlying capacities needed for change. These can be considered minimal interpretations of the concept. They do not imply any need for critical, reflective abilities. They are typified in the UK in the approaches to occupational competence that have shaped much of the discourse about post-school education and training in the 1990s. It has been argued elsewhere that this minimalist interpretation of compet- ence serves the objectives of curriculum modernizers, who have put an emphasis on state intervention to achieve an enterprise economy through a free market where access to knowledge and skill is 'democratized'. The labour market has been redefined in terms of the rationale of competences, collected together as units, elements and range statements, the function being to 'measure the individual against the ideal worker which the skills matrix represents' (Norris, 1991: 230). The concept of competence thus becomes essentially technical, and omits the social meanings and social relations of work. The individualized, technical approach to competence 'de-skills indi- viduals in terms of competences acquired within the informal localized net- works of everyday life' (Giddens, 1991) and thus effectively disempowers them. In this sense it is best understood as part of the broader framework of regulation and control in modern societies. Others such as Issitt *et al* (1995) argue that approaches that equate competence with performance are essen- tially retrospective, reflecting and reinforcing the status quo and therefore reproducing structural inequalities. They have also been shown to be unwork- able for higher levels of professional training.

Generic and cognitive constructs of competence, by contrast, emphasize broad clusters of abilities that are conceptually linked. They involve an underlying generative capacity reflected in a general ability to coordinate resources necessary for successful adaptation (Norris, 1991). These may be seen as maximal interpretations. They imply the need for critical reflective learning and emphasize the development of self-efficacy and shared autonomy and attributes such as judgement. Reflective learning is considered essential if competence is to become future oriented, that is, able to develop the skills of the future (Brown *et al*, 1994; Wellington, 1987) rather than being tied to the performance of narrowly specified tasks.

In the international literature, the concept of capabilities has recently been elaborated in ways that further emphasize underlying abilities and attributes that are important to task performance. These formulations move beyond the surface features of common descriptors in task analysis, into a recognition of the importance of a degree of autonomy, emphasis on taking responsibility, being capable of undergoing and managing change in oneself and one's environment, having initiative and self-reliance. They tend to emphasize individual rather than collective capability, although the latest findings from Europe-wide research into aspects of work process knowledge by Boreham *et al* (2000) are challenging some of the more individualistic formulations and leading into a new generation of work on collective competence and collective intelligence (Brown and Lauder, 2001).

The current positions in partner countries (Germany, Portugal, Greece, the UK) were reviewed at the outset of our research into interrupted occupational and learning careers. None of the current formulations of key competences was found to be adequate for the experiences we were trying to understand. In the UK and German formulations, there is not sufficient attention to motivations, learning abilities nor the ability of people to manage their own biographies in line with personal interests and needs. The German 'action competence square' does not sufficiently recognize the non-formal dimensions of learning outside institutional frameworks in its 'Beruf'-centred training, and the English formulations are split between the general skills which now sit more easily in an educational paradigm and those embedded in work processes, in ways which have compromised their usefulness and have become conceptually confused (Unwin, 2001). In Portuguese models, the approaches to recognition of know-how are interesting and important, but not sufficiently advanced for our purposes here – their development in Portugal has centred to date on the traditional occupational areas.

The research needed to develop a model of key competences that was more future oriented and generative in terms of people's personal and professional projects, given our emphasis on interrupted occupational biographies and learning careers (allowing for a wide range of life experiences and value orientations). Since all possibilities could not be explored simultaneously, the model which came to be known as the 'Starfish' model (or 'l'etoile de mer') for ease of international communication was developed initially on the basis of existing knowledge in the partner countries, and developed heuristically in exploring the tacit dimensions of key competences in work re-entry (see Figure 5.2).

The Starfish model was thus initially developed from a collective review of studies and used as a basis for heuristic investigation, to meet project criteria. The model was one we could test and develop empirically through our investigation of learning and occupational biographies. The model has emphasized broad clusters of abilities coming together in ways that generate growth, movement and future development. That is why the model is not a square or a list but an organism with abilities coming together at its centre. Our evaluation has shown that the model – as elaborated through the investigations in the four partner countries – has value in capturing some of the

- Responsibility
- Tolerance
- Reliability
- Determination
- Resilience
- Principled/ethical
- Awareness of rights

Response to work-content-related demands
- practical aspects of operating in modern work environments
- willingness to carry out a variety of different duties
- updating of skills and knowledge in relation to roles

- adaptability to different learning contexts
- perceptiveness
- openness to learning experiences
- ability to improvise

Competences related to attitudes and values

Content related and practical competences

Learning competences

Methodological competences

Social and interpersonal competences

- organizational ability
- initiative/ability to make decisions fast in critical situations
- crisis, time and budget management
- networking
- planning and problem solving
- discipline -- methodicality
- communication, means and modes
- ability to handle multiple tasks and demands

- communication
- listening
- patience, sensitivity
- deal effectively with routine/everyday life
- social events
- creativity
- ability to encourage others
- awareness of others' viewpoints and circumstances

Figure 5.2   *A biographical approach: key competences identified through biographical analysis of significant non-formal learning experiences and job/role change (Starfish Model)*

features that underlie successful change, adaptation and personal growth in ways that transcend national boundaries. It also has good fit with wider European definitions of CEDEFOP in which key competences are *interlinked and interdependent human actions, involving self-steering capacities, integrated social cognitive and technological dimensions together with underlying capacities for lifelong learning.*

In the Starfish model we identified five clusters of abilities that are important in negotiating changes of work and learning environments. These are *not* de-contextualized 'transferable skills' but abilities which have both structural features and features which are referenced to context. Their structural features may be carried (tacitly) between environments but they have to be situated, underpinned by domain-specific knowledge and developed through social interaction within the culture and context of the work environment. *Learning abilities* included the critical dimensions of perceptiveness, and learning from reflection on experience. *Social abilities* included empathy and promoting feelings of efficacy in others. The *methodological cluster* included being able to handle multiple tasks and demands in complex and sometimes contradictory environments. Competences related to values and attitudes can be argued to be attributes rather then competences, but the standard competences of honesty and reliability often identified by employers are overlaid with responsibility, resilience, determination and awareness of rights as well as responsibilities as ingredients of workplace survival.

Our early research confirmed that naïve mapping of key skills between environments does not work. It has confirmed that the clusters generated from learner perspectives also capture employer and trainer perspectives at the level of the generic 'label'. Employer perspectives, however, ascribe and recognize the key competences at lower levels than the learners, a phenomenon also observed in the Brown and Keep COST review of VET research (1999), while trainers are more likely to recognize key competences at higher levels than employers, but also more narrowly than learners. Attributes of creativity, sensitivity and emotional intelligence often go unrecognized.

Case studies of males and females enrolling in Continuing Vocational Training (CVT) programmes aimed at changes of direction are showing that male and female biographies cluster in the ways they deploy the abilities gained through experience. There are also commonalities of experience associated with gender and class that transcend national boundaries. In our cases, positive experiences were shown to be associated with awareness of ownership of the key competences identified – the 'positive' experience of overcoming setbacks is particularly powerful in these respects. One of the most interested findings is that males and females with long-term occupational breaks view and deploy their skills differently. Females often regard their 'family' skills as highly developed but unrecognized in all areas except 'caring' or other areas of 'women's work', so disregard them in their search for work re-entry in other fields, concentrating instead on new or updated explicit skills. But they do take the structural aspects of these wider skills with them, and point to their importance when applied (tacitly or explicitly) in their new work situations. In practice, employers ascribe 'female skills' to mature women re-entering the labour market, but at a level and in a way that advantages them only in relation to other vulnerable job-seekers, 'women's work' and easily exploitable positions. Males ignore their skills gained outside the economic sphere, no advantages are derived from them and they are regarded as totally separate from the economic domain. Explicit new skills are sought for work re-entry and no advantage is perceived to stem from those informally gained in the family/domestic domain. More generally, those who are able to operate as 'labour force entrepreneurs', moving frequently between jobs in order to improve their position, have forms of know-how which appear to have currency in the labour market despite the fact that they cannot be easily codified (see Table 5.1).

Further analysis of these phenomena is indicating how important 'tacit supplementation' is in the ways in which employers ascribe competences to individuals and delineate requirements for jobs.

Leplat (1990) showed how tacit skills appear important in at least three places: the gap between skills officially required for jobs, and 1) the skills actually required, 2) the skills actually implemented, and 3) between the skills required by preliminary training and the skills actually implemented. Our findings are showing how the processes by which key competences are ascribed to people (often along gendered or class/disability-based lines) align with the tacit (as opposed to official) requirements of occupations, and thereby reinforce workplace inequalities. For example, attributes of 'mature and reliable' often ascribed by employers to women returners have a tacit supplement of 'compliant and undemanding', tacitly seen as equipping them 'better' than younger people or males for low grade and low paid positions with few development opportunities. These processes of tacit supplementation of key competences and jobs continue to reinforce inequalities in the workforce and the systematic undervaluing and underdevelopment of the skills of segments of the population (Ashton *et al*, 2000; Equal Opportunities Commission, 2000).

So, what would happen if a Personal Skills Card or alternative means of 'making learning visible' were to be introduced? Would this increase democratic access to knowledge by making it explicit and distributing and recognizing it more widely? Or would the existence of unequal power relations mean the control of more and more domains of knowledge by the powerful, and the disappearance of the 'protective belt' of tacit knowledge formed in the informal discourses of everyday life, through which individuals and groups can exercise their rights and resist exploitation?

Table 5.1 *Case studies of participants in CVT – job change programmes*

Five clusters of key competences according to . . .	
Advancement-oriented, work-centred attitude	Predominantly males, 'labour force entrepreneur' frequent job moves geared to advancement; high awareness of key competencies and know-how.
Precarious occupational biography in low graded jobs	Predominantly males; awareness of social competencies for adapting to new work situations; little confidence in ability to draw on other experiences or skills in new work situations, or recognition of their relevance.
Return to general job market after occupational break for personal (family) reasons	Predominantly stability-oriented females; awareness of key competencies gained outside work but knowledge that these are seen as equipping for helping/caring occupations or low graded jobs ('women's work'!) For males, awareness of key competencies but these are seen as irrelevant for work re-entry: 'in a different dimension'.
Aiming for self-employment	Both males and females; high awareness of key competencies, used with confidence to pursue chosen business opportunities – does not rely on accreditation by others.
Resuming high skilled professional career after career break	Focus on regaining lost technical skills and updating them – importance of key competencies gained outside work. Valued retrospectively, but irrelevant to work re-entry process.

The possibilities can usefully be explored in the context of Coffield's two scenarios for the future of lifelong learning, mentioned earlier – the technocratic and the democratic versions of the learning society. The technocratic model envisages continuation of the present policy lines, emphasizing individuals' responsibility to maximize their competitive position within markets. The democratic scenario emphasizes the individual, social and political rights that are minimum conditions in a democracy.

In the *technocratic* model, short-term gains might be made in providing a basis for more equitable rewards for those whose skills currently go under-recognized and underpaid, but continuation of current policies would mean that the onus would still fall on individuals to negotiate and sell their skills in market places in which the strong dominate. Longer term, will those same markets operate in ways which reward individual investment (by people acting as private agents) in securing expanded forms of know-how as the new 'knowledge currency'? Does this fuel still further the processes of polarization as the advantaged are able to expand their ownership of all four kinds of economically valuable knowledge through engagement in knowledge-rich and experience-rich environments and 'know-who' networks which are denied to those with fewer resources and less social capital?

The *democratic* scenario would reassert the four domains of knowledge as public goods to which anyone should have access, through the twin principles of education provided as a public and collective responsibility and social audit of enterprises and their policies in relation to skills development and relationships with their communities. It would also reassert the wider importance of learning in, through and for all domains of life (Coffield, 2000b). It would prioritize the inclusion of those who are currently the 'knowledge poor', and its emphasis in 'making learning visible' would be to strengthen the self-assurance of those who have skills and knowledge which presently are unrecognized or exploited.

The knowledge-based economy raises fundamental questions about what counts as knowledge and who owns, manages and controls it. This is reflected in the contested nature of the Recognition of Prior (Experiential) Learning. Two projects involving documentation of the experiences of workers in the mining and motor industries, reported by Evans (2000), showed that these became highly problematic because management and unions had entered the process with completely different agendas, with management wanting a skills audit while the union saw the process as 'part of a move towards improved job grading and wages for workers' in the first instance and improved access to further education in the second. In both cases, neither improvement in wages nor improved educational access was forthcoming, with consequent deterioration in industrial relations. This led the researcher to comment towards the end of his book that, 'what has become clear is that RPL cannot be separated from the broader epistemological, political and ethical issues'. This is obviously so. In our ESRC Tacit Skills and Knowledge network project (Evans and Sakamoto) and in the wider network of which it is part, our agenda is to explore adult learning processes within these frameworks.

Johnson and Lundvall (2000) have argued that a much more satisfactory mapping of the knowledge base is needed, and that such a mapping has to capture the competencies and competence building of individuals, organizations and regions, 'in order to understand what is learnt, how and by whom, in different contexts and to construct better indicators of different kinds of knowledge' (p 18). By focusing on competence building in interrupted occupational biographies and the implications of accrediting non-formal learning, this chapter has aimed to bring questions of social inequality closer to the centre of the debate.

Note

1. These findings are from pilot work carried out in European funded research on aspects of gender and qualification (Evans, Hoffmann and Saxby-Smith) and in the ESRC-sponsored Teaching and Learning Programme Research Network project, 2000–2003 (Evans and Sakamoto, 2000–2003).

References

Ashton, D, Felstead, A and Green F (2000) Skills in the British Workplace, in Coffield, F, *Differing Visions of a Learning Society*, Policy Press, Bristol

Barnett, R (1994) *The Limits of Competence – Knowledge, higher education and society*, Open University Press, Buckingham

Bernstein, B (2000) *Pedagogy, Symbolic Control and Identity*, Rowman and Littlefield, Maryland, USA

Billett, S (2000) Performance at Work: identifying smart work practice, in *Training for a Smart Workforce*, eds R Gerber and C Lankshear, Routledge, London

Boreham, N (2000) *Final Report of TSER Project on Work Process Knowledge*, European Commission, Brussels

Brown, A, Evans, K, Blackman, S and Germon, S (1994) *Key Workers: Technical and Training Mastery in the Workplace*, Hyde Publications, Bournemouth

Brown, A and Keep, E (1999) *Review of Vocational Education and Training Research in the United Kingdom*, European Commission, Brussels

Brown, P and Lauder, H (2001) *Capitalism and Social Progress*, Palgrave, London

CEDEFOP Press release based on *Making Learning Visible* by Bjornavold, J (2001) CEDEFOP, Thessalonica

Coffield, F (2000a) *Differing Visions of a Learning Society*, Policy Press, Bristol

Coffield, F (2000b) *The Necessity of Informal Learning*, Policy Press, Bristol

Cowan, W M, David, P A and Foray, D (2000) The explicit economics of knowledge codification and tacitness. Paper originally presented at the DRUID International Conference on National Systems of Innovation, Rebild 1999 and subsequently published in *Industrial and Corporate Change*

Dewey, J (1993) *How We Think – A restatement of the relation of reflective thinking to the educative process*, Heath, Boston, MA

Ellstroem, P E (1997) The many meanings of occupational competence and qualification, *Journal of European Industrial Training*, **2** (6/7), pp 266–74

Engestrom, Y (2000) *Training for Change*, International Labour Office, London

Equal Opportunities Commission (EOC) (2000) *Attitudes to Equal Pay*, EOC, London

Eraut, M (1999) Theoretical and methodological perspectives on researching workplace learning. Unpublished manuscript

Evans, K (1998) *Shaping Futures – Learning for competence and citizenship*, Ashgate, Aldershot

Evans, K, Brown, A and Oates, T (1986) Developing Work-based Learning, *Manpower Services Commission Research Report*, 39, Sheffield

Evans, K and Sakamoto, A (2000–2003) 'Tacit Knowledge and Work Re-entry', Project 2 in 'Incentives to Learning to Work', Award no L139251005, ESRC, Swindon

Evans, N (2000) *Experiential Learning around the World*, Cassell, London

Further Education Unit (FEU) (1979) *A Basis for Choice*, FEU, London

Gerber, R and Lankshear, C (2000) *Training for a Smart Workforce*, Routledge, London

Giddens, A (1991) *Modernity and Self-Identity: Self and society in the late modern age*, Polity Press, Cambridge

Heidegger, G (1997) The social shaping of work and technology as a guideline for vocational education and training, *Journal of European Industrial Training*, **2** (6/7), pp 238–74

Issitt, M, Hodkinson, P *et al* (1995) *Competence, Professionalism and Equal Opportunities in the Challenge of Competence*, Cassell Education, London

Johnson, B and Lundvall, B-A (2001) Why all this fuss about codified and tacit knowledge? Paper presented at the DRUID International Conference, Aalborg

Kusterer, K (1978) *Know-how on the Job: The important working knowledge of 'unskilled' workers*, Westview Press, Boulder, CO

Lave, J and Wenger, E (1991) *Situated Learning: Legitimate peripheral participation*, Cambridge University Press, New York

Leplat, J (1990) Skills and tacit skills: a psychological perspective, *Applied Psychology: An International Review*, **39** (2), pp 143–54

Norris, N (1991) The trouble with competence, *Cambridge Journal of Education*, **21** (3), pp 331–4

Polanyi, M (1967) *The Tacit Dimension*, Doubleday, New York

Ryle, G (1949) (1963) *The Concept of Mind*, Penguin, Harmondsworth

Schon, D (1983) *The Reflective Practitioner: How professionals think in action*, Jossey-Bass, San Francisco, CA

Unwin, L (2001) Key skills for work. Paper presented at the Key Skills For All? Conference, Institute of Education, University of London, London

Wellington, J (1987) *Skills for the Future*, University of Sheffield, Sheffield

Chapter 6

Developing pedagogies for the contemporary workplace

Alison Fuller and Lorna Unwin

Introduction

The relatively recent recognition by social scientists that the workplace is a major site for learning is stimulating researchers from different disciplinary backgrounds to investigate the nature of this learning within the context of changing workplace conditions. As Stern and Sommerlad (1999: 1) argue, workplace learning is not a new concept, but 'it has acquired visibility and saliency' because 'it sits at the juncture of new thinking concerning the nature of learning about new forms of knowledge, about the transformation of the nature of work and about the modern enterprise in a globalized economy'. The concept of the 'learning organization' has been one attempt to capitalize on this new awareness of the latent potential of workplace learning, and empirical studies are providing evidence that training is now more likely to be carried out in the workplace itself rather than in an off-the-job setting (see Raper *et al*, 1997).

In becoming more visible, workplace learning is being articulated through new discourses that attempt to capture the complex processes involved when people (and organizations) learn in a workplace setting. The very notion of what constitutes a 'workplace' is, in itself, problematic. For example, many people still work in Fordist style organizations where work is highly routine and offers little scope for creativity or personal autonomy; increasing numbers of people are working from home; and some people work alone while others work in teams. We also need multiple definitions of what people learn at and through work. For example, people learn to perform competently but also to 'beat the system'; they learn about personal relationships and about power; and they learn about their own potential and the extent to which the workplace can fulfil or restrict their aspirations.

In this chapter, we are concerned with how people learn from and teach others about work tasks. As such, we are concentrating on one aspect of people's workplace experience. We want to argue that the very act of learning to do one's job in the workplace is worthy of close attention, and that much of this learning occurs through explicit pockets of activity which make use of a range of pedagogical methods. We also want to argue that pedagogical skills can be found in all types of workplaces, at all levels in an organization and that they are not restricted by age. This latter point is of particular importance because we believe it challenges the traditional conceptions of 'novice' and 'expert' which are generally associated with models of skill formation and, in particular, apprenticeship.

The use of the term 'pedagogies' in our title and throughout the chapter is deliberate. In recent years, most of the research on workplace learning has pursued one of two approaches. The first, which has close ties to and often arises out of the adult education tradition, sees learning in the workplace as primarily an informal, learner-centred and experiential activity, while the second, which arises out of a human resource development (HRD) tradition, is more concerned with improving off-the-job training effectiveness, often through the use of new technologies. The experiential approach uses terms like 'facilitation' and 'reflection' to capture the self-directed and informal nature of the process and so pedagogical skills are played down (Fuller and Unwin, 1998). In contrast, the HRD approach examines how trainers and training packages can be organized as scientifically as possible to meet predetermined goals. In this approach, pedagogical skills are important but tend to be homogenized in an attempt to create a uniform or corporate approach. Our current research, on which this chapter draws, suggests that people are constantly put in the position of having to teach (a word that can be interchanged with show, instruct, coach, etc) a colleague how to improve their practice.[1] This often happens *informally* in the sense that the need arises in a naturalistic and unplanned way.[2] The act itself, however, involves a *conscious* and *explicit* process in which skills and knowledge are passed from one person to another or others using a range of pedagogical skills, which may or may not reflect knowledge of experiential or didactic approaches to teaching and learning. In addition, and importantly, the act is usually instinctively collaborative as the parties recognize that each has something to bring to the occasion.

This chapter is divided into four sections: the first examines five dominant theories of workplace learning and pedagogy; the second discusses the distribution of knowledge and skills in the workplace; the third presents initial findings from our research in the UK steel industry; and the fourth comments on the implications of the research for organizations and the direction of future studies on learning at work.

Existing models of workplace learning and pedagogy

Attempts to describe and conceptualize the nature and practice of learning and pedagogy in the workplace currently tend to coalesce around five theoretical models. It should be noted, of course, that the boundaries between the five models presented here have become more and more fluid, though they can all be seen in their pure form in many organizations.

The first of these is the transmission model in which skills and knowledge are passed on in a formal manner within a hierarchical framework either in the workplace itself or in an off-the-job setting. This model is synonymous with the growth of Taylorist approaches to work organization with its emphasis on clearly defined and demarcated job roles, uniform practices, and an acceptance that decision making is solely a function of managers (see Marsick and Watkins, 1999). This model relies on what Lewis (1997: 5) has called 'an act of faith approach, dependent on. . . the trainer's belief in the efficacy of training'. Although this model has come under sustained attack due to the growth of interest in experiential learning and the recognition of the importance of informal learning (as described below), it is alive and well and has been nourished by the development of new technologies specifically designed for the education and training market (see Rylatt, 1994). A challenge for our research is to explore the extent to which workers can be said to recreate the transmission model in their informal interactions in the workplace.

The second model, and one which could be said to be the mirror image of the transmission model, concerns the acquisition of so-called tacit skills through informal processes of learning. This model has acquired a particularly elevated status within research on workplace learning (see, inter alia, Eraut *et al*, 1998; Garrick, 1998; Marsick and Watkins, 1990). The concept of informal learning is, ironically, attractive to two seemingly very different interest groups. The first consists of those researchers and educators from an adult education background who position informal learning in the workplace in the tradition of experiential, learner-centred and reflexive learning, which places the learner rather than the teacher (or trainer or manager) in control. The second group, consisting of policy makers, human resource managers and others who take a human capital perspective and want to harness informal learning as part of their mission to improve workplace performance, are trying to find ways of codifying and accrediting the informal alongside formal training episodes (see Evans, 2001; Garrick, 1998). Both groups tend to view workplace learning through the lens of an education paradigm that dislocates action from context and theory from practice and, furthermore, conceives of learning as primarily an individualized activity. In their study of technicians, managers and professionals, Eraut *et al* (1998) showed that informal learning was inseparable from the work context so that learning grew out of purposeful social interactions. Our research is showing that this finding is also applicable to employees at lower levels of the workforce hierarchy.

In Eraut *et al*'s work, we see a direct link to Lave and Wenger's (1991) concept of communities of practice in the sense that learning is as much a collective as an individual activity. This concept arises out of a social theory of learning, which combines aspects of both the transmission and tacit models, and provides our third model for the workplace. Lave (1995: 2) describes her theoretical perspective as taking learning to be 'an aspect of participation in socially situated practices' and an activity which is historical and dialectical. We regard the historical and dialectical dimensions as being of vital import-ance for any understanding of how workplace learning occurs, why it is stimulated or restricted, and who participates. These dimensions help us to paint a picture of the nature of the community of practice in terms of its historical development, the internal structures which determine how people interact, struggle and cooperate, and its relationship to the wider community outside the workplace's walls (see Fuller and Unwin, 2001, and Ashton's chapter in this volume).

In complete contrast to the social theory of learning, our fourth model, which we refer to as the competence-based model, detaches the outcomes of learning from the learning process and so could be regarded as being a-pedagogical in nature. In this model, teachers and trainers *facilitate* and *guide* learning and may have a role (along with specialist assessors) in the assessment of learners' competence against performance criteria prescribed by standard-setting bodies. The learner, armed with the list of competences to be achieved, is in complete charge and may not need to call on the services of a teacher or trainer at all. The competence-based model, alternatively referred to as the outcomes-based model, has been seen by some adult educators as being empathetic to the experiential tradition in its privileging of the learner. Gilbert Jessup, the English civil servant who pioneered the introduction of the model in the UK, claimed that his advocacy of the outcomes-based approach stemmed 'from a concern that individuals should be given the opportunity to realize their potential' (Jessup, 1991: 6). As the many subsequent critiques of the model have shown, however, it is far more likely to be used by policy makers as a means to regulate workplace activity, to exert tougher control over education and training providers, and to ensure providers meet the needs of employers (see, inter alia, Hodkinson and Issitt, 1995; Raggatt and Williams, 2000). This latter claim has been shown to be particularly spurious in the UK context, where employers have generally rejected the model on the grounds that it leads to occupational outcomes or competences that are too rigid and narrow in scope, and that it is particularly unsuitable for young people who need to acquire skills and knowledge beyond the confines of their current job role in order to progress. The notion of being 'competent' in the workplace is, of course, an important one when considering how people learn at work (see Eraut, 1994). We need, however, to rescue the term from its rationalistic straitjacket and redefine competence for the contemporary workplace (see Sandberg, 2000).

Our fifth and final model of workplace learning embraces 'activity' theory and, in particular, the work of Yrjo Engestrom. Activity theory recognizes the extent to which people learn in social situations and through interaction, while at the same time proposing that their knowledge and understanding can be further advanced through structured teaching and learning. Engestrom (1994: 48) argues:

> although there are many occasions of productive learning in everyday situations, most of everyday learning consists of conditioning, imitation and trial and error. Investigative deep level learning is relatively rare without instruction or intentional self-instruction. For that very reason, instruction is necessary. Its task is to enhance the quality of learning, to make it purposeful and methodical.

The importance here is that Engestrom reclaims a central role for teachers and trainers within the landscape of vocational education and training, a role that has been diluted by the parallel influences of those who advocate informal learning, the outcomes-based approach, and experiential learning. His concern is to enhance the routine teaching and learning that occurs on a daily basis in the workplace. In his development of a theory of 'expansive learning' at work, Engestrom (2001: 137) goes further and argues that workplace learning 'violates' presuppositions that knowledge and skill are stable and reasonably well-defined commodities and that there is a 'competent "teacher" who knows what is to be learned'. He continues: 'People and organizations are all the time learning something that is not stable, nor even defined or understood ahead of time' (p 137). We support this view but would argue that we must not lose sight of the everyday pedagogical interactions, for they provide the vital bridge to the expansive learning stage that Engestrom is anxious to reach.

Two further and related elements of Engestrom's work are important for this chapter. First, he argues that it is more useful to conceptualize workplace learning as horizontal in nature rather than, as is common in formal education settings, to see it as a vertical process. We would add that a vertical, top-down conception of workplace learning is also inherent in the conventional understanding of how skills are transmitted in the workplace. Secondly, Engestrom observes that people move in and between multiple activity systems in the workplace and thus, as of necessity, often cross boundaries which may be both real and virtual (see Engestrom *et al,* 1995). In our view, it follows that the same worker can be seen as novice, competent or expert (and therefore also as a 'teacher') depending on the situation and task under consideration.

Distribution of knowledge and skills

Around the world, policy makers and commentators are telling us that public and private sector organizations now need 'knowledge workers' as we enter the 'knowledge economy' (see, inter alia, DTI, 1998; Seltzer and Bentley, 1999). At its most extreme, this vision implies that only certain jobs require knowledge (see, for example, Thompson, 2001) and to get these so-called knowledge jobs, people will have to embrace that equally slippery concept of lifelong learning. The vision of the knowledge economy has been critiqued elsewhere in terms of its relationship to the real world of local and national economies and labour markets (see, inter alia, Keep, 2000; Rees, 2000). It should be noted, however, that Felstead *et al* (1999) have found evidence, by surveying workers across the UK, that upskilling has and is taking place across occupational sectors.

The debate on skills demand and the changing nature of the economy is clearly pertinent to the study of workplace learning. In this chapter we are concerned with the way in which knowledge and skills are acquired and shared as part of an ongoing process in the workplace. In addition, we would argue a further four points. First, knowledge and skills are not only the preserve of some workers, but that all workers, regardless of level and qualifications, have knowledge and skills which they can potentially share. Second, skills and knowledge are located in all workplaces and settings regardless of sector and type. Third, skills and knowledge gain their meanings and value at work within the context of everyday work activities: it follows that these meanings may change in line with the changing imperatives and priorities of the workplace. Fourth, given the last point, policy makers and educationalists should be wary of codifying tacit knowledge and skills for the purpose of allocating them to a level within the hierarchical straitjacket of the national qualifications and skills framework.

Many people in the workplace can be regarded as having a specialism(s), a chunk of knowledge or know-how. In some cases this specialism has cross-workplace importance and the specialist will be called upon to instruct others in the skills and knowledge he or she possesses. A classic example of a cross-workplace specialism that will be familiar in many public and private sector organizations is that of the photocopying guru. This is the person (and there may be more than one) who understands the mysteries of the copying machine and who, by sharing his or her knowledge, can dramatically cut the often excessive amounts of time that colleagues spend in attempting to make the machine work for them. These mini-specialisms are often too small to be identified within the formal structure of workplace knowledge and skills but they can be passed on in a conscious and explicit way that is naturalistic and which bypasses traditional hierarchies. For example, we can all identify or imagine moments when we become stuck on some aspect of our work, then remember that a colleague was recently working on the same thing or something similar and can be called on to provide help. This support might be executed using a variety of pedagogical methods including an explanation, a demonstration, coaching and so on. Importantly, such inter-actions indicate how knowledge and skills that may previously have been conceptualized as tacit can be openly expressed by the individual as part of the pedagogical process situated in the work context. Such learning processes are often very effective as, by their nature, they happen on a 'need to know' and 'just-in-time' basis and when the learner is highly motivated to learn.

Some people, of course, are not inclined to pass on their expertise. This may be because they are not team players but it could be because of fears of losing their job (particularly to younger people) or other barriers that their employer has created (Rainbird *et al,* 2001). In their writing on apprenticeship, Lave and Wenger (1991: 115) point out that, over time, the 'newcomers' will displace the 'old-timers' and that this can be a source of tension between generations: 'The different ways in which old-timers and newcomers establish and maintain identities conflict and generate competing viewpoints on the practice and its development.' Nevertheless, Lave and Wenger go on to argue that this conflict is an important source of learning for both apprentices and experienced workers as they participate together in everyday practice:

> Shared participation is the stage on which the old and the new, the known and the unknown, the established and the hopeful, act out their differences and discover their commonalities, manifest their fear of one another, and come to terms with their need for one another. (Lave and Wenger, 1991: 116)

At this stage, our research suggests that Lave and Wenger are right in so far as work conceived as a participative process is more likely than not to involve people sharing their expertise.

Research findings

In attempting to capture how people learn in the workplace, we have devised a number of research instruments. The two we draw on here are, first, a questionnaire survey of employees' attitudes to learning and, secondly, an individual 'learning log'. These instruments are being used in four companies in the UK's steel industry and we report here on emerging data from our research. In addition to the surveys and logs, we are also carrying out individual interviews and holding group discussions with our research participants to explore their survey and log responses in more detail. We decided to develop the learning log in order to help people try and capture their teaching and learning activities in a systematic way over a period of time. Our concern was that, in interviews, individuals would remember some of aspects of their workplace learning but the more 'everyday' incidents might be forgotten. On the other hand, using the log on its own would have been equally restrictive. For example, an apprentice in one of our companies had not recorded in his log any incident of helping someone else to learn. In discussion with his fellow apprentices, all of whom had recorded incidents where they had passed on skills and knowledge to a colleague, he said, 'Oh yeah, I do that. I do it a lot because I know stuff from being an apprentice that some of the men on the shop floor don't know.' When asked why he hadn't recorded these incidents in his log, the apprentice said, 'Well I didn't record them because I thought I was the one being learnt.'

As the data from the surveys, logs and interviews emerge, we are finding that our research participants are often surprised by the detail in their log entries and this, in turn, has enriched the interviews.

Survey data

The survey of employees' attitudes to learning contained a set of questions designed to elicit respondents' experiences of, and attitudes to training or helping others to learn. Company A, which employs some 200 people on a sprawling site in Wales, turns large blocks of steel into rods and bars. The factory is hot and noisy. The survey responses from this company showed the following:

- Nearly half the respondents (43 per cent) agreed that 'training/helping others' takes a lot of their time.
- Only 3 out of 10 agreed that 'it's rare for me to have to show someone how to do something'.
- Only 13 (15 per cent) of the respondents agreed that they 'haven't got time to show someone else how to do tasks'.
- About half (48 per cent) of the respondents agreed that they 'would like to spend more time training others'.
- The vast majority (81 per cent) agreed that 'more people should be involved in training others' at the company.

We would argue that these findings are illustrative of two key points. First, they show that, for many employees, helping others is routine: it is part of their daily experience at work. Second, they indicate that many respondents have a positive attitude towards helping others. Most agreed that they had the time to help others and about half would like to spend more time training others. This is despite findings elsewhere in the survey which indicate that the workplace 'climate' is more likely to discourage than encourage positive attitudes to learning and support. In this regard, we found:

- Nearly two-thirds of respondents (63 per cent) agreed that their 'workload is very heavy'.
- Only a third agreed that 'the company has a strong commitment to training'.
- Over two-thirds (68 per cent) agreed that 'you don't get any recognition for training new staff'.
- Less than 1 in 10 of respondents (8 per cent) agreed that 'morale at work is high'.

Company B is a steel 'stockholder' based in the English Midlands employing some 100 people. Its prime function is buying and selling steel from and to customers throughout Europe. The survey here revealed the following:

- Over 3 out of 10 (35 per cent) agreed that 'helping others takes a lot of my time'.
- Half agreed that it is 'rare for them to have to show someone how to do something'.
- About a third (32 per cent) agreed that they would like to spend more time training others.
- About two-thirds (68 per cent) agreed that 'more people should be involved in training others'.

In some similarity to the previous company, the findings for company B indicate that for many staff (up to half) helping others to learn is a common experience. While fewer staff than at company A indicated that they would like to spend more time training others, the climate for providing inter-staff support may be more positive at company B. The following findings are illustrative:

- 70 per cent of respondents agreed that 'the company has a strong commitment to training';
- the vast majority (79 per cent) agreed that 'experienced workers are happy to answer questions';
- 38 per cent of respondents agreed that the company doesn't give employees any recognition for training new staff. This is a much lower proportion than at company A, where it was 68 per cent.

Learning log data

Individual employees in all the companies have been keeping a written log of their workplace learning for periods of eight weeks at a time. The learning log includes a section on *helping others*. Findings from four experienced male production workers (aged between 40 and 60) at company A showed that in nearly two-thirds of the weeks in which the log was completed, respondents reported helping another to learn. The log goes on to ask respondents about what their help has involved and in which areas they were able to help someone learn.

Table 6.1 indicates that respondents were able to employ a range of pedagogical skills to help others learn and that the activities of *showing* and *explaining* were the most frequently used.

Table 6.1 *Range of pedagogic activities – company A*

Question	Number of times option ticked
What has this involved?	
Showing someone/others how to do a task	18
Explaining how to do something	18
Giving someone/others the information he/she/they need to solve a problem	4
Working with another/others to solve a problem	6
Other	0

In Table 6.2, respondents report helping others in various specific ways. Here, we see that *job-related craft skill* was the area in which respondents were most likely to act as 'teachers'. This is probably unsurprising as the focus of activity at this firm is on practical skills.

Table 6.2   *Focus of pedagogic activities – company A*

Question	Number of times option ticked
In which area(s) were you able to help someone learn?	
Job-related craft skill	15
Job-related technical skill	3
Managerial skill	2
IT/Computer	0
Communication	5
Maths	0
Other	0

In company B, three employees (a 20-year-old male apprentice in business administration, a female sales assistant in her early 20s who has just completed a part-time degree in business studies, and a woman in her mid-30s who is the company's personnel and training manager) have completed learning logs. The *helping others* section in their logs showed that in the majority of the weeks for which the log was completed, respondents reported helping another person to learn. It was particularly interesting to note that the apprentice reported helping another to learn in five out of the seven weeks in which he returned a completed log. What the logs showed, in terms of pedagogical skills, is given in Table 6.3.

Again we see that the activities of *showing* and *explaining* were the most frequently used. The apprentice reported that he had *shown* someone how to do a task on five occasions and *explained* how to do something on five occasions, indicating that he was differentiating between two teaching methods.

Table 6.4 shows that respondents were helping others in various areas of work activity, but particularly in regard to tasks involving information technology (IT) and communication. The majority of employees at company B are involved in administrative and sales functions and rely heavily on the company's IT systems to carry out their jobs. The apprentice has quickly gained a reputation for being able to solve computer problems and to provide colleagues with ongoing support. This helps explain why he reported helping

Table 6.3   *Range of pedagogic activities – company B*

Question	Number of times option ticked
What has this involved?	
Showing someone/others how to do a task	8
Explaining how to do something	15
Giving someone/others the information he/she/they need to solve a problem	0
Working with another/others to solve a problem	2
Other	0

Table 6.4   *Focus of pedagogic activities – company B*

Question	Number of times option ticked
In which area(s) were you able to help someone learn?	
Job-related craft skill	0
Job-related technical skill	1
Managerial skill	1
IT/Computer	10
Communication	7
Maths	0
Other	0

someone to learn in the area of IT in five out of the seven weeks in which he completed the logs. The lack of help being provided in job-related craft skills is indicative of this area not being a focus of activity at this company.

Company C manufactures and supplies domestic products made from steel, and is based in the English Midlands. Learning logs have been completed by a group of male engineering and steel processing apprentices, and one experienced male production worker who is acting as a mentor to one of the apprentices.

The *helping others* section in the log yielded the following findings. The apprentices reported helping others in nearly half (44 per cent) of their completed weekly logs. In relation to the question *'What has this involved?'*, we found that respondents were most likely to indicate that they had been

Table 6.5   *Range of pedagogic activities — company C*

Question	Number of times option ticked
What has this involved?	
Showing someone/others how to do a task	17
Explaining how to do something	14
Giving someone/others the information he/she/they need to solve a problem	11
Working with another/others to solve a problem	9
Other	0

involved in *showing* and *explaining* activities (see Table 6.5). They also reported helping others via: *giving someone/others the information they need to solve a problem,* and *working with another/others to solve a problem.*

The most popular areas in which respondents were involved in teaching were job-related craft and technical skills. This reflects the nature of the work in this manufacturing and engineering firm and the respondents, who were all involved in technical and engineering activities. The apprentices indicated that they helped someone learn in job-related craft and technical skills in 15 out of the 31 weeks in which they had completed logs. The mentor was also most likely to tick these areas.

At company D, which polishes steel and employs some 40 people in the English Midlands, three male steel production apprentices are keeping learning logs. Initial data from these logs show that in the *helping others* section, respondents are reporting doing this for a quarter of their time, largely through *showing* and *explaining* in relation to the craft and technical skills necessary to operate the polishing machines (see Table 6.6).

Conclusions

Overall, our research is beginning to show that experienced and inexperienced employees in a variety of companies are involved in 'teaching' a wide range of knowledge and skills needed in the workplace. These include practical craft-related tasks, interpersonal and IT skills, as well as help in an area such as mathematics, which is more normally associated with subject teaching in classrooms. Moreover, there is evidence that people are teaching each other across traditional workplace boundaries of age and status, and across departments and work activities.

Table 6.6   *Focus of pedagogic activities — company C*

Question	Number of times option ticked
In which area(s) were you able to help someone learn?	
Job-related craft skill	15
Job-related technical skill	12
Managerial skill	1
IT/Computer	2
Communication	4
Maths	4
Other	0

Although the research is still at an early stage we suggest that our analysis and findings on workplace learning challenge conventional ways of thinking about teaching and learning at work. In particular, we would argue that the concept of pedagogy and pedagogic practice is relevant to all types of employee, all types of workplace (factories, shops, offices, etc) and to a broad and inclusive interpretation of what counts as knowledge and skill. This perspective implies that organizations need to find ways of encouraging people to share their expertise as a matter of course and to explore how this aspect of their practice can be improved. In a recent study, Billett and Boud showed how employees selected for their technical expertise and natural aptitude gained new pedagogic skills in 'guiding' learners to develop through everyday work activities (Billett, 1999; Billett and Boud, 2001). The strength of their approach to improving pedagogic practice was to embed it in the dynamic and changing requirements of the workplace. Our reservation would be that selecting certain individuals and preparing them as 'guides' still reinforces the idea that pedagogical skills and roles are restricted rather than being applicable to the whole workforce.

We have found it useful to think through our ideas and findings on pedagogy at work in relation to the five models of workplace learning outlined earlier in this chapter. However, we would argue that for us the modelling of workplace learning can be problematic in the sense that the lens that a model provides is inevitably limited and even ring-fenced. For example, processes are conceived as formal or informal, planned or unplanned, didactic or learner-centred. In this regard, we have found the work of Lave and Wenger, and Engestrom particularly helpful in that their approaches to understanding and conceptualizing workplace learning are situated in practice. Recent empirical research by Eraut and colleagues (1998) has also taken a situated perspective and has produced important insights into the development of knowledge and skills in higher-level occupations such as engineering and management. We have discussed elsewhere the strengths of Lave and Wenger's social theory of learning, and Engestrom's concept of expansive learning, which stresses the importance of teaching (Fuller and Unwin, 1998).

Prior to the construction of any new models, more empirical studies are required in order to generate better pictures of what constitutes teaching and learning in the workplace. In our view, such studies should examine the ways in which workplace pedagogy is a boundary-crossing activity that occurs within and between people operating in communities of practice. From a research perspective, it is important that ways are found of opening up the 'black box' of the phenomenon of pedagogy at work. The learning log, supported by follow-up interviews and group discussions, which we have developed for the case studies reported in this chapter, appears to be a particularly promising tool in this respect.

Notes

1. This chapter draws on our current research project, funded by the ESRC, exploring workplace learning in the UK steel industry. This project is one of five which form a Research Network (Improving Incentives for Workplace Learning) under the ESRC's Teaching and Learning Programme and which are due to report in April 2003.
2. See Hodkinson *et al* (2001) for a discussion on the differences between planned and unplanned learning opportunities.

References

Billett, S (1999) Guided learning at work, in *Understanding Learning at Work*, eds D Boud and J Garrick, Routledge, London

Billett, S and Boud, D (2001) *Participation in and Guided Engagement at Work: Workplace pedagogic practices*, Conference Proceedings, 2nd International Conference on Researching Work and Learning, 26–8 July, University of Calgary, Canada

DTI (1998) *Our Competitive Future: Building the knowledge driven economy*, Department for Trade and Industry, London

Engestrom, Y (1994) *Training for Change: New approach to instruction and learning in working life*, International Labour Office, Geneva

Engestrom, Y (2001) Expansive learning at work: toward an activity theoretical reconceptualisation, *Journal of Education and Work*, **14** (1), pp 133–56

Engestrom, Y, Engestrom, R and Karkkainen, M (1995) Polycontextuality and boundary crossing in expert cognition: learning and problem-solving in complex work activities, *Learning and Instruction*, **5,** pp 319–36

Eraut, M (1994) *Developing Professional Knowledge and Competence*, Falmer Press, London

Eraut, M, Alderton, J, Cole, G and Senker, P (1998) Learning from other people at work, in *Learning at Work*, ed F Coffield, The Policy Press, Bristol

Evans, K (2001) The challenges of 'making learning visible' – will codifying tacit knowledge and hidden abilities reduce inequalities in the workplace? Paper presented at Working to Learn Seminar, Institute of Education, University of London

Felstead, A, Ashton, D, Burchell, B and Green, F (1999) Skill trends in Britain: trajectories over the last decade, in *Speaking Truth to Power: Research and policy on lifelong learning*, ed F Coffield, Policy Press, Bristol

Fuller, A and Unwin, L (1998) Reconceptualising apprenticeship: exploring the relationship between work and learning, *Journal of Vocational Education and Training*, **50** (2), pp 153–72

Fuller, A and Unwin, L (2001) *From Cordwainers to Customer Service: The changing relationship between apprentices, employers and communities in England*, SKOPE Monograph No 3, Oxford and Warwick Universities

Garrick, J (1998) *Informal Learning in the Workplace*, Routledge, London

Hodkinson, P and Issitt, M (1995) (eds) *The Challenge of Competence*, Cassell Education, London

Hodkinson, P, Hodkinson, H and Senker P (2001) Problems measuring learning and attainment in the workplace. Paper presented to Working to Learn/SKOPE Seminar, University of Warwick

Jessup, G (1991) *Outcomes, NVQs and the Emerging Model of Education and Training*, Falmer Press, London

Keep, E (2000) *Learning Organisations, Lifelong Learning and the Mystery of the Vanishing Employers*, SKOPE Research Paper No.8, Oxford and Warwick Universities

Lave, J (1995) Teaching as learning in practice. Sylvia Scribner Award Lecture, Division C, Learning and Instruction, American Educational Research Association, Annual Meetings, San Francisco, CA

Lave, J and Wenger, E (1991) *Situated Learning: Legitimate peripheral participation*, Cambridge University Press, Cambridge

Lewis, P (1997) A framework for research into training and development, *International Journal of Training and Development*, **1** (1), pp 2–8

Marsick, V J and Watkins, K (1990) *Informal and Incidental Learning in the Workplace*, Routledge, New York

Marsick, V J and Watkins, K (1999) Envisioning new organisations for learning, in *Understanding Learning at Work*, eds D Boud and J Garrick, Routledge, London, pp 199–215

Raggat, P and Williams, S (2000) *Governments, Markets and Vocational Qualifications: An anatomy of policy*, Falmer Press, London

Rainbird, H *et al* (2001) Improving incentives to learning at work. Paper presented to Working to Learn /SKOPE Seminar, University of Warwick

Raper, P, Ashton, D, Felstead, A and Storey, J (1997) Towards the learning organisation? Explaining current trends in training practices in the UK, *International Journal of Training and Development*, **1** (1), pp 9–21

Rees, G (2000) Can a learning society produce a learning economy?, in *The Learning Society and the Knowledge Economy*, eds W Richardson and L Unwin, NACETT Sponsored Lecture Series, Learning and Skills Council, Coventry

Rylatt, A (1994) *Learning Unlimited*, Business and Professional Publishing, Sydney

Sandberg, J (2000) Competence – the basis for a smart workforce, in *Training for a Smart Workforce,* eds R Gerber and C Lankshear, Routledge, London

Seltzer, K and Bentley, T (1999) *The Creative Age: Knowledge and skills for the new economy*, Demos, London

Stern, E and Sommerlad, E (1999) *Workplace Learning, Culture and Performance*, Institute of Personnel and Development, London

Thompson, P (2001) Half truths and high roads knowledge: learning and skill in the contemporary workplace. Conference Proceedings, 2nd International Conference on Researching Work and Learning, 26–8 July, University of Calgary, Canada

Chapter 7

An approach to learning at, for and through the workplace: a trade union case study

Jim Sutherland

This chapter draws on the author's experience and practice as Director of Education and Training with Unison, the UK's largest trade union, and his chairmanship of the Workplace Learning Task Group established by the Secretary of State's National Advisory Group for Continuing Education and Lifelong Learning (NAGCELL). It is, essentially, a practitioner's perspective on how the learning needs of both employees and employers can be satisfied and, simultaneously, benefit the consumers of products and services through flexible and cost-effective learning methods.

The approach devised by the author was based on a clear philosophy with a number of underlying principles. First, the promotion of individual learning and personal development as a lifelong activity; secondly, the opportunity for all members of the union, including non-traditional learners, to have access to learning opportunities at a level which allowed them to learn at their own pace, to fit their learning around their domestic and employment commitments and to obtain satisfaction from and recognition for their efforts. Agreements were negotiated with employers to ensure that learning opportunities could be accessed during working time in addition to open and distance learning provision. The union operated, mainly, as a broker between members, employers and learning providers in ensuring a wide range of provision, competent and empathetic tutors and flexible methods of accreditation.

Introduction

Trade unions and workers throughout the developed world are experiencing the consequences of a major revolution in economic and social development. This revolution is generated, largely, by developments in information technology and the impact of economic globalization. The ability of unions and workers to respond individually and organizationally to its impact on job opportunities and job security depends, increasingly, on human capacity and intellectual capital. This, in turn, requires radically new approaches to learning in general and workplace learning in particular.

In the UK, the increasingly insecure nature of employment, the privatization of public services, the internationalization of company ownership, the remoteness of decision making and the growing pool of part-time employment is demanding of trade unions a different approach to the question of flexibility. Historically, trade unions have legitimately opposed demands from employers for flexibility and multi-skilling as such developments have usually led to job losses or the intensification of work activity. Today, however, it is workers as much as, if not more than, employers who need the flexibility that a wide range of skills and knowledge can provide in order to ensure future employability.

Learning at, for and through the workplace is, therefore, a key component of trade union organizational strategy. It should have as high a priority as pay and conditions bargaining both in profile and internal resources. The trade union approach to learning at, for and through the workplace has to be driven by three particular considerations: the immediate interests of the membership, the quality and reliability of public service provision of goods and services produced, and the wider issue of citizenship.

At one end of the membership spectrum of many unions is a significant cross-section of that part of the population that has suffered greatest disadvantage from the inadequacies of the compulsory education system. Most are women, the majority of whom work part-time. Many come from minority ethnic communities and significant numbers are employed in low paid and low status manual occupations. These are the very people who need access to high quality learning if the UK is to have an economy based on high value-added production and services. At the other end of the spectrum are many technicians, managers and others who are in the front line of economic and structural change and who require support in developing their capacity to respond to change.

On the question of service and product quality, trade unions have traditionally been largely concerned with the interests of producers, their members, and only tangentially with the interests of consumers. However, increasingly in the public services, trade unions recognize that if the public do not value the services they receive, they will not value those who provide them. Low pay and low status will be the norm and the privatization of public services will continue with little opposition, if not direct support, from consumers. In the private sector there is greater recognition among unions that if customers are not satisfied with the quality or after-sales service of the products they buy, companies will go out of business and jobs will be lost. It is not a one-way street, however. Employers cannot expect low status or insecure workers to concern themselves with quality unless they are provided with the necessary tools and incentives enabling them to respond to those challenges. Learning opportunities are the tools and the incentives can come from greater security of employment and potential improvement in pay and working conditions deriving from public support for public services and customer satisfaction with goods and services generally.

On the issue of citizenship, trade unions have historically been in the vanguard of social change. If they are to continue to be in the forefront of creating a thriving democracy with cultural wealth and economic health they have to ensure their strategies on workplace learning contribute to wider policy making aimed at enabling the whole population to become continuously engaged in learning. It is not simply a matter of developing the skills and competence for task-specific, job-related purposes of a short or medium-term nature, but also of learning that provides real choices in employment and lifestyle.

In seeking to satisfy the immediate and personal needs of individual members, in contributing to improvements in the quality and delivery of goods and services with a potential for greater job security, and in maintaining their historic drive towards a fairer and more equitable society, trade unions need to develop a coherent framework within which to pursue initiatives and improvements in learning at, for and through the workplace. This framework has to include clear principles and objectives, flexible methods of access, a coherent approach to accreditation, a broad range of provision and be firmly grounded in partnership.

Developing a framework

The framework should be based on a clear set of principles and objectives that ensure that learning at, for and through the workplace:

- is supported by a strong foundation of provision that develops learning skills and widens participation in learning through equality of opportunity;

- ensures the updating and enhancing of skills, competence and knowledge within a continuing learning culture;
- provides for the consolidation and progression of learning;
- enables individuals to develop within and derive job satisfaction from their employment, make choices on future employment and engage in opportunities for personal development;
- is underpinned by impartial learning and career guidance;
- encourages the development of centres of learning within workplaces and the wider community;
- is supported by structural and funding mechanisms that create incentives for widening participation;
- is developed in partnership with the appropriate stakeholders;
- has links with citizenship and family learning and community development in pursuit of social cohesion;
- has links with programmes of work experience for unemployed people and others so as to ensure as seamless a transition as possible into work and workplace learning.

Too many learning providers offer what they can offer rather than seek to discover what learners need. Predetermined lists of courses and prospectuses are sold like washing powder, and employers frequently commission training which meets their immediate task-specific production or service needs with little thought given to medium to long-term transferable skills provision and employee development.

To meet those deficiencies, thorough learning needs assessment in determining the content of the curriculum offer will be crucial to the success of learning at, for and through the workplace. Development reviewing, practised by many organizations, offers one example of a useful methodology for this. It is a continuing process based on one-to-one sessions with potential learners, which take place as part of an annual development cycle. It does not directly concern itself with employee performance, nor is it an appraisal interview. The aim is to give each member of staff the opportunity to focus on how they can enhance their contribution to helping the organization achieve its aims and objectives through developing the skills, knowledge, experience and competence each individual brings to his or her job and provide the individual with new opportunities for personal development. Development needs identified in the review session could relate to employees' current tasks, broader long-term objectives of a team, or possibilities for enhancing a work role, increasing transferable skills and/or developing beyond the scope of their current employment.

Development reviewing can benefit all parts of an organization. The outcomes from the review sessions can be amalgamated in each team/ department/organization so that common themes are drawn out. This assists the organization in ensuring that development activity is fairly distributed and linked to its priorities. The process also gives individuals some ownership of their personal development. The overall result is a wealth of information that can be used to develop all staff in pursuit of individual and organizational goals. In too many organizations learning opportunities have been captured by, or frequently only provided for, those who have a tradition of learning and often are well placed in the hierarchy of the organization. If non-traditional learners are to be encouraged to engage in personal development, any structure for learning at, for and through the workplace should provide ease of access for individuals in a wide variety of occupations. In particular, it should enable individuals to enter at a level appropriate to their current state of learning, learn at a pace suitable for them, receive recognition for their efforts, use a variety of routes and ladders for progression where desired, and develop an enthusiasm for, and confidence in, learning. This will require a structure of provision sensitive to the needs of all the stakeholders. It must not be skewed towards the needs of any particular group, or set of occupations, unless this is determined by a system of learning needs analysis and employee development review acceptable to all the stakeholders.

While professional grades have long had access to professional qualifications it is only relatively recently that there has been the realization of the importance of accreditation for all employees. The growth of National Vocational Qualifications (NVQs) for employees whose work, too frequently, has been undervalued and not recognized through formal accreditation, has been a significant development. However, much still has to be done to ensure that NVQs, and the occupational standards on which they are based, form the basis for a coherent and progressive learning strategy, and offer truly transferable skills, competence and knowledge rather than simply being the accreditation of prior learning and an end in themselves.

The introduction of the national Open College Network (OCN) system of accreditation into the workplace has enabled disadvantaged learners to gain access to forms of accreditation that have been of great value both inside and outside the workplace. It has proved to be of particular value in accrediting episodic learning not linked to traditional examination systems and is now widely used in learning initiatives pioneered by trade unions. The Credit Accumulation and Transfer system of accreditation in certain universities has opened up further opportunities for flexible learning capable of responding to the specific needs of workplace learning and should be incorporated into workplace learning strategies.

The successful creation of a comprehensive employee development strategy will depend to a great extent on the support it receives from the various stakeholders. Too often the development of the notion of 'partnership' has taken the form of partnership between employers and learning providers with little if any involvement from the principal stakeholders, the learners themselves. If the development of innovative and effective workplace learning is to take place it has to take account of all the stakeholders and their distinct, if complementary, needs. Three particular sets of stakeholder interests have to be considered. Employers will, naturally, wish to see any investment in workplace learning contribute to increased efficiency and productivity. Government is concerned to have a workforce and potential workforce capable of responding to economic and technological change. Individuals and trade unions want learning opportunities which not only improve their capacity to retain their existing employment but which also give them choices in employment and lifestyle. In addition, the involvement of trade unions, as stakeholders, will assist in legitimizing the purposes and processes of workplace learning in the eyes of their members and facilitate take-up. It will also help defuse suspicion and apprehension about the consequences of improved efficiency and productivity for job security. Their direct involvement in shaping the learning process should encourage long-term planning which, through the identification of future skills needs and the early introduction of appropriate learning programmes, will minimize the impact of economic and technical change on job security and aid restructuring when necessary.

In responding to the needs and interests of the different stakeholders, a workplace learning strategy should provide for a variety of learning. Three broadly defined categories of learning can reasonably be identified as the range of provision to be made:

1. Task-specific or job-related learning designed to improve the competence, efficiency and productivity of the workforce within their current occupations. This form of provision would apply across all occupations, from the lowest status jobs to the most complex.
2. Parallel and transferable skills learning designed to create a more flexible workforce, responsive to the changing nature or short-term staffing needs of the workplace. This form of provision would enable individuals to obtain experience from 'acting up' or 'acting across' in other occupations or tasks, both solving short-term staffing difficulties and enabling them to seek career progression with confidence when vacancies occur.
3. Personal development learning designed to provide the knowledge, skills and competence necessary to enable individuals to make employment

and career changes not limited to progression within the hierarchy of their present employment and also to create opportunities for personal fulfilment. This form of provision has a number of purposes. It will contribute significantly to the perception of a holistic workplace learning culture, thereby motivating and generating commitment and loyalty from staff at all levels. Linked to effective long-term and continuous learning needs assessment and employee development reviews, it will help defuse suspicion and fear about the consequences of improved efficiency and productivity for job security. It will also offer employees the opportunity for developing marketable skills which will enable them to seek employment elsewhere and so minimize the impact of restructuring occasioned by economic or technological change.

The categories broadly defined above do not necessarily require three different types of learning opportunity to be provided. In any one learning programme there can be individuals seeking to improve their skills and competence for task-specific purposes, others engaged in the same programme acquiring parallel/transferable skills for application within the organization, and others seeking to make career changes or in pursuit of personal fulfilment.

A comprehensive, coherent and holistic strategy for learning within a continuing learning culture can also contribute significantly to solving future staffing problems. A structure which provides access for all employees, encourages an enthusiasm for learning, offers recognition for all forms of learning, creates a variety of routes and ladders for progression, will provide the basis on which employers can begin a process of 'growing their own' staff where appropriate or necessary, as evidenced in the Unison experience.

The Unison open college

It was within the framework outlined above that the Unison open college approach was developed, deliberately avoiding placing all its emphasis on seeking greater access to learning opportunities from employers through the traditional collective bargaining process. Instead, the union adopted a brokerage approach. This offers solutions rather than making demands. Its methodology transcends the vagaries of day-to-day collective bargaining and allows learning development to bypass the legitimate, if short-term, industrial relations conflicts between employers and unions.

The Unison model was designed for its members and is, therefore, mainly for people in work. Nevertheless, it has the capacity to provide the basis for

that part of a 'learning society' strategy concerned with economic performance and the enhancement of employment opportunities. The range of
successful provision and the creation of genuine partnerships between a trade
union, employers and education and training providers on a voluntary basis
suggest what might be achieved universally with government action and
support. It is a model of provision that could be offered through the University for Industry. It is defined as much by method as content. Its underlying
philosophy is the promotion of individual learning and personal development
as a lifelong activity. Its aim is to provide stimulating opportunities for
personal and career development through a mixture of flexible, workplace,
distance, taught and supported open learning. Learning opportunities are
offered in four phases. This phased structure and the methods it employs,
are designed to enable members to enter learning at a level appropriate to
their current state of learning, proceed at a pace suitable for the individual,
fit their learning around their domestic and employment responsibilities,
obtain satisfaction from and recognition for their efforts, and appreciate that
learning is a lifelong activity.

Phase 1 *of the open college is designed to introduce individuals to learning skills.
Among the options available are modules on literacy, numeracy, communications and
confidence building. In addition to tutor-supported study groups operating in the
learners' own time, partnership agreements are increasingly being established with
employers for the delivery of the modules in working time. In many circumstances
these modules are used for providing the necessary underpinning knowledge for NVQs
and SVQs. Where modules are delivered solely by Unison, the union bears all costs.
Where they are delivered in association with the employer, the union develops and
provides the materials and is responsible for brokering the tutorial support and quality
assurance. The employer provides the appropriate paid time off work for students and
meets the tutor costs. The fundamental principle is that there is no cost to the individual.
Accreditation is provided for these modules through the National Open College
Network.*

Phase 2 *is designed to encourage individuals to re-enter learning and to engender
the confidence required to begin to realize their potential. The courses and projects are
more demanding than Phase 1 and encourage individuals to recognize that while
learning can be exciting and rewarding, it also requires an organized and disciplined
approach. The flagship course in this phase is Return to Learn (R2L). It is based on
a 180-hour directed study, nine-month programme involving personal assignments
from workbooks, small, tutor-supported, evening study groups in the immediate vicinity
of the student's home, two weekend seminars, or two pairs of linked days, with the
first a participative but diagnostic seminar early in the course and the second an
opportunity to apply learnt skills towards the end of the course.*

To date, more than 10,000 members have completed R2L and around 2,000 members now undertake the programme each year at no cost to the individual. Independent research has shown that 80 per cent of participants are women; 42 per cent work part-time; 90 per cent left school at the first opportunity; 60 per cent are without any kind of qualification; 80 per cent are over the age of 35 (with 50 per cent more than 45 years old) and 76 per cent earn less than the Council of Europe's decency threshold. Yet, notwithstanding these apparent disadvantages, 59 per cent have gone on to further and higher education, 30 per cent have taken on additional responsibility or been promoted at work and 25 per cent have become more active in the union, providing members with higher quality representation than through traditional routes.

Unison has a partnership agreement with the Workers' Educational Association (WEA) for the necessary tutorial support and has been extending those learning opportunities into the workplace through a growing number of partnership agreements with employers. Around 200 employers are currently working in partnership with Unison to provide R2L, and other courses for employees, in the workplace. In these cases the employer contributes the tutorial costs of R2L, together with 60 hours paid release to enable the 12 evening study group sessions and the two weekend schools to take place in working time. The partnership is based, therefore, on the employer providing 60 hours paid time off plus tutor costs, the individual contributing a further 120 hours of their own time in completing the workbook assignments and the union having borne, and continuing to bear, the development costs of the programme, including materials, tutor training and quality assurance. A similar framework operates for other courses in this phase. Accreditation for these courses is provided through the Open College Network.

Phase 3 *is designed to enable individuals to make choices, to take stock of their prior learning and life experience and to explore and identify further learning and development opportunities. Processes for the Accreditation of Prior Learning (APL) and the Accreditation of Prior Experiential Learning (APEL), linked to provision in Phase 4, are offered in this phase within a framework entitled 'Making experience count'. An access course has been validated on the theme of 'Public services in a changing world', creating a direct link between R2L and higher education courses by providing the opportunity for achieving the necessary credits for university entrance. Student members are then offered three routes of progression into Phase 4: an industrial relations/trade union studies strand, a general education strand leading to university degrees, and a vocational qualifications strand.*

Phase 4 *is designed to provide opportunities for lifelong development through the three strands referred to above. Individuals are encouraged to transfer between strands throughout their lifetime so that they can refresh their learning through mixing and matching between vocational-specific and broader learning opportunities.*

From micro to macro – developing the strategy

A key objective is to take the Unison experience and seek to demonstrate how the four-phase model can provide a means of access to all learners and particularly non-traditional learners, and offer methods of progression which can be undertaken collectively as well as individually. At present, more than 4,000 members, annually, are engaged in Unison's four-phase programme supported, in many cases, by their employer. Partnerships have been established with employers, government agencies and education and training providers. These partnerships encourage a joint approach to meeting medium and long-term staffing needs as well as providing individuals with the opportunity for personal development. The government acknowledged the contribution made by the Unison model to government policy in launching its Trade Union Learning Fund in 1998.

Growing their own

The four-phase model is being used to encourage employers, through such partnerships, to 'grow their own' staff. This has particular benefits for individuals but also has some significance for trade union organization in developing a new bargaining agenda and demonstrating trade union relevance to members and potential members. There is an agreement between the union and the Scottish Health Executive, which has provided finance for R2L to be offered in every health trust in the country. More than 2,000 non-traditional learners participated in these courses over the past 18 months and progression routes are being developed for ancillary staff in particular. In England similar initiatives have taken place. The development plan for the NHS has identified the need for all staff to have access to learning opportunities. An ILA scheme, based on the DfES model, providing more than £7 million in the first year, has been established and funded by the NHS nationally for the development of a learning programme for staff without professional qualifications. A Unison officer has been seconded, nationally, to the NHS to develop the scheme throughout all NHS trusts. An NHS employee has been seconded in each of the eight regions to work with a WEA tutor/organizer, financed by the NHS, to develop the project at local level.

A two-phase programme of courses has been designed. The first, entitled 'Pathways to the future', develops a range of learning skills and begins the process of creating a personal development plan for all participants. The second, entitled 'Improve your study skills', builds on NVQ developments and is particularly appropriate for helping health care assistants and others moving into nurse training or similar programmes. It is expected that this initiative will produce between 8,000 and 10,000 new learners in the first year. The two-phase programme will be funded by the NHS, and the DfES funding will be used to provide all those who complete the courses with an ILA for further progression.

A further example of the impact of the open college approach is located in the Coventry Health Care NHS Trust. An agreement between the trust, Unison, the WEA and Coventry University has established a programme whereby individual employees undertake the R2L course concurrently with achieving an NVQ level 3 in health care. On completion they automatically move on to the university's Diploma in Nursing with three years paid release from the trust and a guarantee of a job at the end of the course. The first cohort includes health care assistants and administrative workers wishing to move into direct care. Anyone failing the course will return to their old or similar post. The trust recognizes the stability of staffing that an initiative of this kind gives in that most participants will be established employees in the trust, with no illusions about the nature of health care, and with families in the district and unlikely to be chasing a career elsewhere. For individuals it removes age, confidence and knowledge barriers to career change.

In local government there have been a number of similar developments. In Suffolk the County Council is committed, through an agreement with Unison, to the four-phase model across the county with a particular focus on social services. They are funding Phase 1 communication skills courses and a generic Phase 2 R2L programme. Phase 3 introduces R2L participants to social work through a WEA/OU designed 'Working in care' course, which introduces participants to the theoretical and underpinning values of social work. At Phase 4 a Diploma in Social Work, CETSWA and OU validated, and delivered part-time in the workplace, has been introduced for home carers and residential carers without formal qualifications, so providing new employment opportunities to non-traditional learners. The first cohort was 18 strong and there has been a 100 per cent completion of the programme. The County Council has now adopted the model as its method for recruiting social workers in future, with the probability of a new cohort being established at two-yearly intervals. In eight local authorities R2L is being used as the springboard for classroom assistants to acquire the OU Specialist Teachers Assistant Certificate. The union has now created a learning hub under the auspices of the University for Industry (UFI) covering Health & Social Care. Pilot projects run by the hub in Yorkshire and Humberside have around 500 participants, with between 200 and 300 involved in the South East. It is expected that within a year similar programmes will be running in all 12 regions of the union with much of the learning material going online.

If provision of this type and partnerships of this kind were replicated throughout the UK and across employment sectors – particularly of the Return to Learn variety – the UK would be on the verge of creating a truly learning society.

However, given the scale of the challenges posed by the information revolution, the increasing insecurity of employment experienced by many citizens and the unwillingness of many employers to engage in innovative approaches to learning, there is a need for some encouragement.

Stimulating the further development of learning at, for and through the workplace

To date, the success of the largely voluntary approach to promoting learning at, for and through the workplace operating in this country, has been patchy. Some employers invest extensively in staff learning, while others make very little provision. Reluctant employers have to be encouraged to recognize that investment in learning will not only meet short-term needs but also lay the foundation for long-term success. Individuals who have been discouraged from learning have to be convinced that it can be rewarding in reinforcing employment and career prospects, as well as contributing to personal fulfilment and social wellbeing. Particular effort needs to be directed towards supporting lifelong learning in small businesses and among those who are self-employed.

A minimalist legislative framework

The stimulation of workplace learning should stress responsibilities as well as rights and encourage a holistic and integrated approach. It should encourage partnership in identifying needs and wants, delivery solutions and funding provision. There is a role therefore, if a minimalist one, for a legislative framework in this area. One tried and successful approach from another area of activity that could be adopted here is that applied to health and safety in the workplace. There is substantial evidence from the experience of the

Health & Safety at Work, etc Act that enabling legislation can have a dramatic effect in improving the voluntary approach to workplace issues. Before the 1974 Act insufficient attention was paid to workplace health and safety by employers and employees alike. The legislative requirements introduced by the Act for Health and Safety Policy Statements from employers, the creation of safety representatives and the encouragement of safety committees, among other developments, transformed the approach to workplace health and safety.

A similar approach should be adopted for workplace learning in larger workplaces. The statutory framework would have two principal components for encouraging partnership: policy statements produced by employers clearly setting out not only a commitment to workplace learning but also an indication of how it is to be achieved; and learning committees with equal representation from employers and trade unions with responsibility for developing and monitoring progress in achieving the objectives of the policy statement. From this process learning agreements could evolve, defining rights and responsibilities in relation to workplace learning, for employees and employers. In order to provide guidance to the stakeholders and to encourage smaller workplaces to develop new approaches to learning, a Code of Practice for Workplace Learning should be developed. The Code, following the legislative proposals, would set out guidelines and minimum standards for the promotion of workplace learning. The Code could become a factor in the allocation of contracts between government, public authorities and contractors and a benchmark of quality in contractual relationships between employers. A further important measure of the commitment of employers to workplace learning will be the arrangements they make for, and the proportion of their expenditure they invest in, learning opportunities for their employees as well as the volume and nature of provision offered. They should be required to account for their investment in learning in their annual reports and publish a statistical report on the volume and nature of learning provided.

Funding workplace learning

A key question in developing workplace learning is who should pay for what. In developing approaches to funding learning at, for and through the workplace, consideration has to be given to the various and proportional responsibilities of government, employers and individuals for the existence of current learning needs. Also required will be an assessment of the financial, economic and personal benefits that will accrue to each, with those factors reflected in the financial and other contributions expected from each.

The levy-grant system established following the 1964 Industrial Training Act was successful in increasing the quantity and quality of training. It had merit in that it provided for some equity between those who did invest in training and those who did not, although the process often degenerated into a paper chase with training officers spending more time chasing grant, avoiding levy or seeking exemption than in providing training. Nevertheless, variants of the levy-grant system still operate within the Engineering Construction and Construction Industry Training Boards, local government and the National Health Service, with a voluntary levy system in broadcasting. These approaches continue to be reasonably effective in ensuring equity and quality of learning on a national basis, as evidenced by what has happened in the Unison–NHS partnership developments referred to above. Consideration should be given to widening the use of such systems based on the experience of existing models.

Individual Learning Accounts (ILAs)

The creation of ILAs, contributed to by government, employers and individuals, with their twin core principles of shared responsibility and shifting the emphasis of support to learners themselves and away from learning routes or institutions, provided a significant opportunity for promoting the interests, and widening the constituency, of learners.

The original intention of the government was to give individuals £150, provided they contributed a further £25 to the account, with the employer encouraged to add to the total. Industries, sectors and workplaces would be targeted, with the accounts channelled through the employer.

The TUC and some unions, notably Unison, developed strategies in association with employers, with the NHS scheme mentioned above a notable example. Those strategies were based on effective learning needs analysis with guidance and support for individual learners. They ensured that non-traditional learners were targeted and enabled ILAs to be collectively used by groups of employees to utilize economies of scale in establishing new learning opportunities.

Unfortunately, the ILA scheme was suspended in the autumn of 2001 when it was discovered that some learning providers were engaging in fraudulent practices. This problem could have been avoided if government had not handed over the ILA scheme to providers but had maintained the original intention of channelling support through employers. The NHS scheme is continuing and government would be well advised to consider the lessons from that in devising any new approach. In particular, lessons can be drawn about the successful identification of need, the provision of guidance and advice to individuals, and the nature of the partnership between the employer and union.

Conclusion

Much more could be said on this topic. If the UK is to have a thriving democracy with cultural wealth and economic health, if employees are to acquire the skills and knowledge enabling them to make choices about employment in an insecure future, there has to be better and wider access to a new range of learning opportunities.

New learning opportunities have to be linked to individual and organizational learning needs within the context of the impact of future economic and technological change. This chapter demonstrates how trade unions can take initiatives, make a significant contribution to the development of a new learning culture and, at the same time, demonstrate their relevance to both existing and potential members. The University for Industry could do worse than adopt this approach as a principal plank in its strategy.

Further reading

Kennedy, H (1995) *Return to Learn. Unison's fresh approach to trade union education*, Unison, London

Chapter 8

Education and training for small and medium-sized enterprises

Peter Senker

Small firms are extremely diverse. They range from small retail outlets such as fish and chip shops, newsagents, hairdressers and hi-fi shops, car repair workshops and a great variety of manufacturing firms, to hi-tech firms developing applications of new materials or biotechnology, designing complex instrumentation or writing complex software.

> The SME population is highly differentiated. . . from. . . the simple craftsman and small service business. . . to the sophisticated manufacturing business operating in complex and uncertain markets, to a wide range of 'professional' small firms offering services directly to the consumer and to industry and commerce. (Gibb, 1996)

This chapter considers the various ways in which firms can learn. It identifies some of the principal sources from which firms can draw the new knowledge that they need to access and considers why SMEs (small and medium-sized enterprises) need to innovate. The vast majority of SMEs operate in traditional sectors and find it extremely difficult to access the knowledge they need, and the nature of these difficulties is outlined. One UK government-supported scheme, the Teaching Company Scheme, provides a powerful mechanism for enabling SMEs to acquire and use the knowledge they need. Its mode of operation is outlined, and the reasons for its success analysed briefly. Some prominent features of current and proposed government training arrangements are then presented, and their contribution to SMEs' performance together with some of their limitations are then reviewed. In conclusion, some approaches to solving the serious problems identified in the chapter are considered briefly.

Why SMEs need to innovate

International competition is intensifying and is based increasingly on firms' ability to develop consistently new products of high quality and to manufacture them efficiently and cheaply. The complexities of the new product development processes, shortening product lifecycles, the transformation of production processes, the growing use of computer and telecommunications-based innovations such as the Internet and e-commerce, together with organizational innovations such as total quality management, all demand that firms learn to do things in new ways in order to sustain and enhance their ability to compete (Dodgson, 1993). It is often essential to improve quality systems in order to remain competitive in world markets and to reduce import penetration from foreign competitors.

The application of scientific and technological knowledge can help companies in many ways, including:

- to ensure that products meet ever more stringent quality requirements, dictated both by customer demand and by regulation;
- to develop new product ranges to meet the needs of changing markets, and to develop and use the most suitable available technologies for that purpose;
- to use efficient methods for controlling production so as to maximize the company's ability to meet the needs of its customers, for example by shortening lead-times, and to reduce work-in-progress and inventories and thereby reduce the costs involved in carrying them;
- to introduce process control, which reduces raw materials and energy costs.

There are huge opportunities for SMEs to use new technology and new knowledge to increase productivity and/or to increase quality – just a few examples are the application of Computer Aided Design in foundries, the use of computer-controlled cutting in garment production, the use of production control in food and drink production and in crockery manufacture, and the use of computers to control stocks in retailing.

Which SMEs need to innovate

Firms in traditional sectors

Several studies have found that UK manufacturing firms face serious problems at a certain stage in their development: as firms grow, the problems they face become too diverse to be controlled successfully by one or two people. In order to continue to be successful, growing firms need to change from 'entrepreneurial', based mainly on the knowledge and experience of one or two founder/proprietors, to 'managerial'. Serious threats to a company's long-term viability may also be presented to firms which fail to employ graduate level staff with scientific and management training who are capable of using technology and modern management and marketing methods properly and systematically (Senker, 1981). University trained staff also have 'knowledge of knowledge', ie when they are confronted with technical problems beyond their capability, they know how to seek out external information to solve such problems (Gibbons and Johnston, 1974).

Where firms in traditional sectors use new technology, they often use technology produced by their materials and equipment suppliers, and sub-contractors rely on their customers for precise specifications (Rothwell, 1991). Studies have shown that small food manufacturing firms are also assisted by the activities of some large food retailers, which act as brokers between the science base and their small firm suppliers when necessary (Senker, 1986). There may be a similar relationship between large garment retailers and their suppliers (Braham, 1985). There is, however, extensive evidence that firms that do not employ qualified scientists or engineers (QSEs) have great difficulty in absorbing knowledge from such external sources. Studies of the plastics processing industry suggest that lack of QSEs and technicians can restrict their ability to use technical information available from their suppliers, and can affect the quality of products they produce (Rigg *et al*, 1989; Walsh *et al*, 1980).

Many firms in traditional sectors such as construction, food, plastics, clothing and mechanical engineering were originally founded by practical people, few of whom yet recognize or understand the need for graduates or technicians in scientific, technological or management disciplines. If there is nobody in a firm who can understand the knowledge generated in universities and research institutes, then the firm cannot use such knowledge. Firms cannot innovate effectively unless they employ staff who understand science, technology and modern management methods, and are able to apply them.

The principal factor constraining firms' demand for scientific and technological knowledge is their own lack of scientific and technological capability. Universities play important roles in producing new knowledge and in educating students. But firms can only gain access to such knowledge if they employ people capable of reading the textbooks, journals and manuals in which it is published, and communicating directly with the people who produce it. There is a considerable amount of empirical research data which demonstrate that this capability is related to the educational level of a firm's staff – in particular to the employment of QSEs able to understand the output in terms of books and papers produced by universities and research institutes which generate new technology (Entorf and Kramarz, 1997; IRDAC, 1991). Qualified staff can also participate in personal discussions with people who generate new knowledge. In principle, the higher the level of knowledge and understanding within the company (the more elevated its skills profile), the more its staff become aware that new knowledge could help their business, and the better they are able to use new knowledge to improve the company's competitiveness.

Cooperative research associations were originally established to assist smaller firms in industrial sectors that were unable to support in-house R&D. However, it has been found that large firms have more contacts with research and technical associations than SMEs. To some extent this is related to the fact that large firms have the time and personnel to make such contacts (Rothwell, 1975). A survey of Sussex companies' interactions with higher educational institutes found that interaction increases with QSE employment and with firm size (Lowe and Rothwell, 1987). Another study found that the in-house laboratory and contract research organizations are comple-mentary to each other, and cooperative research associations cannot therefore substitute for the lack of in-house research by firms (Mowery, 1983). A study of government support for industrial R&D in Norway throws further light on the problems encountered by small firms that do not employ QSEs and yet attempt to access the expertise within research institutes. On the one hand, such SMEs have difficulty in specifying their needs in the technical manner required by the research institutes. On the other, those that manage to surmount this hurdle seldom implement the results of projects undertaken for them by the institutes. This is often because such firms do not employ staff with the capability necessary for comprehending and applying the results to their products and processes (Senker, 1997).

However, the learning process may also be constrained by a firm's culture – it is generally conservative and sustains existing structures of belief (March et al, 1991). There is a tendency also for organizations to socialize new recruits to adopt their pivotal or central assumptions, and firm culture is taught to new members as the correct way to perceive, think and feel (Schein, 1985). This has implications for firms trying to transform themselves by adopting a more scientific approach to management, or indeed introducing technology that is new to them. The new approach may demand cultural change in the company. To be integrated successfully into the organization, all new recruits have to assimilate company culture to a very considerable extent. But there is also a need for company culture to accommodate itself to the new knowledge being introduced. This holds true whether the knowledge relates to management techniques, the introduction of new technology, or the application of science. It is likely to involve recruiting and/or developing people able to integrate a firm's accumulated knowledge about its products and processes with the new knowledge being introduced. During the process of integration, problems beyond the capability of the new recruits may emerge, demanding interaction with external experts. Senior management also needs to be involved in the process of integration, learning about the wider implications of adopting a new approach. For instance, studies of firms involved in automation implementation showed that they very often failed to secure the anticipated benefits from their investment largely as a consequence of senior management failure to understand the need to manage new technology introduction according to a strategy which covers work and its organization in addition to technical aspects (Bessant and Haywood, 1988; Senker, 1984; Senker and Simmonds, 1991).

Small hi-tech firms

While the vast majority of SMEs operate in traditional sectors, small hi-tech companies have great significance in contributing to innovation, productivity and growth of the economy as a whole. However, there is no convincing evidence that lack of training is a major problem for these firms.

The main barriers to technology transfer for companies in hi-tech sectors which do employ QSEs are that it is difficult for the small number of people they employ to have sufficient time and a sufficiently wide range of knowledge and experience to cope with the numerous problems these firms face; and these firms are also often very short of financial resources. Some government programmes appear to help these SMEs to overcome these obstacles, but the design of other programmes does not seem to have taken the specific needs of SMEs or particular technologies into account. Programmes for technology transfer in scientific instruments and advanced engineering ceramics appear appropriate for SMEs, but are less relevant in relation to biotechnology. In ceramics, lack of investment in public research can be a major barrier to technology transfer from academe. This has been overcome to some extent by relying on transfer of technical knowledge from supplier and buyer firms (Senker, 1997). Similarly, many biotechnology SMEs are intimately connected with larger firms as suppliers of intermediate products, research materials and equipment, and they report that they have benefited from such links in a number of ways.

The main method by which SMEs overcome barriers to technology transfer is by building good informal relationships with academics and this includes bartering goods and services in exchange for access to university expertise. Companies offer lectures to students, or give valuable materials in return for university information, advice and help. The expertise needed by SMEs takes many forms, including market information (in parallel computing), use of university instrumentation (in advanced engineering ceramics and biotechnology) and scientific knowledge.

How firms learn

Firms can learn by a variety of means – for example, by conducting research and development (R&D), by training their own staff, by hiring individuals from outside, by reverse engineering, by installing capital goods and by imitating inward investors. In addition to R&D, learning can also take place in many other company activities including design engineering, manufacturing, marketing and management. It is important for firms to learn continuously and to base their learning on multiple sources of knowledge (Tiler and Gibbons, 1991).

The acquisition of knowledge by firms is a complex process, however, and it is necessary to draw a sharp distinction between individual learning and organizational learning. It is not sufficient for a firm to access useful knowledge. It has also to organize methods for the internal diffusion of new knowledge, to ensure that knowledge that is received from external sources is communicated and utilized effectively throughout the organization. For example, research has shown that for individuals to learn about Information Technology (IT) is not enough. Indeed, it is dangerous for an organization to rely on individual IT experts (Dale, 1986). The organization as a whole must learn to use IT, so that it can draw upon the complex blend of skills and talents over which it has control, locating and drawing upon the strengths in its knowledge base. A key part of the learning process is concerned with the identification of information that can add value to the business, and integrating new knowledge with a company's existing accumulated knowledge (Tiler and Gibbons, 1991).

Sources of new knowledge

A study of over 2,000 UK SMEs enquired into their use of external technical information and support. Sixty per cent of the firms in the sample made use of such external information. As shown in Table 8.1, trade and professional journals together with suppliers and customers were by far the most

Table 8.1 *External sources of technical information used by SMEs*

External Source	Local %	National %	International %
University/higher education	12.5	12.2	3.3
Private research institutions or consultants	9.4	22.4	5.6
Government research establishments	2.0	11.6	2.6
Suppliers or customers	22.2	54.3	23.0
Other firms	10.7	23.9	9.6
Trade or professional journals	12.4	59.1	24.0
Total responses (No.)	1172	1172	1172

Source: The State of British Enterprise, 1992, Small Business Research Centre, Department of Applied Economics, University of Cambridge, p 65.

important sources, and universities and government research establishments the least important.

But universities play a significant role in producing new knowledge and in providing access to the stored knowledge developed over time. For SMEs to innovate, they need to be able to access this information more effectively. A great deal of this knowledge is published in textbooks and journals, but it can often be applied only by graduates who have absorbed the associated tacit knowledge and skills. Polanyi (1966) encapsulates the essence of tacit knowledge in the phrase 'We know more than we can tell', and provides clarification by giving such commonplace examples as the ability to recognize faces, ride a bicycle or swim without even the slightest idea of how these things are done. Tacit knowledge is heuristic, subjective and internalized and is not easy to communicate. Winter's taxonomy of knowledge recognizes that knowledge may or may not be observable, teachable and articulable (Winter, 1987). This is helpful in understanding that it may be possible to acquire tacit knowledge which is observable but non-articulable by working closely with experts and learning through example and experience. Winter also points out that the non-articulation of articulable knowledge (for instance the non-documentation of revisions to a computer program) may pose a greater barrier to the transfer of knowledge than tacitness itself. Well-established practices of recruiting QSEs enable firms to apply scientific knowledge – both formal and tacit – to solve their technical problems.

There are significant differences between university and industrially trained problem solvers in their use of external sources of knowledge. Those who lack a university education, but who have had industrial experience, education and training, tend to rely more on their existing education and experience to solve technical problems. In contrast, those with a university education are more inclined to use it to extend their knowledge resources. University-trained problem solvers make frequent use of information in the scientific literature and also utilize direct personal contacts with scientists in the public research sector. Industrially trained problem solvers tend to ignore this resource. These findings have two explanations: that university educated problem solvers have acquired 'knowledge of knowledge', ie the ability to recognize when available internal resources are inadequate to solve particular problems *and* where and how to find the necessary information. It also seems that industrially trained problem solvers experience a barrier to the use of scientific sources, and this can inhibit them from transferring scientific knowledge to industrial applications (Senker, 1997).

There has been rapid growth in the number of graduates produced by universities in the UK in the last two decades. This growth has resulted in graduates in numerous disciplines being recruited to fill posts in industry previously held by less highly qualified people. Unfortunately, there are no data on how this has affected SMEs. Nevertheless, the increased employment of graduates does raise relevant questions, in particular, to what extent are the additional skills and knowledge acquired by graduates wasted? To what extent are jobs being changed so as to permit the use of the additional skills and knowledge acquired by graduates to improve productivity and product and service quality?

In manufacturing, while QSEs in the shape of graduate engineers are being employed as supervisors and upgrading supervisory skills, foreign language graduates are also being used to help to increase export scales. Many non-QSE graduates have entered the service industries and there are many cases in which they have played significant roles in expanding the range and quality of services offered by their companies (G Mason, 'Learning for labour', *The Guardian*, 18 February 1997). For example, in the steel and financial services industries, product ranges have been widening considerably and job roles have been broadened to take advantage of graduates' 'skills, knowledge and presumed greater analytical capacity and ability to undertaken non-routine work'. So graduates are not necessarily being under-utilized if they are employed in jobs for which university degrees have not been required traditionally.

In financial services, there is a mixed picture. There has been an increasing tendency to stream graduates into several layers of employment. As in manufacturing, some jobs in which graduates were not normally employed in the past now employ them and utilize the extra skills and knowledge they possess. However, while it is difficult to draw hard and fast distinctions, it seems likely that some graduates who 'are lacking both in technical expertise and in inter-personal skills are regarded as well-suited to routine, clerical-grade type of jobs'. In some such cases it may be realistic to regard their university education as 'wasted' to some extent (Mason, 1995).

Present UK government policies and their limitations

For the last several decades, governments have been anxious both to promote innovation in small firms and to stimulate training in them. The two departments most involved in these efforts currently are the Department for Education and Skills (DfES), responsible for promoting training as well as education (until recently the DfEE – the Department for Education and Employment), and the Department of Trade and Industry (DTI), responsible for promoting innovation. The DfEE introduced Modern Apprenticeships (MAs) and National Traineeships (NTs) now re-branded as Advanced and Foundation Modern Apprenticeships, and the DfES is very keen that SMEs should adopt them. However, recent research found that the barriers that restrained take-up and use of MAs and NTs by SMEs were related to the business culture of SMEs and particular sectors. Driven by short-term business imperatives, and operating within slim profit margins, SMEs tended to provide in-house training for immediate requirements, which often made them unresponsive to adopting external training initiatives, and many SMEs did not have the infrastructure and staff to introduce and manage training initiatives, including liaison with external bodies and related administration (Sims *et al,* 2000).

The DTI has numerous schemes to promote innovation by firms, with a range of special schemes for SMEs and, increasingly, Science and Engineering Research Council (SERC) policy has been directed at increasing support for research with industrial relevance. Schemes such as the Teaching Companies Scheme have been helpful to SMEs in learning the value of R&D and innovation, and of collaboration with academia (Senker and Senker, 1994).

The Teaching Company Scheme

Several studies have demonstrated the success of the Teaching Company Scheme (TCS) in terms of encouraging technology transfer and training in both large and small firms mainly operating in traditional sectors (Senker and Senker, 1994). Established in 1975, the TCS sets up partnerships between academic institutions and companies to bring benefits to industry and to develop a group of high quality, young, technical managers. Its objectives include facilitating the transfer of technology and the diffusion of technical and management skills, and encouraging industrial investment in training, and provision of industry-based training, supervised jointly by academic and industrial staff, for young graduates intending to pursue careers in industry; enhancing the levels of academic research and training relevant to business by stimulating collaborative research and development projects; and forging lasting partnerships between academia and business. The terms on which TCSs operate are far more favourable for SMEs than for larger companies. Accordingly, a high proportion of schemes take place in SMEs.

The scheme operates through programmes in which academics in universities join with companies to contribute to the implementation of their strategies for technical or managerial change. Each partnership, called a TCS programme, involves academic participation with company managers in the joint supervision and direction of the work of a group of young graduates. The graduates, known as TCS Associates, are recruited by the academic department concerned and are normally based full-time at the company. TCS Associates also undertake supporting courses, covering both personal development and enhancing their skills where necessary.

The scheme makes a grant towards the basic salaries of the TCS Associates and provides the academic department with the costs of a Senior Assistant who takes over a proportion of the normal workload of the academics so they can spend time at the company. Industrial and academic partners interested in setting up a programme are advised by a TCS regional consultant.

It was suggested that a TCS programme could put in place an organizational mechanism that initiates knowledge transfer from academia to firms that have not previously recruited graduate scientists or engineers. It could also play a significant role in creating more favourable attitudes to the recruitment of such graduates. In a company that already recruits scientists and engineers, a TCS programme can facilitate transfers of a specific ensemble of scientific, technological or management knowledge which may be critical to the company's future.

The placement of a TCS Associate within a company not only acts as a conduit to bring in new knowledge: he or she is also able to adapt the new knowledge to the needs of the firm by absorbing certain aspects of company culture. The case studies show that TCS programmes are most successful when the company need no longer rely on external experts, because organizational learning has taken place, enriching the company's existing knowledge.

Organizational learning resulting from TCS programmes has sometimes been so extensive that it is justifiable to refer to it as 'cultural change'. This can involve transformation of a company's attitudes and procedures from a basically 'craft' mode of operation to a 'scientific' mode of operation; or radical changes involving the use of more scientific methods for ensuring quality in processes and products. There are strong indications that some TCS programmes have played major roles in such processes. This is important because company culture needs to change in order to accommodate new technology or managerial methods.

It is interesting to reflect on the success of some TCS programmes in inducing 'cultural change' in SMEs. The TCS Associate enters the company not as a new employee, but as an employee of the university department with which the company is cooperating in the programme. Thus the TCS Associate absorbs the company culture to a considerable extent by virtue of working in the company and being jointly supervised by a member of the company staff. However, his or her absorption of the company culture is limited to the extent that his or her work is controlled by a Local Management Committee (LMC) on which university academics sit; and by virtue of the fact that the TCS Associate is jointly supervised by academics in addition to company managers. Thus, in comparison with a graduate recruited by the company in accordance with its normal procedures, who absorbs the company culture, the TCS Associate is encouraged and supported in the acquisition of knowledge and cultural norms deriving from the academics and university department by whom he or she is employed (Senker and Senker, 1994). TCS Associates can take up knowledge held by the academics, and derived from the network of knowledge production in which the academics are involved, and are in a privileged position to 'inject' this knowledge into the companies (Tiler and Gibbons, 1991). This 'injection' is less likely to be rejected by the company, insofar as it does not come directly from an external source (as it would if the academics themselves were acting as temporary consultants to the company). Thus the potential of TCS Associates to change company culture is greater than that of new graduate recruits with comparable knowledge, skills and experience. This enhanced potential is derived from the supporting infrastructure provided as part of TCS programmes, and by virtue of the possibility that TCS Associates will be perceived by company employees as insiders – as colleagues rather than as outside academics or consultants.

TCS Associates are in an interesting, no doubt sometimes difficult position, of being both part of the company and absorbing its culture; and at the same time, through the direction of their work by a LMC, which includes academics as well as company managers, also being partially independent. TCS programmes can be seen as mechanisms 'whereby firms can "self-adjust" their knowledge bases'. But there are difficulties in integrating graduates into small firms not used to employing them: small firms, especially traditionally run companies in industries using mature technology, may be wary of graduates (Tiler and Gibbons, 1991). Indeed, one of the significant cultural changes, which TCS programmes have the potential to induce in small firms, is changing reluctance to employ graduates into enthusiasm about their recruitment.

Lifelong learning policies

Government policies focus on encouraging individuals to learn throughout their working lives. This is very necessary to foster economic development, but it is not sufficient by itself. Increasing the capacity of SMEs to locate relevant new knowledge and technology and to apply it appropriately to their businesses has been relatively neglected. Particularly in less prosperous regions, one of the principal problems detracting from the UK's competitiveness is failure of SMEs in traditional industries to modernize their products and processes by using new technology. The vast majority of training programmes operate by increasing the supply of suitably educated and trained people, but the failure of SMEs to demand highly qualified workers is of at least equal significance to their competitiveness (Senker, 1999).

Modern Apprenticeships

The minimum requirements for Modern Apprenticeships (now re-branded as Advanced Modern Apprenticeships) are: 1) a formal training programme compatible with the framework developed by the sectoral National Training Organisation (NTO); 2) training aimed at the acquisition of a National Vocational Qualification (NVQ) at level 3 or above, including acquisition of relevant key skills (numeracy, communication, etc); and 3) a formal training contract between the apprentice and the sponsoring employer. Unless the relevant NTO framework stipulates off-the-job instruction, none is required. Most Modern Apprentices work under frameworks without such a requirement and, although most do receive at least some off-the-job instruction, much appears to have little educational content.

But there are serious questions about the feasibility of reviving apprenticeship via Modern Apprenticeship Schemes in the unregulated environment of the UK. In summary, these are the low educational attainments of many potential apprentices, widespread youth preference for full-time schooling, low employer demand for apprenticeship when it is regulated by market forces alone, dangers of employers free-riding on the training efforts of others, low quality in work-based training and under-training in the face of high payroll costs for apprentices (Ryan, 2000).

The National Vocational Qualifications (NVQ) system

The NVQ system was originally intended to simplify the structure of qualifications and a senior official of the Qualifications Curriculum Authority (QCA) has admitted that it has manifestly failed to do this. What the introduction of the NCVQ (the National Council for Vocational Qualifications, the predecessor of the QCA in terms of responsibility for vocational qualifications) did was 'to *add another set of qualifications* to an already confused system' (emphasis in the original text). In 1998, 446,000 NVQ certificates were issued. A similar number (447,000) were issued for non-NVQ qualifications, mainly delivered in publicly funded colleges (Stobart, 2000).

Few small firms have adopted NVQs, largely because of the complexity of the system and the work involved in implementing assessment processes. In effect, instead of having a choice of learning pathways leading to nationally recognized qualifications, employees, especially those in SMEs, are generally denied access to qualifications. Incentives to train are reduced substantially by the considerable amount of paperwork employers have to complete to qualify for NVQ funding. Lack of employer and employee interest in NVQs derives from the lack of incentives to acquire them, to the poor design of the qualifications and of the standards that underlie them. It is of little value to offer SMEs standards and qualifications for their employees to aspire to without giving them sufficient information on how to achieve them. Pressure from the NCVQ and the earmarking of funds forced ITOs to concentrate on Lead Body and Awarding Body functions of producing standards and qualifications. Constraints on the resources available to ITOs resulted in reduction in their efforts to produce, modernize and market guidance on training processes, curricula and courses (Senker, 2000).

To the extent that the training system responds to the training needs of employers, it responds mainly to the needs of large employers. Perhaps partly because the training systems have been designed by government bureaucrats in consultation with representatives of large firms, they do not take sufficient account of the extreme difficulties small firms have in dealing with paperwork, and their inability to afford to employ people to deal with it. For example, NVQs and the standards that they are based on have been influenced by employers, but almost exclusively by large employers, if only because few small employers have the time to serve on the committees which design NVQs. As a consequence, the NVQ system is far too complex and paper-driven to meet the diverse needs of small firms.

A large number of studies show that 'the NVQ system has largely failed to achieve its objectives in stimulating training and upskilling in the SME sector' (Matlay and Hyland, 1997). In 'Working to Learn' we argued that small employers:

cannot cope with the complexities of current narrowly focused training approaches, let alone a programme with wider objectives. Their role is and should remain central, but there is a need for structures to support and enhance the contribution that such employers can reasonably be expected to make. (Evans *et al*, 1997: 12)

The constraints on small firms need to be recognized: unaided, they cannot deal with bureaucratic demands from funding and other bodies. The practical training and work experience that small firms can provide represents a potentially valuable but neglected national asset: there are far fewer training opportunities available for trainees in small firms than there should be. But small firm training needs to be supplemented by broader skill training and general education, which can be provided in partnership with other organizations such as group training schemes and further education colleges (Evans *et al*, 1997).

As mentioned above, recent research has suggested that the culture of SMEs is inappropriate for coping with Modern Apprenticeships and National Traineeships (Sims *et al*, 2000). It is suggested that it is the bad design of such programmes and the absence of appropriate intermediate institutions to help SMEs to cope with their complexities which is at fault, rather than the culture of SMEs.

National Training Organizations

Industrial Training Organizations (ITOs), which became National Training Organisations (NTOs), have also been diverted from designing training programmes to help SMEs cope with technological change and be more competitive. NTOs have been forced by funding constraints to deploy a high proportion of their efforts to the design of standards, qualifications and assessment methods to comply with inappropriate guidelines imposed centrally, first by the NCVQ, and then by the QCA. The NCVQ promoted the idea that employers in each industry design qualifications standards and assessment methods. This is by no means the whole story as the NCVQ, followed by the QCA, imposes inappropriate methodologies on Lead Bodies and Awarding Bodies that are responsible for devising standards and qualifications (Senker, 2000).

Government proposals do not seem to be based on any coherent understanding of why small firms do what they do, for example why they train less than they should – if, indeed, they should train more. Storey (1999) suggests three possible sets of reasons why small firms may not train very much, and the evidence for all three is plausible:

1. Because the owners and managers of small firms are stupid and ignorant and do not appreciate the benefits of training. There is some evidence for this, insofar as the government's Teaching Company Scheme has subsidized the employment of graduates (mainly scientists and engineers) in some small firms that have never employed them before. In many cases, the pre-existing attitude of owners and managers is that graduates are just over-paid 'crown princes' with nothing to offer. Indeed, recent research has indicated that a significant consideration for SMEs is to recruit new staff who could get on with their existing workforce. The ability to work together in a small company was often regarded as more important than new recruits having previous experience or qualifications (Sims *et al,* 2000).
2. Because the benefits of training accrue to other firms to a large extent, and not to the firms which train. In contrast to large firms, there is a very restricted internal labour market in small firms, so a high proportion of those who are trained in particular small firms may leave them and exploit their training for their own benefit by setting up their own small firms, or move to employers other than those which have trained them.
3. Because learning derived from experience may be more important than formal training. This is probably true in large firms (see for example Eraut *et al,* 1998), and may be even truer in small firms.

The reorganization of training

Individual Learning Accounts and the University for Industry are designed to reinforce individual responsibility for learning, on the one hand, and offer solutions in the form of the supply of training, on the other. But these initiatives will not be adequate to overcome the substantial barriers to small firm training. In addition, it is necessary to reform the institutional structure so that it encourages small firms to train rather than, as at present, on balance tending to discourage them. Indeed, there are proposals in 'The Learning Age' Green Paper that are likely to *increase* the barriers to training provision in small firms. In discussing mechanisms for sharing investment in skills with employers, the Green Paper states, 'from next September, for employee training which directly benefits individual employers, further education colleges will share these costs equally with employers by increasing fees' (DTI, 1999). Increased fees will not encourage small employers to invest in training.

At the time of writing, the organization and delivery of work-based training (WBT) is under review. Unwin (2000) argues, however, that, 'Whilst a process of whole-scale "re-branding". . . will take place, young people and adults are unlikely to see much improvement in the WBT programmes available to them.'

The Labour government has initiated a 'major overhaul of post-16 funding mechanisms, institutional architecture and contractual arrangements'. The language has changed extensively, in particular the terms 'education and training' are being replaced by 'learning and skills'. But changes in substance are far more difficult to locate: 'one of the key reasons for change is the government's dissatisfaction with the disparate funding streams for post-16 education and training'. TECs are being abolished because the post-16 education and training market 'seemed out-of-control'. But higher education and school sixth forms have not been affected substantially by the reforms, and like the abolished TECs and the arrangements for the new central and local Learning and Skills Councils, 'see the same faith placed in people from the "business community" and in the merits of consumerism that has characterized education and training policy since the late 1970s' (Unwin, 2000).

The Small Business Service

In 1999 DTI undertook consultation about a new Small Business Service (DTI, 1999). The following year, the government published its response (DTI, 2000). The objectives of the Small Business Service (SBS) are:

- acting as a strong voice for small business at the heart of government;
- simplifying and improving the quality and coherence of government support for small businesses;
- helping small firms deal with regulation and ensuring small firms' interests are properly considered in future regulation.

A Small Business Council will report to the Secretary of State for Trade and Industry on the needs of existing and potential small businesses and the effects of government and the SBS on such businesses.

The SBS will promote the benefits of being recognized as an Investor in People to SMEs, as a basis for improving learning at work. Learning and Skills Councils will work closely with the SBS to encourage businesses to invest in their workforce through learning in development. It will be involved in encouraging small businesses to provide Modern Apprenticeships and National Traineeships and to go for Investors in People recognition (DTI, 1999, pp 17 and 26).

The 'Learning to Succeed' Green Paper (DfEE, 1999) provides for small businesses to be represented on the National Learning and Skills Council.

It also mentions the initiation of a new Small Business Service (by the DTI). In 'Learning to Succeed' the government recognizes that the actions of individuals, especially the millions of small businesses, will have a major impact on the skills that individuals develop and on productivity in the economy (p 64): 'in the digital age, learning must take place "on-site" in small and medium sized companies as well as in large businesses' (p 13). However, recruitment difficulties are currently at about the same level as in 1990 and they are particularly acute in small businesses. 'Learning to Succeed' seems to be merely a change in structure as far as small firm training is concerned. Government policy seems very much 'the mixture as before'. Local Learning and Skills Councils' plans will be developed in conjunction with the new SBS, for example by arranging for the Service to provide 'a seamless service to small and medium sized businesses and to integrate skills development with enterprise and business competitiveness' (p 10). It is envisaged that the Learning and Skills Council and the SBS will work very closely together, for example in relation to workforce development services and programmes. But the absence of 'joined up thinking' by the government is demonstrated on pages 26 and 27 of the DTI's consultation document (1999) which lists 'Some of the Government Services to Small Business that will be accessible via the Small Business Service' by the Department offering the service (eg, DfEE services followed by DTI services). These and other initiatives have just been piled on top of each other by successive governments (and of course several have been abolished for various reasons, good and bad).

If the DfEE (now DfES) and the DTI have problems in cooperating at national level, it seems unlikely that the DTI will be able to set up 'a seamless service' at local level. Government policy is based on the assumption that no special incentives are needed to encourage small firms to train; that government has no responsibility for lowering the barriers to them training caused by the complex system of training provision which was created by previous governments and continued by the present one (perhaps even more complicated by the addition of Individual Learning Accounts and the University for Industry). There is no evidence of any coherent government thinking about what is needed to encourage and stimulate small firms to train more; nor is there any new thinking about why small firms should be encouraged to train more from a national point of view.

It is a high priority for the SBS to help reduce the burden of regulation and red tape on small firms. But this aim is unlikely to be realized, at least partly as a consequence of the lack of 'joined-up thinking' in government. While the DTI is committed to reducing the burden of regulation on small firms, the DfEE (now DfES) policies are increasing training paperwork through the highly bureaucratic and small-firm-unfriendly NVQ system.

Some approaches to solutions

The present system of education and training in England and Wales is not delivering the high quality learning we need as a society and economy. Factors which contribute to our poor national performance include: low expectations of what people can achieve; an education system which produces young people who are disillusioned with formal learning; a widespread belief that many are destined for unemployment or low skilled work; and well-founded cynicism about the poor quality of government-financed training schemes for the unemployed (Evans *et al*, 1997).

Provision remains fragmented and incoherent. A-levels are too narrow, specialized and old-fashioned, and it is clear that the introduction of AS levels has not succeeded in solving deep-rooted problems with the system. Nevertheless, the Education Secretary Estelle Morris, while admitting that 'the new AS has more than its fair share of problems', has ruled out fundamental overhaul of the new sixth form curriculum (W Woodward, 'AS overhaul fails to satisfy unions', *The Guardian*, 1 July 2001).

Vocational training is too job-specific, low level and poorly coordinated. Inadequate education and training has deprived young people of opportunities for earning an honest living. The costs to them and the rest of society – not least in terms of youth crime – have been very high. Foundation training standards are way below those needed to enable the workforce to become competitive. Youth Training Schemes have been revamped frequently, but overall must be judged to have failed (Evans *et al*, 1997). There is no solid reason to suppose that the latest version – Foundation Modern Apprenticeships, the re-branded National Traineeships – will prove an exception.

Market approaches are cumbersome and expensive to administer. Colleges are forced to give too much priority to short-term financial considerations and too little to provision of courses which meet current and anticipated local labour market needs. Changes in the ways in which education and training are organized and funded have resulted in the continuation of an absurdly complex, expensive and incomprehensible system.

Recent experience and extensive research demonstrate that market forces cannot form the basis for effective national education and training strategies. We need an industrial strategy based on achieving a high-skill, high-productivity economy. The broad-based skills required by the economy cannot be produced through full-time schooling and mass higher education alone. We also need effective work-based education and training which embraces academic, vocational and practical elements. We need to move from the failed market-based model of provision to one based on *partnership and entitlement*. Partners should include central government, employers and their representative organizations, employees and their representative organizations – the trade unions, local authorities and Local Delivery Partnerships, the Careers Service, colleges and voluntary bodies (Evans *et al*, 1997).

Addressing small firms' demand for training could involve giving them advice on product and market strategies, giving them better access to investment capital and different forms of shared facilities which can contribute to the quality of goods and services. The most effective government scheme at present for increasing small firms' innovation, their demand for more highly skilled workers and the supply of relevant training is the Teaching Company Scheme. Several studies have demonstrated its value in terms both of encouraging technology transfer and training in SMEs. The TCS has been extended to include technicians, and the resources devoted to it have increased steadily. But expenditure on the TCS is extremely small in relation to its proven potential. An obvious solution to increasing small firms' demands for skill and their investment in training would be to develop more TCS-style programmes, to expand the resources devoted to them substantially, and to extend their scope considerably.

More structures are needed to promote cooperation between small and large employers, and among small employers at local level; and to remove or at least reduce some of the bureaucratic burdens that engagement in training currently entails, so as to enable SMEs to contribute to the quality of the trainees' learning experience. More and stronger intermediate institutions are needed. In the engineering industry in particular, Group Training Schemes (GTS) fulfil such roles – acting in effect as training officers for member firms as well as training providers. In addition to helping companies to plan training in line with their business goals, they help them to recruit trainees, supervise their training, provide NVQ assessment services and generally help firms to deal with the excessive paperwork generated by the NVQ system. As the Confederation of Group Training Schemes points out, 'the time taken for Group Training Schemes to bid to gain, manage and administer. . . contracts is many times greater than the time they allocate to training' (letter to the author, June 1998). The financial pressures on these organizations are substantial. Many have gone out of business, many more have converted themselves into private companies, though a significant number still remain which operate as companies limited by guarantee, and aim to increase the amount and effectiveness of their (mainly small firm) members' training. There has, however, been some progress in the last few years.

In some sectors, policies designed to sustain and resuscitate existing GTS and stimulate the creation of new ones could constitute part of the solution to deficiencies in small firm training. Such roles may need further public support beyond that offered by the market and such support can be justified and even required by society's interest in supporting training in small firms. However, it is important to note that the promotion of cooperative solutions should be carefully tailored to the needs of particular sectors. Research has indicated, for example, that there is strong resistance to the idea of GTS in construction (Senker *et al*, 1998), and other cooperative solutions need to be initiated in such sectors.

The principal influences on training provision at present are the government and large employers. Securing more participation by small firms in training requires small firms themselves to be more involved in its design and governance; and requires that the bureaucratic burdens involved in engagement in the current system of government-supported training be reduced substantially.

References

Bessant, J and Haywood, B (1988) Islands, archipelagos and continents: progress on the road to computer-integrated manufacturing, *Research Policy*, **17** (6), pp 349–62

Braham, P (1985) Marks & Spencer: a technological approach to retailing, in *Implementing New Technologies. Choice, decision and change in manufacturing*, eds E Rhodes and D Wield, Basil Blackwell, Oxford

Dale, A (1986) *Organisational Learning about Information Technology: A manager's guide and strategy*, Management Development for Information Technology, (MANDIT) Report Part 2, Unit 6, Aids to Development, Manpower Services Commission

DfEE (1999) *Learning to Succeed. A new framework for post-16 learning*, DfEE, London

Dodgson, M (1993) Organizational learning: a review of some literature, *Organization Studies*, **14** (3), pp 375–94

DTI (1999) *The Small Business Service: A public consultation*, June, Department of Trade and Industry, London

DTI (2000) *The Small Business Service: Summary of consultation replies and the government's response*, Department of Trade and Industry, London

Entorf, H and Kramarz, F (1997) Does unmeasured ability explain higher wages of new technology workers?, *European Economic Review*, **41** (8), pp 1,489–509

Eraut, M, Alderton, J, Cole, G and Senker, P (1998) *Development of Knowledge and Skills in Employment*, University of Sussex Institute of Education, January

Evans, K, Hodkinson, P, Keep, E, Maguire, M, Raffe, D, Rainbird, H, Senker, P and Unwin, L (1997) *Working to Learn: A work-based route to learning for young people*, Institute of Personnel and Development, London

Gibb, A (1996) *Training for Enterprise. The role of education and training in small and medium enterprise (SME) development*, Durham University Business School discussion paper, 28 May

Gibbons, M and Johnston, R (1974) The roles of science in technological innovation, *Research Policy*, **3**, pp 220–42

IRDAC (1991) *Skills Shortages in Europe*, Industrial Research and Development Advisory Committee of the Commission of the European Communities, Brussels

Lowe, S and Rothwell, R (1987) *The Sussex Technology Transfer Centre. A background report*, Science Policy Research Unit, University of Sussex, Brighton

March, J, Sproull, L and Tamuz, M (1991) Learning from samples of one or fewer, *Organization Science*, **2** (1), pp 1–13

Mason, G (1995) *The New Graduate Supply-shock: Recruitment and utilisation of graduates in British industry*, National Institute of Economic and Social Research, London

Matlay, H, and Hyland, T (1997) NVQs in the small business sector. A critical overview, *Education and Training*, **39** (9), pp 325–32

Mowery, D (1983) The relationship between intrafirm and contractual forms of industrial research, 1900–1940, *Explorations in Economic History*, **20** (4), pp 351–74

Polanyi, M (1966) *The Tacit Dimension*, Routledge and Kegan Paul, London

Rigg, M, Christie, I and White, M (1989) *Advanced Polymers & Composites: Creating the key skills*, a report prepared for the Skills Unit of the Training Agency by the Policy Studies Institute, Training Agency, Sheffield

Rothwell, R (1975) Information patterns in innovation, in *Scientific and Technical Information Needs in R&D Laboratories*, eds A Robertson and R Rothwell, Science Policy Research Unit, University of Sussex

Rothwell, R (1991) External networking and innovation in small and medium sized manufacturing firms in Europe. Paper prepared for Network of Innovators Workshop, May 1–3 1990, Montreal, Canada

Ryan, P (2000) The institutional requirements of apprenticeship: evidence from small EU countries, *International Journal of Training and Development*, **4** (1), pp 42–65

Schein, E (1985) *Organizational Culture and Leadership*, Jossey-Bass, San Francisco, CA

Senker, J (1986) Technological co-operation between manufacturers and retailers to meet market demand, *Food Marketing*, **2** (3), pp 88–100

Senker, J (1997) Overcoming barriers to technology transfer in small and medium sized firms, in *Managing Technological Knowledge Transfer – Proceedings COST A3*, ed S Campodall'Orto, Office for Official Publications of the European Communities, Luxembourg

Senker, P (1981) Technical change, employment and international competition, *Futures*, June, pp 159–70

Senker, P (1984) Implications of CAD/CAM for management, *Omega*, **12** (3), pp 225–31

Senker, P (1999) Education and training for innovation: individual and organizational learning, *The IPTS Report*, November, pp 20–25

Senker, P (2000) The relationship of the NVQ system to learning in the workplace. Céreq Seminar, The Certification of Vocational Qualifications in France and the United Kingdom, 8–10 March, Marseille

Senker, P and Senker, J (1994) Transferring technology and expertise from universities to industry: Britain's Teaching Company Scheme, *New Technology, Work and Employment*, **9** (2), pp 81–92

Senker, P and Simmonds, P (1991) Changing technology and design work in the British engineering industry, *New Technology, Work and Employment*, **6** (2), pp 91–9

Senker, P, Gann, D, Clarke, L *et al* (1998) *Strategic Review of Construction Skills Training*, Construction Industry Board/Thomas Telford, London

Sims, D, Golden, S, Blenkinsop, S and Lewis, G (2000) *Barriers to Take-up of Modern Apprenticeships and National Traineeships by SMEs and Specific Sectors*, National Foundation for Educational Research, London

Stobart, G (2000) Can a single standard of vocational certification impose itself in the UK? Paper prepared for Céreq Conference, 8–10 March, Marseilles

Storey, D (1999) *Changing the Agenda for Training in Small Firms*, Manufacturing Brief, London, Institute for Manufacturing, June

Tiler, C and Gibbons, M (1991) A case study of organizational learning: The UK Teaching Company Scheme, *Industry & Higher Education,* March, pp 47–54

Unwin, L (2000) Work-based training programmes in England: musical chairs, pass the parcel, snakes and ladders, and other nursery pastimes in the new world of learning and skills. Paper presented to the ESRC Seminar, 'Home Internationals' Comparison of Work-Based Training Programmes in England, Scotland, Wales and Northern Ireland, University of Edinburgh, 3 November

Walsh, V, Townsend, J, Senker, P and Huggett, C (1980) *Technical Change and Skilled Manpower Needs in the Plastics Processing Industry,* Science Policy Research Unit, University of Sussex, Brighton

Winter, S (1987) Knowledge and competence as strategic assets, in *The Competitive Challenge. Strategies for industrial innovation and renewal*, ed D Teece, Ballinger, Cambridge, MA, pp 159–83

Chapter 9

The dynamics of workplace learning: the role of work organizations

David Ashton

Introduction

Within sociology the topic of workplace learning, while having only recently come into prominence, nevertheless has its roots in the work of the founding fathers. Marx, with his concern for the conditions of the working class, sought to demonstrate the impact of work on the workers' experience of the world. His work on alienation has been picked up and developed by Blauner in the 1960s, although there it became almost synonymous with work satisfaction (Blauner, 1964). Durkheim (1893/1964) used the division of labour as one of his central themes, highlighting the impact of the 'abnormal' forms in limiting the opportunities for learning that were available to workers. Both of these were concerned with showing how the way in which we organize work conditions the worker's experience of the world. The mechanism through which workers acquire their specific perceptions of the world is, of course, the process of learning. Thus, while not specifically concerned with the process of learning, both revealed the fundamental proposition, that the way in which we organize work shapes and conditions the individual's perception of the world.

This theme was further developed with more of a focus on learning by the work of Kohen in the 1970s. Using a longitudinal methodology he studied the impact of work organization on the personality of the worker. What his early work demonstrated was that workers who moved through a series of jobs, characterized by routine tasks and limited autonomy, with little or no opportunity to exercise discretion, and subject to close supervision, did not develop their skills, especially their intellectual skills. Indeed, for this group there was a greater probability that these intellectual skills would actually decline over time. In contrast, workers who moved through a series of jobs which did provide autonomy, which did offer the opportunity to exercise discretion and were not subject to close supervision, improved their intellectual skills over time (Kohen and Schooler, 1983). This work, originally conducted in capitalist US, was later replicated in socialist Poland (Kohen and Schooler, 1990) where the same results were found,[1] suggesting that it was the organization of work, especially job conditions, and not market relations, which had such a profound impact on the worker's ability or capacity to learn.[2]

Today, this long tradition of sociological enquiry into the ways in which the organization of work conditions what we learn and how we perceive the world has been swamped by a series of more recent sociological and social psychological studies focusing on how we learn at work. The work of Vygotsky (Cole *et al*, 1978) generated important insights into the social basis of learning, the significance of culture and the role of others in the process of learning. Lave and Wenger (1991) moved on to locate the process of learning in communities of practice. Consequently, we are starting to understand the mechanics of how we learn, the role of the mentor or significant other and the ways in which the process of learning is intimately related to the formation of identity. More recently Engestrom (1994) and Eraut *et al* (1998) have revealed the significance of informal learning in the workplace and the ways in which that occurs. These are all important contributions to our knowledge.

As with most significant advances in our knowledge there have been costs associated with them. To make the advances on how we learn, researchers have narrowed the focus to concentrate on how learning takes place in the process of interaction between individuals and groups: Vygotsky on the process of interaction between the teacher and novice through which culture is transmitted; Lave and Wenger on the ways in which the occupational community is reproduced through the learning process, and Engestrom and Eraut on the informal nature of the processes involved. One major cost of these advances has been the loss of the earlier focus on what is learnt and how the (work/job) context shapes the learning. The aim of this chapter is to help rectify the balance.

The argument is that we cannot fully understand the process of workplace learning unless we locate it in the context of the underlying structural relationships that underpin the process. These underlying relationships determine the range of opportunities for learning, the knowledge that is made available to be learnt, the support available for learning and finally the rewards that are available for successful learning. These are all crucial in influencing the extent to which workers can learn at work and the demands it makes on their intellect. We demonstrate this through a comparison of workplace learning in Taylorist organizations and high performance work organizations (HPWOs).[3]

Workplace learning in Taylorist organizations

Taylorist forms of work organization tend to be personified by mass production companies. There, the organization of work is determined by managers. Tasks are broken down into their constituent elements with each worker performing one limited set of operations, whether that is placing one component on a car as it moves down the assembly line, stitching the collar onto a garment or sweeping up peas as they fall off a belt conveying them to the freezing unit. This leaves operators on the line with little or no room for independent decisions about work tempo, order or method. Only in non-routine situations may operators, within certain narrowly defined limits, take decisions themselves. The tasks can often be learnt in minutes, although it may take hours and sometimes days of practice to learn to coordinate the motor operations involved, in order to get the execution of the task up to the speed required by the line, or to make a minimum level of pay, if employees are paid by the piece. There are no further formal opportunities for the development of skills or learning.

The knowledge requirements are minimal. There may be a literacy requirement to enable the worker to read safety instructions. Beyond that there are no requirements for the worker to understand how the production process operates or how the company is organized or indeed how it is performing in the market. However, through their everyday activities workers do acquire tacit knowledge about the machines they operate and the social context within which they work (Darrah, 1996).

Of course, this description refers only to the distribution of knowledge in the formal organization. In reality there will also be an informal culture, which may or may not be at variance with the formal organization,[4] but which will also be important in providing access to knowledge about the workshop or office, how it operates and what the politics of it are. Darrah's work has explicated the significance of this culture and its importance as a source of learning. Knowledge of this may take longer to acquire than that required for the formal work task.

As there are few formal opportunities for learning it is not surprising that there are few supports for learning. In these organizations the line managers or supervisors decide what the workers need to know. That small fraction of knowledge and information is then transmitted from the expert 'trainer' to the novice or trainee. Training is highly structured and task-specific and usually occurs in a classroom situation or, if the task is very basic, on the job. Workers are given information on a 'need to know' basis, providing them with just enough information or knowledge to perform their clearly defined task.[5] Krogt and Warmerdam (1997: 92) describe training in two such food processing companies in the Netherlands as follows:

> Training is primarily seen as an instrument for providing the skills and attitudes required for the proper functioning of the production process: it is pre-designed by experts, with the subject matter supplied in the small portions required for specific tasks, planned beforehand and monitored during the training process. Having had the need for training identified by the departmental manager, the trainer draws up the training plan and implements the programme.

In this entire process the workers tend to play what the authors term 'a consuming role', with short courses being delivered to them in a somewhat coercive manner.

Rewards are almost exclusively in the form of payment for the task performed or for the hour worked. This tends to focus the mind of the worker on the immediate operations and the narrow tasks they perform. Few other rewards are available through the formal structure of the organization.

The same Taylorist techniques of work organization are also applied to much clerical work. The extensive use of the division of labour means that many clerical tasks are broken down into individual components with one clerk responsible for just part of the overall administrative process. Sometimes this may mean just inputting specific forms of data, handling specific types of phone calls with a predetermined script, or just recording enquiries. However, some clerical work has not yet been fully standardized, and there one is more likely to find opportunities to develop broader skills.

This was revealed by our own research into the process of learning in a branch of a large multinational corporation in South East Asia. The company saw itself as a 'learning organization' and did indeed implement many of the latest human resource development practices, such as a comprehensive appraisal system, systematic training, multi-skilling for technicians, line management responsibility for training and the use of trainers as learning consultants. It was widely regarded as one of the leaders in the region when it came to training, although it still retained a traditional, hierarchical form of organization. We interviewed 195 employees (10 per cent of the total) representing all job grades, from mail boy to function heads. The semi-structured interviews lasted between 40 minutes and 1 hour and 40 minutes. They covered how the person learnt, who they learnt from and what barriers they encountered in learning.[6] One of the most important findings was that even here, the rigid, hierarchical character of the organization created many barriers to the development of clerical workers' skills. There were a number of reasons for this.

First, unlike new or trainee managers for whom there was a clear developmental plan aimed at providing them with an overall knowledge of the organization and how it functioned, for clerical workers there was nothing. They learnt their immediate tasks and that was it. In some instances they were moved to other departments and hence learnt new skills, but these were usually unrelated to the skills and knowledge they may have acquired in their previous job. There was nothing cumulative about their learning.

Second, within their existing jobs any new opportunities for learning additional skills were sometimes denied by their managers. 'They don't want to help you achieve.' 'They protect their own interests. It helps them if they are the only people who know.' This sometimes took the form of the manager denying the employee access to relevant knowledge. As one of the interviewees remarked, 'Managers are not cascading information. Knowledge is power and people are selfish – more so at the middle and lower levels.' Even in this organization, which was very conscious of the need to inform its employees and made extensive use of newsletters, bulletins, etc, for the individual clerical worker wishing to broaden his or her skills, being deprived of more information in this way effectively denied them the opportunity to develop and tied their skills to those required for the immediate tasks.

Third, although some managers were conscious of the need to support learning, many were ineffective in this role and either could not, or did not want to provide effective feedback. As one clerk remarked, 'She (her boss) is very temperamental, sometimes she is nice but usually with other people. I would have preferred some explanations rather than relying on guesswork and constantly being referred back to the files.' Describing how she learnt her job, one employee said that her first boss just gave her manuals and things to do. If she did not do them well she was not given anything new. She found this 'ineffective' for herself. Her second boss gave her 'guidelines on what to do, discusses and explains with me'. This she found far more effective.

The fourth reason was the failure to reward learning. Here again there were limits imposed by the use of hourly wages to reward clerks, but it was not always the financial reward that employees looked for. What was evident from the interviews was that one of the most significant rewards sought by clerical employees for learning was just a mere acknowledgement from their bosses or supervisors. In the words of two of the employees, 'I prefer proper recognition, something personal, even a letter', or 'I would like acknowledgement by the management.'

This brief examination of clerical work reveals that while much of it is subject to the same constraints as manual work, there may be, because of the more individualized nature of the relationship with the boss or supervisor, more opportunities to develop other skills. However, the learning process is fragile. It requires opportunities to develop skills, access to knowledge in order to learn the skills, support in the learning process and finally some form of reward for successful performance. In conventional hierarchical organizations, the case of the clerical workers shows how difficult it is to bring all these together. In contrast, organizations that have systematically introduced high performance work practices are succeeding in bringing these various components together. There they are developing the workplace as a source of continuous learning and skill acquisition.

Workplace learning in high performance work organizations

We define HPWOs as those that make systematic use of bundles of high performance work practices. At the moment there is still some debate over precisely which practices comprise these bundles, but using the existing literature, as well as analysis of case studies, we have identified four dimensions as the basis for the bundles.[7]

The first is what we have termed the *work design/employee involvement dimension*. This comprises practices that seek to broaden workers' skills and involve them in determining the organization of production. Workers' skills are broadened through practices such as multi-skilling, job rotation and team working. Worker involvement can be delivered through self-managed work teams, quality circles, total quality management and various forms of worker consultation, all of which involve workers in the decision making process about how their immediate work tasks are organized and how they can most effectively meet the objectives of the organization. In terms of learning opportunities, these workers are faced with the possibility of acquiring a range of different skills, while their involvement in the decision making process in the workplace means that they are continually facing new problems and challenges. This creates the possibility of continuous learning.

The second dimension we refer to as the *support for performance practices*. These comprise the practices that support the process of learning and performance improvement. They include the use of formal training programmes and structured on-the-job training to deliver the technical skills and coaching programmes, and action learning to deliver the softer skills. They also include appraisal and mentoring schemes to provide feedback on the acquisition of skills and work performance. These are all a means of institutionalizing feedback to ensure that skill enhancement is not left to the vagaries of the individual supervisor, as was evident in the case cited above. The use of these practices is not essential to ensure that effective feedback is provided. Indeed, in many small enterprises high levels of workplace learning and skill formation are accomplished without the use of formal practices. We use them here as indicative of an attempt by the company or organization to institutionalize feedback.

The third dimension we refer to as consisting of *information/knowledge sharing practices*. These are practices designed to provide the employee with knowledge of the business, its performance and the ways it operates. These include practices such as regular team briefings, meetings of the whole workforce, newsletters, and the regular distribution of financial information. Their purpose is to ensure that all employees have as full a knowledge as possible about the company and its current objectives, because this is necessary for them to make effective decisions about the organization of their own work and their contribution toward the achievement of organizational objectives. Again, management can ensure that these objectives are achieved through the course of everyday interaction, but in larger organizations these practices, or others akin to them, are used to institutionalize the distribution of knowledge. Once again we would stress that the absence of formal practices, especially in SMEs, does not necessarily mean that these objectives are not being achieved.[8]

The final set of practices we refer to as the *rewards dimension*. These consist of payment systems geared toward rewarding performance, sometimes at the individual level in variants of performance-related pay, but also at the group level, in the form of gain-share schemes, profit sharing or group bonuses. There are of course other ways of rewarding performance, including the use of company awards for achievement, employee citations and the numerous ways in which an organization can provide 'perks' for individuals or groups who have demonstrated a significant achievement. The important point here is that the company systematically rewards performance and ensures that the workers obtain their share of the gains from any improvements. Without that reward, the sustained effort and application required to generate continuous improvements are unlikely to occur.

Case studies

Thorn Lighting Ltd

We illustrate how these practices (broadly defined) are used to generate higher levels of learning, skill and improvements in performance, through the use of two case studies undertaken for the International Labour Office.[9] The first is that of Thorn Lighting Ltd, a UK manufacturer of lighting components and systems. This is a company that had a history of conflict between management and workers and operates in a very competitive market. Previously, the production system had been based on traditional Fordist lines with Taylorist techniques used for work organization. Following a management buy-out, steps were taken to restructure in an attempt to halt a threatened decline and improve market share. If the company were to survive then higher levels of performance had to be achieved by the workforce. Crucially, the workers had to be won over by the management, work reorganized and the system of industrial relations transformed.

What appeared crucial was the transformation of the culture of the company. If workers were to commit themselves to the company then the old culture of conflict had to go. To this end the company threw open its financial accounts to the union and worked through the business plan with union representatives. They also asked all employees to go through a two-day course in which they participated in simulated business activities, the 'UK Team Building' exercise as they called it. It took four and a half years to put all their employees through it. The aim was to build trust on the basis of which changes in work organization could be introduced. This was a mammoth task. It meant realigning and integrating the workers' culture with that of management, in the process of which both would need to change. At the level of the individual worker it meant changing their frames of reference and building trust between themselves and their supervisors.

As we saw above, trust between the learner and the person teaching is an important, if not essential, basis for learning within an organization. In the case of the clerical workers cited above, once trust between themselves and their supervisor was lost, employees could not risk trying out new ideas or taking on new tasks lest they be criticized by their supervisor and any failures in performance held against them. Similarly at the organizational level in Thorn, unless workers' representatives could see that management were being open and not hiding anything, they could not move forward to collaboration on joint activities.

On the basis of that trust, the old Fordist division of labour was replaced by a system of 'cellular production'. The layout of the factory was changed so that all operations relating to a product could be done within one area. Production was now organized around teams that had the authority to determine how they organized production and met quality standards. The workers now took responsibility, typically in groups of not more than 20, each with a working team leader. Operators rotated around tasks, although not every operator had been trained in every task. There were also other differences in the organization of teams, reflecting variations in the item produced.

These changes involved a radical transformation of the workers' orientation toward learning. Rather than coming to work to perform the same narrow task day after day, they were now coming to work to perform different tasks. They had to upgrade themselves and acquire new task skills. Of even greater significance from the point of view of learning at work, they were now involved in the decision making process about how work was organized. They confronted new problems when they arrived at work and were called upon to help resolve them. To aid this process, information on business awareness, ranging from cash flow to material inflation and the state of the market, was cascaded down the organization and employees provided with monthly briefing sessions. In addition, facilities were provided for each team to have a room and time to reflect on the process of continuous improvement.

In Vygotskyan terms this represents a massive increase in the zone of proximal development. The worker moves from a situation in which he or she is only concerned with performing a narrow set of operations, focused only on the number of widgets produced, to one in which they are now concerned with maximizing the performance of their group, in the context of the wider business operations of the organization. Now, not only have the demands on their practical skills increased, there has also been a substantial increase in the demands on their intellectual or cognitive capabilities. Similarly, when viewed as a community of practice, we can see that the community is transformed from a small group engaged in the same task on the same machines day after day with only minor involvement of the self, to one in which the worker is now a member of a much larger community, synonymous with the whole organization of 1,000 plus, with a more significant involvement of the self. The work context is making new and increased demands on the worker's ability to learn.

The new relationships also impose demands on the managers. They had to buy into the changes and, as initial team leaders, provide role models for the other employees. In the jargon of the business, it was crucial that they 'walked the talk'. Their relationship with the workers was fundamentally transformed.[10] Like the workers, they required additional training to develop their technical, personal and team leading abilities. When it came to rewards, these had to be re-thought and made appropriate for the new system. They were still negotiated collectively but the management decided against using financial incentives for the teams, as this was thought to detract from the focus on the overall performance of the company. Teams were rewarded in more symbolic forms, for example by using operators and team leaders to represent the company at award ceremonies.

Comfort DC

The second case study is that of Comfort Driving Centre in Singapore. In Singapore the law requires that learner drivers attend a recognized driving school or have a registered instructor to learn. This is a very competitive market with many private instructors and two other Japanese-owned companies all competing for the same business. In the space of three years Comfort DC, starting from scratch, secured a 25 per cent share of the market. It differentiated its product from competitors in a number of ways, first by making the experience of learning to drive a pleasant one, second by speeding up the process of learning, and third through its ability to teach socially responsible driving. The key to success was the commitment from the CEO to transform the relationship between 'instructor' and learner driver.

Instructors were to cease instructing in a didactic manner and instead they were to facilitate the learning process. This involved far more than merely changing the terminology. The vision came from the CEO, the transformation of that into practice came from the newly recruited and trained instructors. They were given the responsibility of thinking through the learning process from the point of view of the trainee. They had to learn how to support the learning process rather than as traditionally done: sit alongside the trainee, issuing instructions.

This transformation was achieved by teams of employees in a number of ways. First, the office was redesigned in such a way as to take the tension out of the process of preparing for the test. Office procedures were designed around the needs of the trainee to eliminate waiting time, not those of the office administrators, while trainees were given a choice of instructors. The instructors underwent a lengthy training process, which included tuition on how to facilitate the learning process. This tuition was grounded in basic learning theory, gearing the learning to the learner's knowledge and skill at the point of entry to the programme and then using explanation, demonstration and practice as the principles to guide the process. The instructors become experts who guide this learning process. It is their activities and behaviour that make the difference to the trainee's experience.

The company also used teams to generate further incremental improve-ments. One such team redesigned the Centre's driving circuit to incorporate motorcycles, after being told by expert consultants that this was not possible because of the lack of space. Another team set to work to develop a computer-based teaching program to deliver the theory component of the course. Although they had only basic secondary education, the team developed a program that delivered the theory in three languages, was easy to follow and, by using graphics, video-clips and animation, made the experience of learning driving theory fun rather than a chore. The program could be accessed from home as well as at the driving centre. This further reduced the time taken to learn and made the learning a more pleasurable experience. The team responsible for the development of the program then continued to meet to seek further improvements in its design.

The impact of these and other changes was that learning time was reduced and the company's pass rate rose to two and a half times higher than that of private instructors. From the point of view of the workers or staff, there was now far more to work than turning up and 'instructing' trainees from the passenger seat. This they still did, but in a different way, which was more demanding on their skills as they sought to facilitate learning on the part of the client/customer. Work was also a place where they developed new skills in programming and designing learning packages, where they took control over the environment as they sought to identify and introduce improvements in the process of learning. They moved away from being instructors and became experts in learning. For these service sector workers, work became a constant source of new learning opportunities and problems that demanded that they too had a knowledge of the business finance, new technology and market circumstances.[11]

Conclusion

The important point about these case studies is that they show it is how the transformation of the broader relationships within work is embedded that is responsible for bringing about radical changes in the demands work makes on the practical and cognitive skills of workers. In both cases this involved the introduction of high performance practices, in Thorn as an explicit set of management techniques, in Comfort DC as an orientation on the part of the founding CEO.[12] It was the use of these techniques, involving a way of organizing the process of production that is different from the conventional Fordist and Taylorist techniques, that has transformed the learning process. The implication is that as long as conventional techniques are used then the opportunities for workers to learn at work will be at best restricted and at worst reduced.

Working in a context determined by these new relationships not only increased the skills of the workers but also offered a challenge to their intellectual development as they mastered the new demands of their business environment, for example the need to master new technology, to understand the operation of markets and the details of the production process.[13] Moreover, by involving workers in the organization of the production process on a day-to-day basis, work became the focus of a process of continuous improvement, a constant source of new challenges about which decisions have to be made. In this way work offers the prospect of lifelong learning. It demonstrates how the way in which we organize work determines its potential as a source of learning.

It follows from this analysis that if we are to further our understanding of the process of workplace learning then we must move beyond a narrow focus on the process of interaction in the immediate workplace that has characterized recent research. While that can tell us much about the mechanisms through which we learn, its role in developing our understanding of the dynamics of workplace learning is restricted. To understand the possibilities of workplace learning in enhancing the broader development of the worker, we must also locate the worker's learning in the context of the wider relations of production.

Notes

1. Kohen's data are used here to argue that the experiences acquired at work, especially job conditions that provide for the exercise of self-direction, have consequences for orientation to self and society, values and cognitive functions. He argues that what is learnt at work is transferred into other areas of social life.

2. This same theme informs much of the early literature on the transition from school to work in the 1970s; see Ashton and Field (1976), Brown (1987) and Willis (1977).

3. There is a considerable debate in the literature on whether these organizations should be termed 'high performance' or 'high involvement' organizations. We use the term 'high performance' here but recognize that performance relates to more than financial performance and includes worker commitment and customer satisfaction as well as a range of other indicators.

4. There is a long tradition of sociological enquiry into the informal culture of the workplace and the role this may play in sustaining workers' control over aspects of the production process and/or resistance to management; see for example Roy (1952).

5. It is no accident that this approach to training was associated with the growing influence of behaviourist psychology. The assumption required to organize training for these types of jobs, the clearly specified objectives in terms of motor activities and the inputs of training required to produce these outputs, closely matched the assumptions the early behaviourists made about the process of learning.

6. Details of this research are available in a paper by D Ashton and L Jones, 'The fragility of the learning process: the impact of organizational structure and practices on learning in the workplace', Centre for Labour Market Studies, University of Leicester.

7. Details of the analysis on which this section of the chapter is based can be found in D N Ashton and J Sung, *Workplace Learning and High Performance Working*, ILO, Geneva, forthcoming.

8. The precise practices that constitute these bundles will vary from one company to another and from one country to another. Moreover, they will only tend to be found in larger organizations. In SMEs they are embedded in the informal working practices of the company.

9. Full details of these case studies are available on the ILO Web site: http://www.ilo.org/public/english/employment/skills/training/casest/index.htm.

10. Given the magnitude of these changes for both managers and workers, there were some who could not adjust to them and preferred the greater 'certainties' of the old system. As in other cases, this means that there is some turnover inevitably associated with these changes, either voluntary or involuntary.

11. Here it is important to point out that we have been focusing on learning in the formal organization on the assumption that formal and informal cultures are more highly integrated in HPWOs, as both groups will have the same values, namely the achievement of organizational objectives. This is another area in urgent need of research.

12. The director of Comfort DC, Haum Chak Koon, was leading a small organization (160 staff at the time of the first interview) and explicit formalized procedures were not in use.

13. Koike (1995) was one of the first social scientists to bring our attention to the importance of studying workers' intellectual skills.

References

Ashton, D N and Field, D (1976) *The Transition From School to Work*, Hutchinson, London

Blauner, R (1964) *Alienation and Freedom: The factory worker and his industry*, University of Chicago Press, Chicago, IL

Brown, P (1987) *Schooling Ordinary Kids: Inequality, unemployment and the new vocationalism*, Tavistock, London

Cole, M, John-Steiner, V, Scribner, S and Souberman, E (eds) (1978) *L S Vygotsky, Mind in Society: The development of higher psychological processes*, Harvard University Press, London

Darrah, C N (1996) *Learning at Work: An exploration in industrial ethnography*, Garland Publishing, London

Durkheim, E (1893/1964) *The Division of Labour*, Free Press, New York (first French edition 1893)

Engestrom, Y (1994) *Training for Change. A new approach to instruction and learning in training*, ILO, Geneva

Eraut, M, Alderton, J, Cole, G and Senker, P (1998) Learning from other people at work, in *Learning at Work*, ed F Coffield, Policy Press, Bristol

Kohen, M L and Schooler, C (1983) *Work and Personality: An inquiry into the impact of social stratification*, Ablex, Norwood, NJ

Kohen, M L and Schooler, C (1990) *Social Structure and Self-direction: A comparative analysis of the United States and Poland*, Blackwell, Oxford

Koike, K (1995) *The Economics of Work in Japan*, LCTB International Library Foundation, Tokyo

Krogt, F and Warmerdam, J (1997) Training in different types of organizations: differences and dynamics in the organization of learning at work, *International Journal of Human Resource Management*, **8** (1), pp 87–105

Lave, J and Wenger, E (1991) *Situated Learning: Legitimate peripheral participation*, Cambridge University Press, Cambridge

Roy, D (1952) Quota restriction and goldbricking in a machine shop, *American Journal of Sociology*, **60**, pp 255–66

Willis, P (1977) *Learning to Labour*, Saxon House, London

Chapter 10

Putting skills in their place: the regional pattern of work skills in Britain

Alan Felstead

The constitutional changes introduced by the present government have heightened interest in regional economic performance in Britain. By mapping the regional pattern of work skills towards the end of the 20th century, this chapter aims to make a timely contribution to the debate. It identifies regional inequalities in the skills possessed and used by workers, assesses the scale of the disparities and tracks how regions have fared over a five-year period in the late 1990s. The chapter's original empirical contribution is based on a comparison of two surveys: one carried out in 1992 that elicited 3,855 responses, and one carried out in 1997 that produced 2,467 responses. The findings suggest that the North East and the East Midlands have fared poorly according to most of the measures examined. Both regions have seen skills demand fall rapidly at a time when other regions have seen the demand for skills rise significantly. The chapter ends by suggesting that more attention needs to be paid to the level of skills demand, and warns against undue concentration on skills supply and skills mismatches about which there are regular and frequent regional analyses.

Regional and national variations

Regional variations in social and economic conditions have aroused considerable interest and controversy for many years. Changes in employment levels, and the associated geography of unemployment and poverty, are high on the list of the issues to attract attention (Fothergill and Gudgin, 1982; Gillespie, 1999; Green and Owen, 1998; Sunley and Martin, 2000; Turok and Webster, 1998). Spatial variations in health have also provoked intense debate and have prompted commentators to claim that 'in sickness and health, as in poverty and wealth, Britain has been split into two nations' – the 'haves' and the 'have-nots', distinguished from one another according to where they live (Acheson, 1998; DHSS, 1980; Townsend and Davidson, 1982; Whitehead, 1987). The traditional equilibrating mechanism of labour migrating from one area to another, however, has itself been weakened by another regional factor – house price variation. The size of the house price divide poses a significant economic hurdle to those wishing to migrate from the poor performing to the high performing regions. 'An Englishman's flat is worth a Scot's castle' is an extreme version of events but is a newspaper headline which captures the essence of the problem (Green, 1988). It is also one that is readily identifiable in the recent teacher shortages in some parts of the country and the government's enhanced housing allowance enticement offered to teachers returning to the profession in high cost areas ('More cash to lure back teachers as government accused of "panic"', *Financial Times*, 13 March 2001). The North-South divide is often used as a shorthand for these and other spatial inequalities such as income distribution, exposure to crime, household composition, car ownership and the like (see The Stationery Office, 2000).

Scottish and Welsh devolution and the establishment of nine Regional Development Agencies (RDAs) in England have heightened interest in regional variations in economic performance in particular. RDAs, set up in April 1999, have a clear remit which crosses the boundaries of local economic development and labour market policy. They are lead bodies at the regional level for coordinating inward investment and regeneration activities, improving the competitiveness of business, raising people's skills and increasing employment. It is not, therefore, surprising that media stories highlight the regional dimension to many of the issues now under the remit of the RDAs. These include comparisons of productivity across the regions of Europe ('Regions placed in lower half of EU rankings of productivity', *Financial Times*, 24 November 2000), access to and the skills required to use the Internet (BBC Online, 'Working from home – is it more stressful?', 19 December 2000; 'Digital divide widens as Internet access grows', *Financial Times*, 20 December 2000), trends in business optimism ('Output shows best growth since 1994', *Financial Times*, 7 February 2001) and the distribution of 'new economy' jobs ('Regions miss out on new economy', *Financial Times*, 12 March 2001). The list goes on. The weekly 'Inside: The UK Regions' section in the *Financial Times*, which ran for much of 2001, and the enhanced airtime now given to regional news on BBC TV also capture the enhanced appetite for the regional dimension that devolution and the establishment of the RDAs have brought about.

Furthermore, many government publications now have a regional slant. For example, the official journal of the Department for Education and Skills (DfES), *Labour Market Trends,* carries a regular 'Spotlight on the Regions' feature that provides labour market information on each of the regions of Britain. The series began in 1997 with one region under the spotlight in, roughly speaking, every fourth issue. In the same year, the Department of Trade and Industry (DTI) published the first set of regional competitive indicators in order to assist those responsible for developing regional economic strategies as well as those with an interest in promoting competitiveness. Originally these were published annually, but since 1999 have been released twice a year and now comprise 14 indicators (DTI, 2000).

The picture this evidence paints is one of uneven economic performance with marked disparities within and between regions. More worryingly, it suggests that, if anything, regional inequalities have increased since 1990. GDP (gross domestic product) per head, for example, has grown significantly faster in the South East and Northern Ireland than the average for the UK, but significantly slower in the North East, North West and Wales. Yet government states that 'ensuring that all parts and all people of the UK achieve their full potential is an economic as well as a social imperative' (DTI and DfEE, 2001: Table 1 and para 1.26). The regional supplements that accompanied the publication of the recent White Paper on skills, enterprise and innovation (DTI and DfEE, 2001), highlight the ways in which each RDA intends to tailor national policies to its own particular circumstances in order to rectify these regional inequalities and fulfil the government's aim.

This chapter is motivated by the desire to add to the existing stock of knowledge on a key aspect of economic performance over which RDAs now preside – skills demand and supply. In tracking how regions have fared over a five-year period in the late 1990s, the analysis identifies and assesses the scale of inequalities and disparities. The review of existing evidence on these issues highlights the relative abundance of data on the supply of skills as predominantly measured by qualifications, and the mismatch between the demand and supply of skills compared to the relative dearth of evidence on the *level of skills* demanded by employers. The two data sets provide new insights. The representative sample of 3,885 employed individuals was questioned in 1992 about their jobs. The second survey was carried out five years later, in 1997.[1] The chapter uses two measures of skills demanded of individuals at work – a broad measure and a particular measure.

The *broad* measure focuses on qualifications required to get and do the job, the length of training, and the time taken to do the job well. The *particular* measure centres on the actual activities demanded of individuals at work. The fourth section plots the regional distribution of skills according to these two measures and examines how the picture has changed over a five-year period – 1992 to 1997. The analysis is carried out for the nine English RDA regions, Wales and Scotland. The chapter concludes with some implications for policy makers and academics.

Existing regional skill profiles

Standard economic theory is based on the principles of demand and supply. Applied to the labour market, this translates into the demand for and supply of labour. The result of these two forces is either an equilibrium wage (price) and level of employment (quantity) or if these forces do not operate, for whatever reason, an over-supply or a shortage of labour. For our purposes, these concepts provide a useful way of summarizing the recent evidence on the regional distribution of skills since much of it focuses on either the supply of skills or the extent of the demand and supply mismatch. This section briefly reviews both sets of evidence.

Skills supply

For many, skills are associated and proxied by the qualifications individuals possess. Many academics and policy-makers agree on this score:

> Because we have no direct measure of skills, it is accepted practice to take certificated education and training outcomes as a proxy for skills. (Green and Steedman, 1997: i)

> The existence of people with qualifications is not necessarily the same as the availability of skills in the workplace – but can be used as a key indicator. (DfEE, 1998: 27)

By definition, then, analyses that focus on qualifications possessed by individuals put the emphasis on skills supply rather than on skills demand (Payne, 1999). Several regional analyses of this type have been carried out in recent years and government systematically publishes some of this material on a regular basis.

One of the prime movers in identifying regional inequalities was the National Advisory Council on Education and Training Targets (NACETT), an independent body set up in 1993 by the previous Conservative government to report publicly on progress towards the National Learning Targets. Since then these targets have been revised, updated and added to on two separate occasions (in 1995 and 1998) as well as being renamed. A further change has been the disappearance of NACETT on 31 March 2001 and the transfer of its responsibilities to the Learning and Skills Council (LSC). However, these institutional changes make little difference to the account that follows.

Shortly after its establishment NACETT signalled its concern over the regional disparities in qualification attainment. Its first annual report highlighted a worry over 'the continuing wide variations in levels of achievement in different parts of the UK' (NACETT, 1994: 13). These were noticeable between the four countries and between the nine regions of England. For example, data on the English regions showed that the highest achieving region (South East) was outperforming the lowest (Yorkshire and the Humber) by eight percentage points with respect to the proportion of young people who had qualifications of at least National Vocational Qualification (NVQ) level 2 or equivalent standard. A regional gap of eight percentage points was also found with respect to the proportion of young people qualified to at least NVQ level 3 or equivalent. Once again, the South East was the best performing English region, but on this measure the West Midlands was the poorest. Disparities were also evident within countries and regions with marked differences at local level (NACETT, 1994: Annex 1). NACETT therefore concluded that it needed to focus its attention 'on specific issues where it believes action should be taken to promote progress towards the Targets, with particular emphasis on tackling *regional* and gender differences in attainment' (NACETT, 1995: 18, emphasis added; for gender differences see Felstead, 1996, 1997). As a result, subsequent reports by NACETT focused attention on the progress made towards narrowing these regional gaps in skills supply. However, the evidence it gathered suggested that the gaps remained stubbornly high. For example, London and the South East were, once again, the highest achieving regions in England in 1996, with 50 per cent of 21-year-olds in each region holding at least an NVQ level 3 or equivalent. This was 11 percentage points more than the East, the lowest achieving region, where 39 per cent met this target (NACETT, 1997: 47).

More recently, NACETT paid rather less attention to regional differences in its reports as these responsibilities shifted to the RDAs (eg NACETT, 2000). Nevertheless, the evidence, reported in places such as *Labour Market Trends'* 'Spotlight on the Regions' features, does not suggest that regional disparities have narrowed. On the contrary, regional differences appear, if anything, to have widened. As Table 10.1 shows, England entered the 21st century with a 15 percentage point gap between the highest achieving region (South East) and the lowest achieving region (North East) regarding the proportion of 21-year-olds holding at least an NVQ level 3 or equivalent. There was also a 10 percentage point gap separating the highest (South East) from the lowest (East Midlands) achieving region in terms of the proportion of 19-year-olds qualified to NVQ level 2 or above.

Similar disparities can also be detected with respect to qualification levels among economically active adults. London and the South East are the only regions to have already met both of the National Learning Targets for adults set to be achieved by the end of 2002 – 50 per cent of adults qualified to a level at least equivalent to NVQ level 3 and 28 per cent of them to be qualified to at least level 4. In Spring 2000, 52 per cent of adults in London and 50 per cent of adults in the South East were qualified to NVQ level 3 or equivalent, and 35 per cent and 30 per cent respectively were qualified to NVQ level 4 and beyond. Some regions fared poorly by comparison. The North East, East Midlands and West Midlands, for example, fell well short of the achievements recorded for London and the South East on both adult targets. It is also worth pointing out that of the countries of Britain, those living in Wales were the poorest qualified. Their qualification levels were on a par with those living in the North East in three out of the four targets considered here. Economically active adults in Scotland, on the other hand, were at least as well qualified as those living south of the border, while young people in Scotland did rather better (see Table 10.1).

An individual's skills are also associated with the training he or she has received, or what the National Learning Targets refer to as 'the learning participation rate'. The implication is that the longer and more frequent the training, the more skilled the worker. Table 10.1 presents the regional variations in the proportion of respondents who reported receiving job-related education or training in the four weeks before being interviewed for the Spring 2000 Labour Force Survey (LFS). The most noticeable finding here is that the variation between the regions is much smaller than it is for qualifications. In England, the South West had the highest incidence of training with 17.7 per cent of respondents reporting that they had received job-related training in the four weeks prior to interview, compared to 15.5 per cent of respondents in the North East, the region with the lowest incidence of training. Similarly, just one percentage point separates the training incidences recorded for England, Wales and Scotland (see Table 10.1).

Skill disparities as measured by qualifications are even higher, the finer the level of spatial disaggregation. In an analysis carried out at the level of the 345 local authority districts and the 46 counties that comprise England,

Table 10.1   *Qualifications and training participation for the regions, Spring 2000*

Region	Qualification Targets for Young People: % of Population		Qualification Targets Economically Active Adults: % of Population		Working Age Employees Receiving Job-related Training
	Aged 19 Qualified to at Least NVQ 2 or Equivalent	Aged 21 Qualified to at Least NVQ 3 or Equivalent	Qualified to at Least NVQ 3 or Equivalent	Qualified to at Least NVQ 4 or Equivalent	
North East	74	45	41	21	15.5
North West	76	52	47	25	16.8
Yorkshire and the Humber	72	50	45	24	16.3
East Midlands	71	50	43	24	15.7
West Midlands	72	54	43	25	16.0
East	74	52	44	25	15.7
London	73	57	52	35	16.9
South East	81	60	50	30	15.9
South West	76	58	46	27	17.7
England	75	54	47	27	16.5
Wales	77	47	39	22	16.0
Scotland	80	58	47	26	15.5
United Kingdom	75	52	43	24	16.1

*All the figures presented in this table are based on the Labour Force Survey, Spring 2000. However, the Welsh, Scottish and UK figures for qualifications are based on the Labour Force Survey, Autumn 1999.
Sources: Office for National Statistics, 2000: Table 5.13; The Stationery Office, 2000: Tables 4.14 and 4.15; and National Assembly for Wales, 2000: Table 5.

Campbell *et al* (1999) found extensive variations in skills supply. Among their findings are the following staggering facts: the proportion of workers who had no qualifications at all was up to four times greater in some areas than others; those qualified to NVQ level 2 in some areas was nearly double that in others; and attainment of qualifications at school at both the age of 11 and 16 varied from the lowest to the highest performing area by roughly a factor of two. These are indeed substantial variations. Their analysis also suggests that localities tend to perform relatively well or relatively poorly across all these indicators of skill supply; poor (good) performance on one indicator tends to go hand in hand with poor (good) performance on all the others.

In a further step in the analysis, Campbell *et al* (1999) go on to link these skill variations with various measures of economic performance such as GDP per head and employment growth. This builds on a similar investigation by Bradley and Taylor (1996) who examined the linkage using data largely extracted from the 1991 Census and 107 Local Education Authorities in England on the educational attainment of young people in their area. Both pieces of research show a strong association between the stock of qualifications and local economic performance. However, simply increasing the stock of qualifications in any of these 'skill weak' areas by no means guarantees an improvement in economic performance – many other intervening variables such as skill demand need to be considered.

While research of this type tells us a lot about the stock of qualifications in an area (supply), it tells us little about the use to which these qualifications are actually put (demand). Boosting the sample size of the LFS will allow information on the stock of qualifications and the incidence of learning and training to be more reliably available at regional and especially sub-regional levels (Bell, 2000; Burke and Williams, 2000). However, these enhancements will not provide information on the regional distribution of skills demand. Surveys of employers' skill needs fail to gauge the level of skills demanded by employers and focus instead on mismatches at the point of recruitment and/or among the existing workforce. Nevertheless, their results are worthy of review, not least because they provide a regional map of demand and supply mismatches, and therefore another important part of the regional skills story.

Skills mismatch

There are many surveys of employers' skill needs in Britain. These have been commissioned by local organizations such as Chambers of Commerce and the now defunct Training and Enterprise Councils (TECs) (eg, East Midlands Chamber of Commerce, 2000; Focus Central London, see Spilsbury and Lane, 2000; Hertfordshire TEC quoted in Blake et al, 2000: Chapter 4), sectoral bodies such as the National Training Organizations (eg, EMTA, 1998) and by central government departments such as DfEE (eg, IFF Research Ltd, 1998). However, interpretation and comparison of these surveys is bedevilled by differences in methodology and terminology. This makes regional comparisons based on the aggregation of local surveys difficult, if not impossible, to carry out.

The most fruitful regional comparisons come from large-scale national surveys, which are extensive enough to allow regional breakdowns. Foremost among these are the Skill Needs in Britain (SNIB) surveys that were carried out annually on behalf of DfEE between 1990 and 1998. Others include the Confederation of British Industry's Trends Survey and the British Chambers of Commerce Quarterly Economic Survey (see Blake et al, 2000 for a review). The SNIB surveys covered medium and large-sized employers (defined as establishments with 25 or more employees) and were intended to provide snapshots of skill needs at the time of each survey for Britain (in the last survey in the series Northern Ireland was added). Every year around 4,000 telephone interviews were carried out with employers drawn from a sample stratified according to region, industry and establishment size. Employers were asked questions about the incidence and cause of any hard-to-fill vacancies they had, and whether there was a gap between the skills their workers possessed and the needs of the business. The published results compare regions on each of these issues and track their respective fortunes over time. In 1998, for example, over a quarter of employers in the East Midlands, North East, South West and London regions reported they had existing vacancies that were proving difficult to fill, compared to just a sixth of employers in Wales. Similarly, Welsh employers were least likely to report a gap between the skills of their existing workforce and those required by the business – only 9 per cent did so. However, elsewhere in the country skills gaps were more prevalent: the figure was double the proportion of Welsh employers in the East, the West Midlands and Scotland (IFF Research Ltd, 1998: Chapters 4 and 5).

For some time, however, there has been a worry about what employers actually mean when they say vacancies are 'hard to fill', they have a 'skill shortage' or they report a 'skill gap'. Researchers, too, have sometimes confused these terms (see Green et al, 1998, and Robinson, 1996 for reviews). The 1999 Employers Skills Survey (ESS), commissioned by the DfEE to replace SNIB but limited to England only, has made major advances in making these distinctions clearer and applying them to the results generated from interviews with around 27,000 employers each year (Hudson, 2000; Mason, 2000). For example, rather than equating hard-to-fill vacancies with skill shortages, the ESS distinguishes between hard-to-fill vacancies that are skill-related and those that are not. The latter may be attributable to company-specific factors such as limited efforts at job advertising or the relatively unattractive salaries or job conditions on offer. This distinction alters the occupational profile of the vacancies involved. Clerical and secretarial, personal and protective service, and sales occupations accounted for the highest proportions of vacancies and hard-to-fill positions, yet they accounted for a much lower proportion of skill-shortage vacancies in 1999. On the other hand, craft occupations accounted for a relatively modest proportion of vacancies (8 per cent), yet they comprised 14 per cent of all hard-to-fill vacancies and 22 per cent of skill-shortage vacancies (Bosworth et al, 2000: 25).

Having said this, a similar regional picture emerges whichever measure is used. Nonetheless, the differences between regions are striking. Vacancies, hard-to-fill vacancies and skill-shortage vacancies are all more commonly found in London and the South East – around two out of five of them are reported in these two regions alone. The North East, on the other hand, accounts for just 3 per cent of each of these three types of unfilled position (see Table 10.2). Obviously these figures do not take into account the relative size of each region in terms of employment. However, when the focus is shifted onto the proportion of employers reporting each type of vacancy, the regional variation narrows but is still evident. For example, in the South East and London, 38 per cent and 36 per cent of employers respectively reported having vacancies compared to 25 per cent of their counterparts in the North East and 29 per cent in the East Midlands. A similar regional pattern emerges with regard to the proportion of employers who reported having hard-to-fill vacancies as well as those who reported difficulty in filling posts because of skills shortages. London and the South East come high on the list on both counts, while the North East and North West come towards the bottom. A similar pattern emerges when the spotlight is put on the incidence of skill gaps reported by employers. Respondents to the 1999 survey were asked to comment on an occupation-by-occupation basis about the extent to which employees were 'fully proficient at their current job'. If they reported that fewer than 'all' or 'nearly all' of them were fully proficient they were categorized as having a skills gap. The regional distribution of skills mismatches, as measured in this way, reveals much the same variation as before, with skill gaps representing more of a constraint to employers in London and the South East, but posing less of a problem for employers in the North East. Triple the proportion of employers in London and the South East than in the North East reported gaps in the proficiency of their employees (see Table 10.2).

Overall, then, the picture painted by the 1999 ESS is one of regional variation in the incidence of skills disequilibria. By and large, disequilibria are more commonly found in the South and less commonly found in the North. In terms of the English RDAs, London and the South East are at one extreme, while the North East is at the other. The policy implication that follows from the identification of a genuine skills mismatch is for the education and training system to supply more of the appropriate skills. However, the absence of a mismatch is certainly not a cause for complacency: in fact it may have far more worrying consequences. Skills supply and demand may be more in line with one another in some regions than in others simply because the demand for skills is exceedingly low and can be met easily from existing skill supplies in the region. In other words, the region may be caught in a 'low skills equilibrium' (Finegold and Soskice, 1988). To make such a judgement, more needs to be known about the *level of skills demanded by jobs* in each region. Apart from proxies such as the occupational profile of a

Table 10.2   *Vacancies, hard-to-fill vacancies, skill-shortage vacancies and skill gaps for the regions, Autumn 1999*

Region	Percentage of Reported Vacancies				Percentage of Employers Reporting Vacancies			
	All Vacancies	Hard-to-fill	Skill-Shortage	Skill Gaps	All Vacancies	Hard-to-fill	Skill-Shortage	Skill Gaps
North East	3	3	3	3	25	10	4	5
North West	11	10	20	18	27	13	5	13
Yorkshire and the Humber	8	9	10	9	29	15	6	10
East Midlands	7	6	7	8	29	14	7	8
West Midlands	10	10	9	10	30	14	7	11
East	11	12	11	11	35	18	8	10
London	20	18	22	18	36	18	10	17
South East	21	22	20	18	38	21	9	16
South West	9	11	10	9	32	18	7	9

Source: Calculated from data contained in Bosworth *et al,* 2000: Tables 2.13, 2.14 and 3.8, and http://skillsbase.dfee.gov.uk/Database/.

region's employed workforce, which can be extracted from analysis of the LFS, there is surprisingly little material on this aspect of the skills story. This is where this chapter hopes to make a substantive empirical contribution.

Surveying work skills

This chapter draws on and compares the results from two separate but similar representative surveys of the employed British workforce in the 1990s. The first was carried out in 1992 and become known as the Employment in Britain (EIB) survey. It was designed to be representative of the British workforce aged 20–60 and covered both those in and out of work. However, the analysis that follows is based on the sub-sample of 3,855 EIB respondents who were in work at the time of interview and who were therefore questioned about their jobs. The second survey was carried out in 1997 and collected information on 2,467 individuals aged 20–60 who were in employment in Britain at the time of interview. Suffice to say, a number of steps were taken to ensure that both surveys contained a representative sample of the employed British workforce (see Gallie *et al,* 1998, and Ashton *et al,* 1999, respectively).

These surveys allow us to examine the regional variation in skills demand in two ways. First, we can examine the abilities and capacities of those in employment by focusing on the requirements of the job. These *broad* skill measures include the qualifications respondents reported they would require to get their current job, the length of training time required for that particular type of work and the learning time needed to learn to do the job well. Furthermore, since identical questions were asked of respondents to both surveys the regional skills profiles for 1992 can be compared with those for 1997. Secondly, the Skills Survey measures the *particularities* of people's jobs by asking jobholders to assess how important certain activities are in their work. Respondents were also asked a number of repeat questions about the job they held five years before the 1997 survey. By comparing these answers with those given for 1997 we can track how the level of skill employers demand changed over the five intervening years. This provides a further insight into how different regions have performed relative to one another over time (assuming limited inter-regional mobility). The remainder of this chapter outlines the findings that emerge from both types of analyses.

Identifying regional variations in skills demand

Previous analyses comparing the answers respondents gave in 1997 to the Skills Survey with those given to the Social Change and Economic Life Initiative (SCELI) survey in 1986 suggest that the jobs people do have become more demanding over the last decade (Felstead *et al,* 1999, 2000; Green *et al,* 2000). On average, better qualifications are now required to get jobs and carry them out. In addition, jobs take longer to train for and to learn to do well. Upskilling has affected young and old alike and all occupations have been upskilled in one way or another. Most industries appear to have benefited from rising skill levels. Women, however, have benefited more than men. The gap between women and men on all of these measures has declined rapidly over time. However, the gender gap remains significant and pronounced. Previous work has also uncovered some groups who have lost out in the upskilling process. These include those in part-time work, the self-employed and those employed in organizations with less progressive management practices (Felstead and Ashton, 2000; Felstead *et al,* 2001; Green *et al,* 2000).

The aim in this section is to examine whether some regions can be added to the list. Unfortunately, it is not possible to carry out a regional comparison of skills demand using SCELI since it collected relevant information, albeit reasonably representative of Britain as a whole, from six travel-to-work areas (Gallie, 1994). Instead comparisons have to be made over a much shorter five-year period based on responses given to the Employment in Britain survey in 1992 and those given to the Skills Survey in 1997. This section plots the regional trends for two measures of skills demanded of individuals at work – a broad measure and a particular measure. These are considered in turn.

Broad measures of skill demand

The demand for skills at work rose over the period according to *all* of the broad skill measures and, in most cases, the movement was significant in statistical terms. The proportion of respondents who reported that some qualifications were required to get the job they held at the time of interview rose significantly over the period; from 66 per cent in 1992 to 68 per cent in 1997 (see Table 10.3). Similarly, degree-level education was more likely to be needed in 1997 than in 1992 to enter jobs. Although the one percentage point movement is not statistically significant, it is nevertheless in the upward direction. Moreover, the finding that skills demand rose over this period is confirmed by the two other independent broad job skill measures: in 1997 people were doing jobs that required longer learning time and training than their equivalents in 1992. For the purposes of presentation we examine the proportions reporting 'short' and 'long' training/learning times, ie the points at either end of the continuum. This suggests an upward movement in skill over the 1992–7 period. For example, the proportion of workers reporting 'short' training times (less than three months) fell from 63 per cent to 57 per cent, while those reporting 'long' training times (over two years) rose from 22 per cent to 29 per cent. Both changes are statistically significant. A similar, but less pronounced, story can be told for learning time: 'short' learning time fell from 23 per cent to 22 per cent and 'long' learning time rose from 21 per cent to 24 per cent (see the last row in Table 10.3).

   This analysis is repeated for each English RDA, Wales and Scotland. The results are contained in Table 10.3. This compares the fortunes of each region in terms of the skills demanded of its residents in 1992 and 1997. Of particular interest here is whether upskilling can be detected in *all* the regions of Britain or whether some bucked the national trend and experienced a skills demand fall. As already noted, all six broad measures moved in directions that suggested skills demand had risen in Britain as a whole over the period. Three regions – Scotland, the North West and the South West – followed this pattern. Furthermore, the increases are statistically significant for at least as many

Table 10.3   *Broad measures of skill demand by region,[a] 1992–97*

Region	Qualifications Required to Get Job[b]				Training Time Need for Type of Work[c]				Learning Time to Do the Job Well[d]			
	None Required		Degree Required		< 3 Months		> 2 Years		< 1 Month		> 2 Years	
	1992	1997[e]	1992	1997	1992	1997	1992	1997	1992	1997	1992	1997
North East	39.4	45.3	7.0	7.2	67.7	72.6	20.3	16.1	26.7	35.0	17.9	12.1
North West	34.4	24.8 ★★★	11.0	13.4	66.4	48.2 ★★★	19.5	36.4 ★★★	20.2	16.2	22.7	30.5 ★★
Yorkshire and the Humber	43.8	42.0	7.8	11.8	67.4	59.6 ★	18.5	27.1 ★★	27.7	32.0	16.0	13.4
East Midlands	27.8	36.2 ★	17.2	10.5 ★	59.3	63.7	22.7	21.7	23.1	26.1	22.0	20.7
West Midlands	33.2	35.2	6.9	12.8 ★★	63.1	62.4	22.5	25.8	20.1	24.0	21.4	26.7
East	36.8	26.9 ★	10.1	15.2	65.1	54.1 ★	20.2	31.4 ★★	24.9	21.6	27.8	25.8
London	27.5	21.2 ★★	23.2	23.3	63.2	58.6	20.9	23.7	17.7	22.7	19.6	22.0
South East	30.1	32.2	19.7	14.4 ★★	59.1	55.4	22.6	29.4 ★★	20.8	17.9	22.1	22.7
South West	40.3	25.6 ★★★	7.5	14.0 ★★	61.8	53.6 ★	22.5	30.9 ★★	21.4	19.1	25.2	29.1
Wales	20.7	34.7 ★★★	13.3	9.5	53.3	59.8	30.6	27.0	17.8	20.2	23.9	24.4
Scotland	48.4	37.1 ★★★	5.0	14.2 ★★★	68.8	55.3 ★★★	17.1	33.0 ★★★	36.9	19.4 ★★★	14.9	26.7 ★★★
Britain	34.3	31.8 ★★	13.1	14.1	62.9	57.3 ★★★	21.5	28.5 ★★★	22.7	22.0	21.1	23.7 ★★

Notes:

a. These regions refer to the nine Regional Development Agencies (RDAs) in England, plus Scotland and Wales. In this analysis, each individual in each of the datasets is allocated to one of these 11 regions according to their travel-to-work area (TTWA), of which there are 322.

b. These categories were derived from the answers respondents gave to the question: 'If they were applying today, what qualifications, if any, would someone need to *get* the type of job you have now?'

c. These categories were derived from the answers respondents gave to the question: 'Since completing full-time education, have you ever had, or are you currently undertaking, training for the type of work that you currently do?' If 'yes', 'How long, in total, did (or will) that training last?'

d. These categories were derived from the answers respondents gave to the question: 'How long did it take for you after you first started doing this type of job to learn to do it well?' If answers 'still learning' ask: 'How long do you *think* it will take?' This question was asked only of employees in 1992 and so the 1997 figures have been restricted accordingly.

e. Chi-squared tests were carried out in each region to assess the significance of the skill changes between 1992 and 1997: ★★★=99% significant, ★★=95% significant and ★=90% significant.

Source: Own calculations from Employment in Britain, 1992 and Skills Survey, 1997.

measures as for Britain; no mean feat given the smaller cell sizes and larger standard errors involved. However, two regions – the North East and the East Midlands – are firmly at the other end of the spectrum. Both saw skills demand *fall* on almost all of these measures. More worryingly still, some of these falls were large enough to be statistically significant. For example, in the East Midlands the proportion of respondents who thought that no qualifications would be required to get the job they had at the time of interview rose significantly from 28 per cent to 36 per cent. At the same time, degrees were becoming less important for jobs in the region – down significantly from 17 per cent in 1992 to 11 per cent in 1997. Across other indicators, too, skill trends in the East Midlands were in the opposite direction to those underway nationally. Other regions fell in between, but were on the whole more in line with the national picture. On at least four out of six skill measures, the other seven English regions, Wales and Scotland reported an increase in skill demand.

Another way of looking at these data is to rank regions by the level of skills demanded at both data points and then to compare their position in 1992 with 1997. The resulting 'league tables' are shown as Tables 10.4 and 10.5. This casts a different light on the change analysis reported earlier since it reveals the relative positions of regions at the beginning of the period of focus and then once again at the end. From this a number of interesting points emerge, especially with regard to regions that appeared (on the evidence above) to have gained most from the upskilling process as well as those that have gained least. Not surprisingly, the regions to have gained most saw their relative skills position improve over the period. However, in some cases the change was dramatic. For example, in 1992, Scotland went from being bottom on all but one of the skills measures to being in the top half of the league table according to all but one measure in 1997. Similarly, the North West moved from a middling position on most indicators in 1992 to topping the league table on four out of six indicators five years later. The story for the South West is less dramatic. Its comparative performance was rather mixed in 1992, but by 1997 had improved on all measures.

The data tell a somewhat different story for regions that gained least from the rise in skill demands. Their relative position in the league table deteriorated markedly. The East Midlands, for example, was in the top three according to four of the measures of skill demand in 1992, but by 1997 had fallen to the bottom three according to five of them. The picture for the North East, however, is particularly worrying. It started the period with low skill demand – occupying one of the bottom four places for each measure – but ended it rock bottom of the league table according to *all* measures of skill demand. The picture does not improve when we examine respondents' accounts of

Table 10.4 *Rank order of regions[a] according to broad measures of skill demand,*
1992

Rank Order of Regions (top to bottom)[b]	No Qualifications Required	Degree Level Qualification Required	< 3 Months' Training Time	> 2 Years' Training Time	< 1 Month Learning Time	> 2 Years' Learning Time
1	Wales	London	Wales	Wales	London	East
2	London	South East	South East	East Midlands	Wales	South West
3	East Midlands	East Midlands	East Midlands	South East	West Midlands	Wales
4	South East	Wales	South West	West Midlands/	North West	North West
5	West Midlands	North West	West Midlands	South West	South East	South East
6	North West	East	London	London	South West	East Midlands
7	East	Yorkshire	East	North East	East Midlands	West Midlands
8	North East	South West	North West	East	East	London
9	South West	North East	Yorkshire	North West	North East	North East
10	Yorkshire	West Midlands	North East	Yorkshire	Yorkshire	Scotland
11	Scotland	Scotland	Scotland	Scotland	Scotland	Yorkshire

Notes:
a. See Note a in Table 10.3.
b. On each of the measures regions were placed in their rank order. Rank 1 indicates that workers in this region had the most demanding jobs in terms of the work skills required of them, while at the other end of the scale rank 11 indicates the region with the least demanding jobs. In some cases, regions were equally skilled; this is indicated by '/' and a merging of the appropriate rows.
Source: Derived from Table 10.3.

what level of skill their jobs actually involve – what we refer to as *particular* skill demands (others, notably DfEE's Skills Task Force, refer to these as 'generic skills'; see DfEE, 2000). It is to these skill demands that we now turn.

Particular measures of skill demand

The abilities demanded by different jobs vary enormously. To capture this diversity the 1997 Skills Survey questionnaire included a wide range of different job activities. Respondents were asked: 'in your job, how important is (a particular job activity)'. Examples of the activities included 'caring for others', 'dealing with people', 'using a computer', 'analysing complex problems' and 'planning the activities of others'. The questionnaire covered 36 activities designed to span the tasks carried out in a wide range of jobs.

Table 10.5   *Rank order of regions^a according to broad measures of skill demand,*
1997

Rank Order of Regions (top to bottom)[b]	No Qualifications Required	Degree Level Qualification Required	< 3 Months' Training Time	> 2 Years' Training Time	< 1 Month Learning Time	> 2 Years' Learning Time
1	London	London	North West	North West	North West	North West
2	North West	East	South West	Scotland	London	South West
3	South West	South East	East	East	South East	Scotland/ West
4	East	Scotland	Scotland	South West	South West	Midlands
5	South East	South West	South East	South East	Scotland	East
6	Wales	North West	London	Yorkshire	Wales	Wales
7	West Midlands	Wales	Yorkshire	Wales	East	South East
8	East Midlands	West Midlands	Wales	West Midlands	West Midlands	London
9	Scotland	Yorkshire	West Midlands	London	East Midlands	East Midlands
10	Yorkshire	East Midlands	East Midlands	East Midlands	Yorkshire	Yorkshire
11	North East	North East	North East	North East	North East	North East

Notes:
a. See Note a in Table10.3.
b. See Note b in Table 10.4.
Source: Derived from Table 10.3.

The response scale ranged from 'essential' to 'not at all important', with 'very important', 'fairly important' and 'not very important' in between. For current purposes, the results are summarized by adding the scores for each of the 36 job activities and then taking an average. The final column in Table 10.6 shows the results by region. Two regions stand out – Wales because its respondents reported that their jobs were significantly more demanding than those living elsewhere, and the North East because job demands there were significantly lower than in other parts of the country. The remaining nine regions of Britain were more or less in line with the situation in the country as a whole (see column 7, Table 10.6).

Respondents to the 1997 Skills Survey were asked a number of repeat questions about the job they held five years before the date of the survey. A total of 15 of these questions were asked, 12 of which focused on skills relating to problem solving, communication and social interaction, team working and computing. Not only are all of these skills said to be of growing importance, but they form part of what the British government refers to as 'Key Skills' ie, the ability to operate in a workplace, alone or with others (see Dench *et al,* 1998: 2–6). For the purposes of this chapter we will refer

Table 10.6　*Particular measures of skill demand by region,[a] 1992–97*

Region	Communication & Social[b]		Teamworking		Computing[c]		Problem-Solving		All 'Key Skills'[d]		All 36 Activities[e]	
	1992	1997[f]	1992	1997	1992	1997	1992	1997	1992	1997	1992	1997
North East	1.78	2.03 *	2.77	2.96	0.66	1.18 ***	2.43	2.57	2.03	2.28 ***	NA	2.25 *
North West	1.86	2.26 ***	2.68	2.92 ***	1.03	1.30 ***	2.46	2.74 ***	2.10	2.45 ***	NA	2.45
Yorkshire and the Humber	1.81	2.16 ***	2.77	2.86	0.78	1.13 ***	2.52	2.73 ***	2.07	2.37 ***	NA	2.34
East Midlands	2.06	2.14	2.67	2.94 **	0.77	0.96 *	2.55	2.72 *	2.22	2.36 *	NA	2.34
West Midlands	1.61	2.10 ***	2.55	2.97 ***	0.91	1.26 ***	2.29	2.59 ***	1.90	2.33 ***	NA	2.34
East	1.87	2.19 ***	2.76	3.15 ***	1.04	1.31 **	2.52	2.89 ***	2.12	2.48 ***	NA	2.46
London	2.06	2.29 ***	2.92	3.02	1.14	1.57 ***	2.57	2.79 ***	2.27	2.54 ***		2.44
South East	1.84	2.23 ***	2.79	3.08 ***	1.14	1.54 ***	2.46	2.86 ***	2.12	2.53 ***	NA	2.44
South West	1.94	2.17 ***	2.53	2.84 ***	0.83	1.29 ***	2.55	2.61	2.13	2.36 ***	NA	2.35
Wales	1.76	2.19 ***	2.75	3.13 ***	0.89	1.26 ***	2.37	2.86 ***	2.03	2.48 ***	NA	2.50 *
Scotland	1.76	2.27 ***	2.65	2.98 ***	0.88	1.30 ***	2.44	2.85 ***	2.02	2.50 ***	NA	2.42
Britain	1.85	2.20 ***	2.72	2.99 ***	0.96	1.33 ***	2.47	2.76 ***	2.09	2.44 ***	NA	2.40

Notes: a. See Note a in Table 10.3.

b. Each respondent was asked to indicate how important particular activities were in their jobs. The response scale was as follows: 'Essential/Very important/Fairly important/Not very important/Not at all important'. Scores of 4, 3, 2, 1 and 0 respectively were allocated to an individual's response, so that those responding 'Not at all important' scored 0 whereas those reporting the activity to be 'Essential' scored 4. Higher skills scores denote more skilled job content. The figures reported here refer to the average skill scores given for each region. For the jobs respondents held in 1992 and 1997, six questions on communication activities were asked, one on team working, one on computing and four on problem solving. To ensure a like-for-like comparison all the 1992 vs 1997 contrasts are based on individuals in work both at the time of interview and five years earlier.

c. Each respondent was asked to indicate, if 'using a computer, PC, or other types of computerized equipment' was part of their job, their level of computer use. Four options were given ranging from 'straightforward' through 'moderate' and 'complex' to 'advanced'. Each was accompanied by a set of concrete examples. To measure the level of computer usage, non-users were given a score of 0 while users were given scores of 1, 2, 3 or 4 according to their level of computer use. The figures reported here refer to the level of computer usage given for each column.

d. This was calculated by adding up for every respondent the skills score for each of the 12 job activities (excluding the level of computer usage) and then an average was taken for each region.

e. This column reports the results of all those in work in 1997 and comprises an additive average score across all 36 job activities (excluding the level of computer usage) for each region. T-tests were carried out to reveal whether the level of skill demands in the region differed significantly from elsewhere in the country: ***=99% significant, **=95% significant and *=90% significant.

f. T-tests were carried out to test the significance of each of the skill changes between 1992 and 1997. The same notation as in Note e was used.

Source: Own calculations from Employment in Britain, 1992 and Skills Survey, 1997.

to them in a similar manner. From information respondents gave on their current jobs allied to information they gave on their job five years ago we are able to track trends in these particular skill demands for those in work over a five-year period. This is achieved by comparing the importance rating given for activities carried out in jobs occupied in 1992 with ratings for the same activities five years later.

Given the nature of the questioning and hence the data, the analysis has to be limited to those in work five years ago (this excludes 15 per cent of the sample). Aside from the point that one is relying on respondents' powers of recall (see Dex and McCulloch, 1998), the nature of the data presents problems that make analysis less than straightforward. The most notable of these is that the data may be subject to biases simply because the cohort has grown older and their job demands have risen as a result. For example, individuals may have more responsibilities placed upon them as they grow older and gain more experience. However, according to the 1997 data, skill demands are only significantly and positively correlated with the age of the respondent in two out of 12 cases. As far as the computing variables are concerned, the relationship appears to be reversed entirely – older people are *less,* rather than more likely to be using computing skills in their jobs. The cohort effect, therefore, appears rather weak. This objection is also blunted by the fact that here we are less concerned with the *overall direction* of change than with patterns of *differential* experience by region.

The results show that the 'Key Skill' demands of jobs rose significantly in all regions of Britain over the 1992–7 period (see column 6, Table 10.6). However, in the East Midlands the upward movement only just reached a reasonable level of statistical significance ($p<0.10$), yet much higher levels of significance ($p<0.01$) were reached elsewhere. Furthermore, the demand for communication and social skills in the East Midlands failed to increase significantly at all. Overall, the 'Key Skills' of jobs in the North East rose substantially over the five-year period. However, the demand for team working and problem-solving skills in the region failed to rise on a significant scale despite the fact that for Britain as a whole these skills were more in demand in 1992 than in 1997 (see columns 2, 3 and 4, Table 10.6).

Conclusion

The present government has done more to change the British constitution than any administration since 1911, when the House of Lords was stripped of its veto over most legislation. Devolved government has been established in different forms in Wales, Scotland and London; most hereditary peers have been ousted from the Lords; and there have been moves towards regional government in England. Each region in England now has an RDA, lightly supervised by a regional assembly composed mainly of coopted local councillors and business people. The Government has also talked about extending the powers of RDAs beyond the remit they presently hold for strategic economic and regeneration issues. It is likely, therefore, that interest in regional issues will continue to grow.

The contribution this chapter makes is to provide evidence on the regional pattern of work skills in the late 20th century; an issue for which RDAs and the devolved governments in Wales and Scotland are responsible and over which they can exercise some purchase. Two general conclusions emerge. The first is that considerable information is now available to map the regional pattern of skills supply, if only proxied by qualifications and recent training experience. Moreover, as from Summer 2001 supplementary LFS interviews with 39,000 people will provide the data for a number of smaller, sub-regional geographies including Local Learning Partnerships, Local Education Authorities, local LSCs and parliamentary constituencies (Bell, 2000; Burke and Williams, 2000). Regional information on skills mismatches is also readily available from the results of interviews with around 27,000 employers every year (Hudson, 2000). Regional analysis of skill demands is, however, hampered somewhat by the relatively small sample sizes involved. The results presented in this chapter are based on surveys comprising 3,855 interviews in 1992 and 2,467 interviews in 1997. Regional comparisons are therefore based on relatively small numbers and the results need to be treated cautiously. Even the 2001 Skills Survey (Felstead *et al*, 2002) comprises a relatively small number of interviews (4,470) compared to the Local LFS and ESS. Having said this, these data sets are the only ones (as far as I am aware) that can provide a regional map of skills demand in late 20th century Britain. This chapter is the first time in which such a systematic regional analysis of these data has been carried out.

The second general conclusion relates to one of the purposes for which RDAs were set up, namely 'to enhance the development and application of skills *relevant to employment in its area*' (clause 4 (1a), Regional Development Agencies Act 1998; emphasis added). One interpretation of this would be the elimination of the immediate skills mismatches employers report. However, this is a short-sighted policy to pursue since equilibrium in the labour market may be the result of employers in the region demanding so little from their workforce in terms of the skills required (Green and Ashton, 1992). It would appear from the evidence presented in this chapter that the North East and the East Midlands fall into this category. In both regions, skills supply is relatively low, skills mismatches are comparatively modest and skills demand is relatively weak. Action will therefore be required on both the supply and the demand side of the labour market in order for these regions to break out of the low skills equilibrium in which they find themselves and move up the rankings of regional prosperity. This will require these RDAs to focus on the *type* as well as the quantity of jobs that employers in the region provide. Other regions, too, will need to monitor how skill demands are changing in their areas and take action through local economic development initiatives (such as inward investment programmes, cf Hill and Munday, 1992) in order to avoid falling into a similar trap. The 2001 Skills Survey will offer some insight into how far this has been achieved in each region, and indicate how skill demands have changed in Britain in the early years of the 21st century.

Acknowledgements

Employment in Britain was funded by the Employment Department, the Employment Service, the Leverhulme Trust and an industrial consortium. I am grateful to Duncan Gallie of Nuffield College, Oxford, for allowing me access to this data set. The Skills Survey was supported by a grant secured under the Economic and Social Research Council's (ESRC) Learning Society Initiative run under the direction of Frank Coffield (L123251032). David Ashton, Bryn Davies, Francis Green and myself designed the survey instrument and the National Centre for Social Research carried out the fieldwork. I am grateful for the comments made by Sally Walters on an earlier draft. However, the usual caveat applies.

Note

1. The 2001 Skills Survey was being carried out at the time this chapter was written. Therefore, 2001 data was not available for inclusion in the analysis reported here (Felstead *et al*, 2002). However, regional analysis of this data is planned in future work.

References

Acheson, D (1998) *Independent Inquiry into Inequalities in Health*, The Stationery Office, London

Ashton, D, Davies, B, Felstead, A and Green, F (1999) *Work Skills in Britain*, SKOPE, Oxford and Warwick Universities

Bell, I (2000) The Local Labour Force Survey for England, *Labour Market Trends*, **108** (5) May, pp 195–9

Blake, N, Dods, J and Griffiths, S (2000) *Employers Skill Survey: Existing survey evidence and its use in the analysis of skill deficiencies*, DfEE, Sheffield

Bosworth, D, Davies, R, Hogarth, T, Wilson, R and Shury, J (2000) *Employers Skill Survey: Statistical report*, DfEE, Sheffield

Bradley, S and Taylor, J (1996) Human capital formation and local economic performance, *Regional Studies*, **30** (1), pp 1–14

Burke, D and Williams, T (2000) Developments in local area Labour Force Survey data, *Labour Market Trends*, **108** (5) May, pp 231–6

Campbell, M, Chapman, R and Hutchinson, J (1999) *Spatial Skill Variations: Their extent and implications,* Department for Education and Employment Skills Task Force Research Paper, No 15

Dench, S, Perryman, S and Giles, L (1998) *Employers' Perceptions of Key Skills,* Institute for Employment Studies Report, No 349

Dex, S and McCulloch, A (1998) The reliability of retrospective unemployment history data, *Work, Employment and Society*, **12** (3) September, pp 497–509

DfEE (1998) *The Learning Age: A renaissance for a new Britain,* Department for Education and Employment, London

DfEE (2000) *Skills for All: Research report from the National Skills Task Force,* Department for Education and Employment, London

DHSS (1980) *Inequalities in Health: Report of a working group chaired by Sir Douglas Black*, Department of Health and Social Security, London

DTI (2000) *Regional Competitiveness Indicators*, August, URN 00/237, Office for National Statistics, London www.dti.gov.uk/sd/rci

DTI and DfEE (2001) *Opportunity for All in a World of Change: A White Paper on enterprise, skills and innovation*, Cm 5052, The Stationery Office, Norwich, www.dti. gov.uk/opportunityforall/

East Midlands Chamber of Commerce (2000) *East Midlands Recruitment and Skills Survey*, East Midlands Chamber of Commerce, Derby

EMTA (1998) *Labour Market Survey of the Engineering Industry in Britain*, Engineering and Marine Training Authority, Watford

Felstead, A (1996) Identifying the gender inequalities in the distribution of vocational qualifications in the UK, *Gender, Work and Organization*, **3** (1) January, pp 38–50

Felstead, A (1997) Unequal shares for women? Qualification gaps in the National Targets for Education and Training, in *Half Our Future: Women, skill development and training*, ed H Metcalf, Policy Studies Institute, London

Felstead, A and Ashton, D (2000) Tracing the link: organizational structures and skill demands, *Human Resource Management Journal*, **10** (3) July, pp 5–21

Felstead, A, Ashton, D, Burchell, B and Green, F (1999) Skill trends in Britain: trajectories over the last decade, in *Speaking Truth to Power: Research and policy on lifelong learning*, ed F Coffield, Policy Press, Bristol

Felstead, A, Ashton, D and Green, F (2000) Are Britain's workplace skills becoming more unequal?, *Cambridge Journal of Economics*, **24** (6) November, pp 709–27

Felstead, A, Ashton, D and Green, F (2001) Paying the price for flexibility? Training, skills and non-standard jobs in Britain, *International Journal of Employment Studies*, April, **9** (1), pp 25–60

Felstead, A, Gallie, D and Green, F (2002) *Work Skills in Britain, 1986–2001*, Department for Education and Skills, London

Finegold, D and Soskice, D (1988) The failure of training in Britain: analysis and prescription, *Oxford Review of Economic Policy*, **4** (3), pp 21–53

Fothergill, S and Gudgin, G (1982) *Unequal Growth: Urban and regional economic change in the UK*, Heinemann, Oxford

Gallie, D (1994) Methodological appendix: the social change and economic life initiative, in *Employer Strategy and the Labour Market*, eds J Rubery and F Wilkinson, Oxford University Press, Oxford

Gallie, D, White, M, Cheng, Y and Tomlinson, M (1998) *Restructuring the Employment Relationship*, Oxford University Press, Oxford

Gillespie, A (1999) The changing employment geography of Britain, in *The People: Where will they work?*, ed M Breheny, Town and Country Planning Association, London

Green, A (1988) The North-South divide in Great Britain: an examination of the evidence, *Transactions of the Institute of British Geographers*, New Series, **13** (2), pp 179–88

Green, A and Owen, D (1998) *Where are the Jobless? Changing unemployment and non-employment in cities and regions*, Policy Press, Bristol

Green, A and Steedman, H (1997) *Into the Twenty First Century: An assessment of British skill profiles and prospects*, Centre for Economic Performance, London School of Economics, London

Green, F and Ashton, D (1992) Skills shortage and skill deficiency: a critique, *Work, Employment and Society*, **6** (2) June, pp 287–301

Green, F, Machin, S and Wilkinson, D (1998) The meaning and determinants of skills shortages, *Oxford Bulletin of Economics and Statistics*, **60** (2), pp 165–87

Green, F, Ashton, D, Burchell, B, Davies, B and Felstead, A (2000) Are British workers getting more skilled?, in *The Overeducated Worker? The economics of skill utilization*, eds L Borghans and A de Grip, Edward Elgar, Cheltenham

Green, F, Ashton, D and Felstead, A (2001) Estimating the determinants of supply of computing, problem-solving, communication, social and teamworking skills, *Oxford Economic Papers*, **53**, pp 406–33

Hill, S and Munday, M (1992) The UK regional distribution of foreign direct investment: analysis and determinants, *Regional Studies*, **26** (6), pp 535–44

Hudson, N (2000) Employer Skills Survey, 1999, *Labour Market Trends*, **108** (11) November, pp 511–15

IFF Research Ltd (1998) *Skill Needs in Great Britain and Northern Ireland 1998*, IFF Research Ltd, London

Mason, G (2000) Skills mismatches 1999. Paper given to the DfEE Skills Research Conference, London, 11 October

NACETT (1994) *Report on Progress*, National Advisory Council for Education and Training Targets, London

NACETT (1995) *Report on Progress towards the National Targets*, National Advisory Council for Education and Training Targets, London

NACETT (1997) *Skills for 2000: Supplement to the report on progress towards the National Targets for Education and Training*, National Advisory Council for Education and Training Targets, London

NACETT (2000) *Aiming Higher: NACETT's report on the national learning targets for England and advice on the targets beyond 2002*, National Advisory Council for Education and Training Targets, London

National Assembly for Wales (2000) *Statistical Brief*, National Assembly for Wales, Cardiff

Office of National Statistics (2000) *Region in Figures*, Winter, No 2, (for each of the nine English regions) Office for National Statistics, Newport

Payne, J (1999) All things to all people: changing perceptions of 'skill' among Britain's policy makers since the 1950s and their implications, *ESRC Centre on Skills, Knowledge and Organizational Performance*, Oxford and Warwick Universities Research Paper, No 1, August

Robinson, P (1996) Skill shortages and full employment: how serious a constraint?, in *Creating Industrial Capacity: Towards full employment*, eds J Michie and J Grieve-Smith, Oxford University Press, Oxford

Spilsbury, M and Lane, K (2000) *Skill Needs and Recruitment Practices in Central London*, FOCUS Central London, London

Sunley, P and Martin, R (2000) The geographies of the national minimum wage, *Environment and Planning A*, **32** (10) October, pp 1,735–58

The Stationery Office (2000) *Regional Trends, United Kingdom,* No 35, The Stationery Office, Norwich

Townsend, P and Davidson, N (1982) *Inequalities in Health: The Black Report*, Penguin, Harmondsworth

Turok, I and Webster, D (1998) The New Deal: jeopardised by the geography of unemployment?, *Local Economy*, **12** (4) February, pp 309–28

Whitehead, M (1987) *The Health Divide: Inequalities in health in the 1980s*, Health Education Council, London

Policy interventions for a vibrant work-based route – or when policy hits reality's fan (again)

Ewart Keep and Jonathan Payne

The new two-year Youth Training Scheme stands comparison with any training scheme for young people in the world. (Lord Young of Graffham, *MSC Youth Training News*, February 1986)

If the two-year YTS fails then we are at the end of the road. (Geoffrey Holland, cited in Evans, 1992: 194)

As the staying-on rate has rocketed, the proportion of 16 and 17-year olds under-taking training in the workplace, whether government funded or not, has fallen steadily. If there is now to be a major expansion of apprenticeships, what is to be the driving force behind such a reversal of recent trends? (Berkeley, 2000: 10)

In many cases, particularly in vocational education and industrial training, we have seen old programmes relaunched under a change of name, but without substantial changes in the patterns of resourcing or incentives for the various participants. (Oates, 2000: 20)

Introduction

This chapter aims to do two things. First, it examines the current policy options for securing a healthy, vibrant future for work-based training in England. The main focus is on initial vocational education and training for young entrants to the labour force (those in the 16 to 24 age group). There are many equally, perhaps more, important issues concerning adult learning in the workplace and how this can best be supported, but to do any justice to these would require another chapter. However, we suggest that there may be considerable merit in trying to link policy on initial VET to wider policy options for adult training and, crucially, for reflection on the role of employers in providing training, both for young entrants and adult workers. In geographical terms, the main focus is upon England, though much of the analysis can, in broad terms, be applied throughout the UK.

Second, the chapter, as a case study in policy process and outcomes, seeks to offer a range of lessons for a wider, international audience. It uses the English example to offer some reflections on the difficulties that surround attempts to develop and sustain work-based learning for the young in a deregulated, voluntarist training system, parts of which have little if any tradition hitherto of providing high quality initial training to young entrants. The tensions created by attempting to use the apprenticeship system as both a vehicle for social inclusion and as a high quality training route are also explored.

The latest twist

Policy in England is undergoing the latest in a long series of reforms. As the first quote at the start of this chapter illustrates, senior policy makers have tended to assume, somewhat prematurely, that they have cracked the problem of youth training, only for their hopes to be dashed. This pattern has been mirrored in other areas of vocational education and training policy formation over the last two decades (see Mansfield, 2000, for an excellent overview of this phenomenon). As we will argue, there is evidence to suggest that this cycle may be about to be repeated yet again.

Although all the details of what is intended have yet to be revealed, the basic outlines of the changes to the apprenticeship system are as follows (DfEE, 2000, 2001). To begin with, despite continuing problems with the quality of much that is being offered via the work-based route, even within the flagship Modern Apprenticeship programme, a major increase in the scale of the work-based route is now planned, with the ultimate implicit aim of offering 16- to 18-year-olds a choice between full-time education or work-based training. The intention is that the current options of work without training, or status zero (those young people outside education, training or work and not in receipt of state benefits), will vanish. Officials have also indicated that they expect some who now go through the full-time education route, pursuing 'inappropriate' courses and qualifications in future to opt for work-based provision. Although the Department for Education and Skills (DfES) has declined to provide any overall figure for the expansion, it admits that it will mean a significant increase in the number of places that will be needed and, given the groups nominated as targets for inclusion, it would seem not unreasonable to suggest a doubling of the numbers involved in the work-based route.

Coupled with this, an 'entitlement' to an apprenticeship place will be offered 'to all young people who have the ability, aptitude and enthusiasm for work-based learning' (DfEE, 2001: 21). The government also expects that some young people may be able to move onto a form of apprenticeship, possibly part-time, from the age of 14. Details of how this would work have yet to be revealed.

Existing National Traineeships (NTs) and 'other training' (the withered remains of Youth Training provision) will be abolished and replaced by Foundation Modern Apprenticeships (FMAs), which will generally aim to provide training to achieve a level 2 qualification. Existing Modern Apprenticeships will be re-styled Advanced Modern Apprenticeships (AMAs). For those entering the work-based route who are not ready to enter direct onto an FMA, Gateway provision (akin to that offered under the government's New Deal scheme for the long-term unemployed) will be made available. It is intended that there will be a ladder of progression, from Foundation on to Advanced Apprenticeship, and from thence to Foundation Degrees and other higher education qualifications. At the same time, the importance of Key Skills and of underpinning technical knowledge and understanding will be boosted within the apprenticeship system, and new forms of certification will support this development. Although the government consultation document on the future of apprenticeships suggested that minimum periods of off-the-job training be specified (DfEE, 2000), it remains to be seen if these will be imposed, or will be left to the discretion of the relevant sectoral bodies – the National Training Organisations (NTOs). The Learning and Skills Council (LSC), as the new funding body with responsibility for non-university post-compulsory education and training, will assume overall responsibility for implementing the expansion of the apprenticeship system. The apprenticeship reforms are linked, in turn, to the government's commitment to boost the status of the vocational route in education, via the abolition of General National Vocational Qualifications (GNVQs) and their replacement by vocational GCSEs and vocational A-levels.

Both the consultation document on the future of apprenticeship (DfEE, 2000) and statements by DfES staff, acknowledge that underlying these policies there are two major tensions. First, that between quality and inclusiveness – a conflict that has been apparent in earlier manifestations of government-sponsored youth training provision, for example the Youth

Training Scheme. Second, there are perceived to be trade-offs between the desire by government to prescribe to employers certain minimum common features and levels of entitlement for trainees, and the desire by employers to maintain maximum flexibility in the design and delivery of a programme which, when it was originally launched, was meant to be 'owned' by industry (Fuller, 1996). These issues will resurface at several points in what follows.

It is also worth noting that what is being proposed raises a number of questions, which at present policy makers have yet to answer. For example, it is unclear how and by what agency (above and beyond the usual, and usually ineffective, device of government exhortation) employers will be persuaded to cease to employ young people in jobs that offer little or no training. The UK's leading employers' body, the Confederation of British Industry, proposed just such a development as long ago as 1989 (CBI, 1989). Their members ignored the suggestion. Nor is it readily apparent how the substantial rise in the number of trainee places needed to absorb the 'zero status' youngsters and others will be achieved. Finally, given current concerns about the quality of existing provision, the means by which quality control can cope with wholesale expansion will pose some interesting problems.

Two scenarios

One helpful device for 'shorthanding' the very different potential trajectories that policy in this area might take, and the results it might produce, is to outline future scenarios of how current strategies could play out. Below are two scenarios for 2005. They present a useful (for the purposes of debate), if probably simplistic, polar dichotomy.

Scenario A – everything is coming up roses

The work-based route has entered a period of fairly major expansion, mainly because of the government's 'entitlement' offer of the place on an apprenticeship to all who want one (DfEE, 2001). As a result there has been a sharp reduction in the number of job opportunities for young people that offer no training, and a major drive to encourage many in the 'status zero' group to participate. There have also been efforts to encourage some young people in schools and colleges to follow the work-based route as one more appropriate to their needs. Despite the introduction of Educational Maintenance Allowances (EMAs – selective grants to students who remain in school or college post-16), and the continuing 'pull' from the education system to encourage more to stay on full-time, more young people have opted for the work-based route. The new Gateway schemes have generally proved successful in preparing many of the disadvantaged and those with learning difficulties to embark upon FMAs. Some then progress to AMAs.

Employers' conceptions of what an apprenticeship might comprise have undergone significant change. There is now much wider acceptance of the value of all of the Key Skills – information technology, communication, numeracy, problem solving, working with others, and improving own performance – and of a relatively substantial element of off-the-job training. Partly as a result, the majority of trainees in most sectors are now achieving level 2 (FMAs) and level 3 qualifications (AMAs), as well as Key Skills certification and technical certification.

The LSC has assumed the task of acting as the overall manager and champion of the work-based route. In taking on this role it has been aided by a revitalized and more uniformly effective and efficient set of sectoral bodies. One of the LSC's successes has been in gaining the support of employers. Firms have generally seen the new funding system for apprenticeships, administered by the LSC, as a positive development that offers them a better funding deal than the earlier Training and Enterprise Council (TEC) system.

Scenario B – on the road to nowhere

The work-based route has entered a further period of decline. Although the number of apprenticeships has held up in those industries where there is a well-established tradition of apprenticeships (such as engineering), in many other sectors the number of places has fallen quite sharply. The quality of the training on offer remains highly variable and completion and qualification rates remain too low – in many sectors below 50 per cent. Many employers continue, as they always have done, to offer employment to 16- and 17-year-olds that provides no training whatsoever. There are a number of reasons for this.

Developments within compulsory and post-compulsory education have continued the trend towards greater full-time post-16 participation in the educational route. These include: government targets for full-time post-16 educational participation, backed by incentives and penalties for LEAs and local LSCs; the introduction of EMAs across the whole of England; growth in the number and take-up of foundation degrees; and the development of a 'vocational stream' (vocational GCSEs, vocational A-levels, foundation degrees), but as largely a stream within the education system.

Outside of a few sectors, such as engineering, the work-based route is increasingly being seen by employers as the means to re-motivate (or alternatively as a dumping ground for) those disaffected with the education system. Employers are unenthusiastic about being left to deal with youngsters the education system has rejected. The introduction of the 'guarantee' of a place on an FMA has heightened this perception. The Gateways have failed to offer adequate preparation for entry on to the apprenticeship and employers are refusing to accept entrants via this route.

Where expansion of provision has been achieved, it has taken place largely in those sectors that have the worst record on training quality and completion (such as retailing). As a result, FMAs have produced low completion rates, high drop-out, failure to achieve qualifications and widely varying standards of training and trainee support. Bad publicity about FMAs is starting to tar AMAs with the same brush. Employers have also failed to heed government exhortation, and are continuing to offer jobs without training to the young.

The abolition of the employer-led, local TECs and their replacement by the LSC removed the one 'product champion' of the work-based route which was willing to go out and sell work-based training for the young to employers. The national LSC has found itself performing a 'funding council plus' role, and this has meant adopting a neutral stance as between the different routes available. It has chosen not to define its task as encompassing any real attempt to actively promote and build up the work-based stream of provision. A few of the local LSCs have tried to adopt a more proactive approach, but their isolated efforts have had limited effect.

At the same time, battles over the funding of work-based provision have been considerable. The LSC's need to develop a simple and relatively uniform set of tariffs, coupled with intensive lobbying by the further education sector against preferential treatment for a 'less cost-effective' work-based route, and random and often none-too-well presented calls from employers for higher levels of support, has led to a situation where no one is happy. Employers, in particular, feel that the transition from TEC funding to the LSC's regime has left many of them worse off.

Despite further re-jigging, 'culling' and a limited amount of additional government support, the sectoral NTOs, in the main, continue to lack the wherewithal to perform a strategic function, or to develop strong links with their membership and with the sectors they are meant to represent and service. Unfortunately, though perhaps unsurprisingly, many of the weakest and most under-resourced NTOs are found in sectors where the tradition of apprenticeship is weak or non-existent and which therefore require the most help and support in delivering a high quality youth training experience.

Although trailed in the final report of the government's Skills Task Force (STF, 2000), the development of a set of locally-focused group training organizations has been very patchy and limited. A number of small-scale experiments have got off the ground, but their coverage is tiny. Again, the initiative lacks a clear champion or adequate funding.

Moves to make Key Skills compulsory and to assess them through examinations have had disastrous effects. Many employers have concluded that Key Skills training is irrelevant to their needs, and both they and trainees have shied away from formal testing – the employers because the tests cost time and money, the trainees because they see them as being more school-style exams that will label them as failures. As a result, Key Skills continue not to be integrated into apprenticeship training and are generally delivered (where they are delivered at all) off the job. Moreover, the vast majority of employers continue to have a very narrow conception of what skills an apprenticeship needs to impart, and remain highly resistant to any attempt to broaden the experience out from a more or less totally job-specific focus.

Which of these scenarios is the more likely to come about? It is our contention that, as things stand, and without a substantial shift in the fundamental direction of policy in this area, the balance of probability suggests that by 2005 it is likely that we will be closer to Scenario B than Scenario A. Some of the main reasons for this belief are outlined in the next section.

Barriers to progress

There is a range of factors which, taken together, suggest that the prospects for the apprenticeship system in England are not particularly bright. Some relate to the absence of some of the fundamental underlying preconditions which comparative research suggests may be needed to sustain a successful system of initial work-based learning. Others are bound up with narrow and more specific institutional weaknesses and failings.

The legacy of past failures

To begin with, it would be far easier to contemplate the future with optimism were the recent past not so littered with the wreckage of earlier failures in the field of vocational training for young people. These include: one-year YTS; two-year YTS; Youth Training; Training Credits (later re-styled Youth Credits and only partially implemented, with much provision soldiering on under the YT banner); and finally National Traineeships, again, only partially implemented, alongside the decaying remains of YT (which eventually simply began to be called 'other training').

Past performance is not always a good predictor of future outcomes, but these earlier failures to create a high quality, permanent 'bridge between school and work' cast serious doubt on the likely outcome of the latest round of 'reform'. Huge amounts of money and political capital were invested in YTS and YT, but the effects were often patchy and disappointing. The scale of financial investment exceeds anything now being contemplated. Between 1983 and 1992, government spending on YTS and YT amounted, in total, at 1992 prices, to £7.86 billion (Employment Department, 1992).

This 20-year legacy means that it is now harder to gather political clout behind the work-based route. Current proposals have nothing like the political salience of YTS when it was first mooted. There are also substantial problems of initiative fatigue among employers, training providers and other players in the field. Finally, failures in the quality of much earlier provision tended to tarnish the reputation afforded the work-based route by parents, teachers and young people. Modern Apprenticeships have gone a long way towards repairing that damage, and have helped establish the value of apprenticeship style training (Unwin and Fuller, 2000), but that reputation remains fragile and could easily collapse if current plans for expansion are not handled carefully.

The lack of legal underpinning or structured trade union involvement

As Ryan (2000) shows, in other EU countries the norm is for the apprenticeship system to be supported by a statutory framework which 'defines what an apprenticeship is and what it is not – ie, provides for the legal definition of its occupational coverage and training content – and provides powers for its governance and its adaptation' (Ryan, 2000: 48). This is the case not only in the Nordic and Germanic countries, but even in Ireland, a state that historically has fallen largely within the ambit of Anglo-Saxon tradition.

Across the whole of the UK, there is no statutory regulation of apprenticeship. It is up to employers to define what they think it is and how it should operate. The only constraint is provided if the employer seeks to gain access to public money by having his or her apprenticeship funded as part of the Modern Apprenticeship scheme. As this chapter suggests, the Modern Apprenticeship provides, at best, a fairly minimalist framework. This absence of public regulation, Ryan argues, is a key difference between the UK and other European states and one that may continue to foster weaknesses and variable quality in what is on offer.

Allied to this, in other European states the legislation normally makes explicit provision for the participation of trade unions in the governance and operation of the apprenticeship system. Again, across the UK as a whole, this requirement is absent. Trade union involvement, where it takes place, is normally at the discretion of the employer: it does not take place as of right. In other systems, trade union involvement helps ensure adequate training quality and aids the legitimization of apprenticeships as a valuable route to young people, their parents and to employees in the workplaces where training is taking place.

Both of these missing elements reflect the UK's tradition of voluntarism in the field of employee relations and its relatively lightly regulated system of labour market governance. Despite some changes, there is a strong element of continuity on this front between the various Conservative administrations between 1979 and 1997 and New Labour's policies since 1997. Although the New Labour government has indicated that it believes trade unions have a valuable, if limited, role to play in some aspects of training, the emphasis has been on adult and continuing training, rather than initial training. In either field, whether at workplace, sectoral or national level, the social partners' involvement tends to take place on a 'grace and favour' basis, ie employers have to agree to it and can do much to delimit its scope.

The problem of educational content

Another element (often enshrined in legislation) found in other European apprenticeship systems but missing in England is its integration into a broader educational context (Ryan, 2000: 53–54). This means an entitlement to part-time vocational education, aimed at supplementing and broadening the learning experiences provided through work-based learning. In the continental countries in Ryan's study, between a quarter and a third of the trainees' time is spent on general education.

The English system is radically different. There is no requirement within Modern Apprenticeships for any general educational element. As Green (1998) details, the UK's overall heritage in apprenticeship places no real emphasis on any component of general education and, as Ryan reports (2000: 53), most apprentices on Modern Apprenticeships do not even receive any off-the-job instruction, never mind general education. Unlike other European countries, where legislation has supported a general educational element, the UK's voluntarist approach has not (Ryan, 2000: 54). Instead, the government has sought to substitute a much more limited agenda, focused around the six Key Skills, as a substitute for general education that is more likely to command support among employers. Even this has proved over-optimistic, with substantial employer resistance occurring.

The problems surrounding firms' attitudes to Key Skills underline the difficulties of engaging with UK employers over VET issues. When consulted on macro level policy, employers and their representatives have appeared enthusiastic about Key Skills (STF, 2000), but experience of trying to introduce and integrate Key Skills in MAs suggests that in practice this enthusiasm is in fact often very limited (Kodz *et al*, 2000; Winterbotham *et al*, 2000). As one NTO Key Skills Coordinator commented, 'We would be better concentrating on their trade skills rather than IT, etc. Why would a modern apprentice welder want basic IT skills and mathematics when he (sic) will never use them in the whole of his working life!'

This type of reaction results, in part, because the Key Skills qualifications that were introduced reflected a very different ethos from the original concept of Key Skills that the government sold to employers. However, it is also true that many employers hold an inherently backward looking and tightly circumscribed conception of what skills and capabilities work does and will entail. These attitudes go a long way towards explaining why vocational skills in the UK remain narrow and low level compared to what is often found in mainland Europe (Green, 1998).

There is the danger that the demands of the assessment system will further reinforce narrowness. Even the existing meagre fare is now in severe danger of being further diluted. Because only three out of the six Key Skills are easily amenable to 'rigorous' assessment through written examinations (IT, numeracy and communication), they are the ones that are now being emphasized by policy makers. Given the tendency to concentrate on activities that generate simple, numerically recordable performance indicators (such as examination passes) there is a strong likelihood that the other three, softer and broader but non-examined Key Skills – working with others, improving own performance, and problem solving – will rapidly be relegated to the bottom of the list of priorities.

Strategic management for the work-based route

There is a long-standing and important dichotomy between the management styles adopted by central government towards the control of education and of training in England (Keep, 1987). Put simply, since the mid-1980s the tendency has been for increasing direct central control and management in detail of education by the government, while a much more laissez-faire, hands-off approach has been adopted towards government-supported training undertaken by employers. Indeed, it would probably be fair to say that whereas much of school education is now micro-managed from the centre, there is relatively loose administration of training schemes. This situation means that there often appears to be little strategic management of training initiatives, and the minimalism of monitoring and control mechanisms often results in the absence of the type of information that is needed to judge overall performance, identify structural weaknesses and trends, and ensure value for money. Two examples of this tendency will suffice.

First, whereas it is entirely possible for the Secretary of State to communicate directly with individual delivery units within the education system (between January and July 2000, the then Department for Education and Employment sent every secondary school 75 separate documents, totalling 2,063 pages – *Times Educational Supplement*, 28 July 2000), this is not possible within the sphere of training. Indeed, the government cannot write to those employers involved in delivering Modern Apprenticeships, because there is no central (or any other) record of who they are. What was the TSC's database (now the Adult Learning Inspectorate) gives details of organizations having contracts to provide government-funded training. The TSC held data on 1,900 training providers, including companies which train their own employees, employers' associations, not-for-profit organizations, private training providers, public bodies (such as hospital trusts and local authorities) and further education colleges (TSC, 2000a: 12). The TSC admitted that 'many of the smallest providers fall outside the present scope of inspection' (TSC, 2000a: 12) and were therefore not covered by the TSC database.

This database, by only covering those with direct contracts to deliver government-supported training, excludes the vast majority of employers who are involved, often as sub-contractors of larger training providers. The DfEE's Learning and Training at Work (LTW) 1999 survey (IFF, 2000) suggested that the number of employers providing government-funded training (whether or not they directly held a contract or were acting as a sub-contractor for a training provider) was far higher than the TSC's 1,900 entries. Even the exact size of this group is unknown.

The LTW survey covered a sample of 4,008 employer establishments having one or more employees at the specific location sampled. All business sectors were covered. Establishments were asked if they had been involved with various training initiatives. The responses suggested that about 4 per cent of employers were involved in the remnants of YT, a similar proportion with Modern Apprenticeships, and about 2 per cent with both National Traineeships and 'other training' (IFF, 2000: 72).

Unfortunately, it is not possible to determine to what extent respondents were simultaneously engaged in several of these schemes, nor whether IFF's sample contains overlap between different establishments of the same company. However, IFF was confident that the 'results are. . . representative

of the 1.8 million employers in England who have 1 or more employees'
(IFF, 2000: 3).

Given the potential for an individual establishment having perhaps two
government-funded training schemes in operation at once (most likely
Modern Apprenticeships and either YT, NT, or 'other' youth training), this
suggests that the likely proportion of employers involved in some form of
government-sponsored initial training might be between 4 and 6 per cent.
The potential size of this population is as follows. If 4 per cent of employers
are involved, this represents 72,000 businesses. If 5 per cent are involved, the
figure is 90,000, and if 6 per cent are involved, the figure climbs to 108,000.
That no one knows what the exact total really is, nor who these employers
are, nor are able to contact them directly, raises a number of questions about
how the government can hope to manage, in any meaningful sense, the work-
based route.

A second example of weak management comes from the TSC's report
on Modern Apprenticeships. As the TSC notes:

> There are no national data showing achievement rates for complete modern
> apprenticeships. . . Without standard approaches to recording retention and
> achievement, little can be said reliably about the success of modern apprentice-
> ships as a national programme or about any differences that may exist among
> different occupational areas or providers. (TSC, 2000b: 21)

This situation, it can be argued, is not acceptable if a high quality work-
based route is to be developed and sustained. Adequate, timely management
information and an ability to communicate directly with those involved in
training delivery are essential prerequisites to making progress.

Selling work-based learning – find the product champion

As Scenario B above suggests, the abolition of the TECs and their replacement
by a national funding council (the LSC) with local arms (the local LSCs)
may result in a position where there is no agency responsible for actively
marketing involvement in government-supported training provision to
employers. It remains to be seen how the LSC and local LSCs will choose
to operate in this area, but it is difficult to see how a funding council can
actively promote any particular route in preference to another. Given the
inherent bias in current government policies towards yet further expansion
of full-time post-compulsory education (see below), unless there is a body

charged with promoting the potential benefits of a work-based route, to both young people and employers, there are liable to be problems. As suggested above, many of the sectoral NTOs remain of limited effectiveness in performing this role.

The role and attitudes of employers

Many of the problems with the work-based route for young people stem from employers' attitudes towards such provision. As evaluations of MA provision have clearly indicated, employers in many sectors have limited comprehension of what a genuine apprenticeship would resemble, and still less ability to provide it (Kodz *et al*, 2000; Sims *et al*, 2000). To give just one example, Winterbotham *et al* (2000: 3) report that only 6 per cent of MAs in retailing attended college as part of their apprenticeship and 'a third appeared to have no formal training of any sort (formal here meaning training beyond merely being supervised while doing day-to-day work)'. It is hard to see that provision of this sort constitutes an apprenticeship in any meaningful sense.

Unfortunately, when faced with these problems the overall keynote of government attitudes towards intervention in the workplace has been anxiety about imposing anything that might be construed as constituting a further 'burden' upon employers. It might be asked why, if the government believes its own rhetoric about skills being the key to economic success, measures to encourage employers to produce a better educated and trained workforce would constitute a burden, but this question is rarely if ever posed in public policy debate.

What is puzzling is how or why policy makers now profess to believe that employers' deep-seated attitudes are about to undergo a sudden and miraculous change for the better. Neither the government's consultation document on the reform of apprenticeship (DfEE, 2000), nor the Secretary of State's speech on the topic (DfEE, 2001), offer any clue as to what major new factor is being assumed will now make employers want to act differently on the value of Key Skills, the value of off-the-job training, the value of full completion of the whole apprenticeship, the costs of offering employment without training to large numbers of young people, and the feasibility of using apprenticeships to provide for the socially disadvantaged and educationally disaffected.

We beg to doubt, on the evidence of what has happened over the last two decades, and given the current state of MA provision (Kodz *et al*, 2000; Sims *et al*, 2000; Winterbotham *et al*, 2000), that this hoped for transformation will occur. They suspect that the result is more likely to be that many of the problems that plagued YTS, YT, NTs and MAs will continue to limit the payoff from the new FMAs and AMAs. Indeed, current proposals for the reform of apprenticeships, as contained in the government's consultation document (DfEE, 2000) and the Secretary of State's speech (DfEE, 2001), may run the risk of obtaining the worst of both worlds by ushering in changes that will discourage many employers from participating, without necessarily delivering a huge improvement. In particular, it remains unclear where the support, help and developmental advice to enable employers to move towards the desired changes are to come from. The consultation document, in its section entitled 'better support' (DfEE, 2000: 15), suggests that local LSCs and NTOs will fill the gap, but whether either will have the time, staffing, resources, expertise or contact with the relevant employers to undertake this onerous role is unclear.

The workplace versus the classroom

A final key issue for the future development of the work-based route is its relative importance vis-à-vis full-time, post-compulsory education. Since the early 1990s policy makers have tended to favour full-time post-compulsory education as the best route to achieving higher post-16 participation. The development of General National Vocational Qualifications and the massive expansion of further and higher education are testimony to this strand of policy. The latest reforms appear to presage a modest expansion of the work-based route, but alongside yet further growth in higher education via the new foundation degrees. The piloting of EMAs may also be followed by their future introduction across England, thereby constituting another major incentive to individuals to remain in post-compulsory schooling.

As some elements of the scenarios outlined above suggest, this situation raises two related problems. First, there is liable to be even greater competition between the education and work-based routes for trainees/students and resources. The LSC and its local arms will be responsible for refereeing this competition, while also promoting work-based learning. How these potentially conflicting roles will be reconciled remains to be seen.

Second, although recent DfES statements emphasize the notion of the work-based route as a high status one, the evidence of past training schemes for the young suggests that the simultaneous pursuit of social inclusiveness, via a guarantee or entitlement to a place for the socially disadvantaged, tends to subvert that status. If the work-based route comes to be associated with 'mopping up' the 'status zero' population, and with offering provision of the last resort to those who are perceived to have failed in education, there are liable to be problems. The DfES plainly hope that by affixing the apprenticeship 'brand' to this type of training, its status can be elevated. The reverse situation – that this kind of provision will drag down the reputation of AMAs – is also possible.

The foregoing suggests that the work-based route of initial training for young people is faced with a number of deep-seated problems. If we assume that current policies are insufficient to address these, how best can they be tackled?

Possible avenues for progress

Developing policies that can successfully bring about fundamental and lasting change will not be easy. A combination of initiative fatigue, feelings of 'been there, done that and it failed', and the now relative marginality of the work-based route, all limit the room for manoeuvre.

In addition, present policies are predicated on a number of problematic assumptions. These include no role for legislative underpinning, no major role for the social partners, and little attempt at systemic capacity building within the infrastructure of the training system. In addition, there is a lack of proper management systems and clear lines of accountability and, most importantly of all, no concerted attempt to confront and incentivize change in employers' attitudes.

This approach, we would argue, needs to change if genuine progress is to be made. We would also suggest that before the route enters into a period of expansion it is vital that we ensure that existing levels of provision can deliver learning opportunities of a uniformly high quality. Unless this foundation is secure, the risks in expansion are considerable. One element in securing the quality of existing provision might be to ask whether the apprenticeship model is appropriate to all sectors or, to put it another way, whether employers in all sectors are currently able to accept and cope with the demands that the full-blown model of apprenticeships place upon them. It may be that there are some sectors that are not ready to be able to offer apprenticeships effectively (Unwin and Fuller, 2000). What data we have on completion rates, percentages of trainees being offered off-the-job training, and the specification of Key Skills levels and their attainment, all suggest that some sectors are experiencing major difficulties. A clear grasp of this picture and realism on its implications would be helpful.

We would suggest that policy options could be conceived of as potentially occurring at three levels:

1. Policies aimed at reform of initial VET provision via the work-based route.
2. Policies linked to reform of adult training in the workplace.
3. Policies linked to broader efforts to stimulate forms of work organization, job design, people management systems and competitive and product market strategies that stimulate the demand for and productive usage of high levels of skill across the whole economy.

We will briefly review each of these in turn, but will argue that while each can be considered in isolation, policy on VET is best framed through an holistic approach operating at all three levels.

Policies on initial vocational education and training via the work-based route

The policies outlined by Evans *et al* (1997) remain a good starting point for exploring how a more robust and higher quality initial work-based route might be constructed. We would highlight the following elements of policy as likely to prove key to making lasting progress.

Coming to terms with the complexity of the youth labour market

There is a real need for those who frame policy to acknowledge and understand the needs, demands and interests of those employers active in the youth labour market. As recent research indicates, these are often complex and underpinned by equally complex motivations. Far from being uniform, employers' requirements for young employees and the training opportunities they are willing to offer reflect both sectoral and occupational differences, and the often strong influences of local labour markets (Maguire, 2000). The interaction of these requirements and local variations in supply and demand (generated, for example, by widely varying staying-on rates in full-time education) produce a range of dynamics. Coupled with this has been the development, rarely acknowledged by the policy community, of a new youth labour market based around students. This means that many part-time and supposedly full-time students in both further and higher education are also holding down one or more jobs. A better appreciation of these factors by policy makers and by the agencies that have to deliver policy across the post-16 system would be helpful.

Systemic capacity building

If the work-based route is to function properly it requires powerful, well-resourced supportive institutions. Where apprenticeship systems flourish abroad, they do so because employers involved in such provision have access to extensive systems of support. In Denmark and Norway (Payne, 2001) this is delivered via the school system and local government; in Germany, via the Chambers of Commerce. In the English context, the minimum requirement is sectoral bodies that are uniformly capable of providing help, guidance and leadership to employers, particularly small employers (Sims *et al*, 2000) in their sector. It also means some form of system of local group training associations that can provide small employers with the economy of scale advantages and expertise of shared training provision. Although group training associations are much talked about, and some very limited sums of seed corn funding have been provided, a concerted attempt to make genuine progress in creating such a system has yet to happen.

The present situation all too often leaves individual employers carrying the burden of implementing forms of training that are simply beyond the resources and expertise they have available. Current policies, aimed at expanding FMAs and using them to cater for groups who may be poorly motivated or have learning difficulties, will only exacerbate these problems. A major investment of time, money and political capital needs to be committed to developing the systemic capacity of the training support systems. This would aid not only youth training policies, but also help support government policies on lifelong learning.

Paying for quality and breadth

It remains to be seen how the LSC will develop a funding system that can encompass the variety of provision found within the work-based route. What is important is that it does so in ways that maximize the number of 'winners' and minimize the 'losers', and that the resultant system offers employers adequate financial support for those elements of the learning package that go beyond their immediate needs. The adequacy of the funding system will become all the more important if the apprenticeship system is to absorb current NTs and 'other' training, because at present such provision makes relatively limited demands on employers and probably offers a reasonably favourable financial deal. FMAs will impose a much more demanding set of requirements, and that is liable to bring with it costs to the employer. Again, if the DfES does prove to be serious about imposing minimum levels of off-the-job training and requirements for education in underpinning skills and knowledge throughout the apprenticeship system, the cost implications for employers in many sectors where this is currently not general practice on what are about to become AMAs, will be substantial.

Employers – strong support, high expectations

If employers need to be provided with more robust and uniformly high quality systems of support, and reasonable funding, they also need to be confronted with their responsibilities. This means funding and support in return for breadth and standards. Those firms and sectors either unwilling or unable to meet agreed quality thresholds, completion rates and attainment targets over an agreed length of time should have their provision cut.

Partnership – let's be clear about who is meant to be doing what

'Partnership' is one of those words without which no government policy document is now regarded as complete, but it often appears to act as a means of spreading confusion about responsibilities. A vibrant work-based route cannot be delivered without the active cooperation of a range of partners: DfES, LSC and the local LSCs, NTOs, employer organizations, trade unions, further education colleges, private training providers, Learning Partnerships, group training organizations, and others. What is missing is clarity about who is meant to be doing what and about the mechanisms through which coordinated cooperation can be concerted. Such clarity needs to be established and with it a clear, general understanding of where the balance of rights, responsibilities and duties lie on any given issue.

Constructing supportive legislation

If the government is serious about seeing an end to full-time employment without training for young people, it will need to contemplate legislation, or at least the threat thereof. As mentioned above, the CBI advocated a voluntary approach to this issue during the tight labour markets at the end of the 1980s, with no visible effect. Many CBI members continued and still continue to recruit young workers to whom they offer little or no formalized training.

A second area where legislative support might be valuable is in regard to sectoral NTOs. Here a case can be made for compulsory membership as a route to creating NTOs that are genuinely representative of their sectors, and as a means of securing adequate resources for their activities.

Policies linked to reform of adult training in the workplace

There is a huge range of issues concerning adult training in the workplace that cannot be dealt with here (for a review of some of the issues, see Keep, 1999, and the various contributions in Rainbird, 2000). What we would suggest is that there is considerable sense in trying to confront employers' approaches towards initial VET in tandem with a reappraisal of their attitudes towards and provision of adult training. Problems in one area are related to those in the other. There is therefore much to recommend a return to the kind of strategic approach originally heralded in the Manpower Service Commission's New Training Initiative (MSC, 1981). The NTI argued for a joined-up approach to training policy that sought to address youth and adult training issues in parallel. Its success in achieving this was very limited, but the underlying logic of such a strategy has not been faulted.

The over-riding issues are what society can reasonably expect of employers, and how they can best be supported to achieve what is needed. Such support might encompass a statutory adult training framework that made clear the rights, responsibilities and duties of all those involved – employers, social partners, state, individuals, the education system and training bodies. Where it is unreasonable or inefficient to rely upon employers, the role of the state and of the education system and individuals needs to be spelt out. Although we know that there are significant weaknesses with employer-provided adult training, particularly for some significant sections of the workforce (Keep, 1999), this is another area where policy makers have been reluctant to disturb the status quo.

Thus the Skills Task Force, set up to investigate skill shortages in the national economy, tiptoed up to the issue of employers' responsibilities, particularly for adult training for those on the lower rungs of the occupational ladder, and then tiptoed away again, unable to agree on the need for any form of statutory underpinning (Keep, 2000a, 2000b; STF, 2000). Subsequently, the CBI issued a document suggesting that there is no problem with UK employers' overall investment in training, and that insofar as a proportion of the adult workforce is receiving limited and narrowly task-specific training, the answer lies with the individual and with state-funded educational provision to remedy the situation (CBI, 2000).

Rather than take these as the last word on the topic, it might be better to treat them as the starting point for a genuine public debate. Such a debate might focus on how external intervention can best aid the creation of workplaces that are conducive to more and better learning (see, for example, IPD, 2000; Rainbird, 2000) and how we can arrive at a balance of responsibilities that ensures that the entire adult workforce has access to levels of training that produce the optimal long-term results for society as whole (STF, 1998: 12).

Policies linked to work organization, job design and competitive strategies (skills and what else. . .?)

We believe that the ability of the workplace to supply high quality learning experiences, whether to young people or adult workers, is inextricably linked to broader issues such as work organization, job design, people management systems and, most importantly, competitive and product market strategies (Keep and Mayhew, 1998). These are topics that rarely figure in the official UK discourse on VET policy. In other policy fora, for example the OECD and the European Commission, and in other countries, for example Canada (see Betcherman and Chaykowski, 1996), consideration of such issues as part of a wider debate about creating high performance workplaces, and thereby the demand for higher levels of skills, is routine. The kind of VET policy that could encompass such issues in the different national contexts existing within the UK has been mooted (Keep, 2000a, 2000b), but whether such a broader perspective can and will be adopted by policy makers remains to be seen.

What is clear is that UK debates about training and the role of employers are framed in a distinctive fashion, in that they often have little to say about the structural and attitudinal environment within which training takes place. This means that, whereas in much of Europe one might expect consideration of training policy to cover topics such as social partnership, industrial relations, collective bargaining systems and co-determination, labour market structures and regulation, and a range of issues concerning industrial policy, such issues are noticeable by their absence in UK debate. In part this mirrors our highly deregulated labour market and weak and atomized system of collective bargaining, but it also reflects a preference for framing policy debate around a narrow range of supply-side issues. The result is discussion that focuses on giving the skill supply system's institutional kaleidoscope another shake in order to see what new and interesting pattern emerges, rather than on confronting structural problems and weaknesses in the demand for and usage of skills. It is our contention that this approach needs to change if we are to make lasting progress. The UK skills debate needs to be framed within wider horizons and encompass broader issues than has hitherto been the norm.

Overview and conclusions

At present, the central thrust of VET policies in England is a further set of supply-side reforms aimed at boosting the supply of skills. These reforms include yet more institutional change and attempts to further amend the curriculum, assessment systems and modes of delivery and pedagogy.

Within this, the latest round of reform of the work-based route for initial VET tries to create a strand of provision that encompasses both high quality technical training and a socially inclusive option for those who dislike or have become disengaged from education. Evidence from earlier rounds of reform suggests that the latter objective has the potential to subvert the status of the former. For a variety of reasons reviewed above, the overall prognosis for the latest attempt to produce a high quality work-based route is not good. In many senses, the current situation is the logical outcome of a combination of earlier policy failures and accepting the basic premises that underlay the previous Conservative administrations' approach to VET policies. There are three points of concern.

One is the continuing belief that institutional restructuring, of itself, will produce fundamental change. The arrival of the Learning and Skills Council and its cohorts of local LSCs is testimony to the view that the failure of the Non-Statutory Training Organisations, the ITOs and the TECs to usher in a transformation of skills supply and usage, as was expected when these institutions were introduced, was just an aberration (or series of aberrations), and that this time the institutional configuration is magically 'right'.

The second is the parallel belief that the failure of earlier re-brandings of work-based training provision for the young was also an accident, and that the latest formulation – FMAs and AMAs – will somehow be different. In particular, there is an implicit assumption that employers will now adopt new and more liberal attitudes – to Key Skills, the need for high quality, structured learning, and significant amounts of off-the-job provision. The evidence to support this assumption is almost wholly lacking.

In both cases, it can be argued that relatively superficial reforms have been chosen to act as a form of displacement activity that helps policy makers avoid the painful task of acknowledging and tackling the underlying structural factors and attitudes that have led to repeated under-performance in both institutional structures and the schemes, initiatives and programmes they are meant to be supervising and delivering. This persistent inability to confront, acknowledge and learn from earlier failures hamstrings our ability to move on and make progress (Mansfield, 2000).

The third problem stems from a fundamental ambiguity about the future role, shape and relative importance of the work-based route vis-à-vis full-time educational provision. VET policy over the last decade suggests that many policy makers see the future route map to high participation in initial VET as being via a mass system of further and higher education, with the work-based route there to cope with a few sectors, like engineering, where apprenticeship traditions are strong, and also as a provider of last resort to those young people who have become demotivated and disaffected within education.

This chapter has argued that the latest round of reforms embodies and reinforces many aspects of these problems and that, while they specify the desired end, they have remarkably little to say about the means by which these are to be achieved. We have suggested an alternative approach to policy that might go some way towards confronting and tackling the underlying causes of persistent failure. Such an approach would also have the benefit of supporting moves to develop the workplace as a source of lifelong learning. Unfortunately, it would also require a radical change in emphasis that at present seems unlikely to come about.

What conclusions might an international audience draw from this rather sorry story? The chief ones concern the immense problems of trying to build and sustain a work-based route for initial education and training in the absence of a supportive political, cultural, legal and institutional framework (Ryan, 2000). Evidence from comparative study of apprenticeship systems indicates that success requires them to be embedded in a rich framework of institutions, expectations and obligations, ultimately supported in many instances by the force of law. As outlined above, many of the main pillars that observers such as Ryan (2000) have concluded are essential to the proper functioning of an apprenticeship system are either partially or wholly absent in our system. These include some element of statutory regulation, this to include elements of quality control in the workplace, a framework for the role of trade unions, and a stronger and more clearly specified general educational element to the apprenticeship programme.

There is also the need for a starting point in terms of a shared set of cultural expectations about what an apprenticeship system and work-based learning for the young should be comprised of and what there is to achieve. In England, at present, policy makers appear to embrace a wide set of expectations that the evidence suggests are often not shared by those who have to deliver the training. The saga of Key Skills is a salutary reminder of this problem. Key Skills are a very thin substitute for the type of general education component found in European apprenticeship schemes (Green, 1998; Ryan, 2000), but even this minimalistic requirement has proved too demanding for many English employers.

As the final draft of this chapter is being written, the UK government is again warning its partners in the EU that they must deregulate their labour market institutions and adopt British-style flexibility if they are to avoid an unpleasant (if vaguely specified) fate. In the area of initial training, on the past and current showing of our apprenticeship system, they would be singularly ill advised to heed this advice. Our tradition of voluntarism, minimal regulation and a willingness to tolerate very limited aspirations on the part of employers has, as has been suggested above, not necessarily served us terribly well in the recent past, nor provided us with the foundations for future success. Others may not wish to share in our misfortune.

For an English audience, perhaps the best way to end this chapter is to go back to where we started, to the series of quotes. Arguably the most important is Geoffrey Holland's view that if two-year YTS did not flourish, the experiment to create a vibrant, mainstream work-based route would have failed. In fact, it did fail, and the echoes of that failure remain with us today. The latest round of reforms is simply yet another attempt to remedy this without addressing its root causes. As some of us suggested a few years ago:

> The effort invested in the creation of institutional mechanisms and modes of delivery that have subsequently been discarded has led to disillusionment and cynicism on the part of some about future developments. If we are not careful, we run the danger that the future, to some extent at least, will be the past, but with fewer options. (Evans *et al*, 1997: 47)

The risk that this will now prove to be the case is greater still.

References

Berkeley, J (2000) A new dawn for the work-based route?, *College Research*, **3** (3), pp 9–10

Betcherman, G and Chaykowski, R (1996) The changing workplace: challenges for public policy, *Strategic Policy Research Papers*, R-96-13E, Human Resources Development Canada, Quebec

Confederation of British Industry (1989) *Towards a Skills Revolution – A youth charter*, CBI, London

Confederation of British Industry (2000) *Fact not Fiction – UK training performance*, CBI, London

Department for Education and Employment (2000) *Modern Apprenticeships – Consultation document*, DfEE, Sudbury

Department for Education and Employment (2001) *Education into Employability – The role of the DfEE in the economy*, DfEE, London

Employment Department (1992) *The Government's Expenditure Plans 1992–93 to 1994–95*, Cmnd (1906), HMSO, London

Evans, B (1992) *The Politics of the Training Market: From Manpower Services Commission to Training and Enterprise Councils*, Routledge, London

Evans, K, Hodkinson, P, Keep, E, Maguire, M, Raffe, D, Rainbird, H, Senker, P and Unwin, L (1997) Working to learn, *Issues in People Management,* No 18, Institute of Personnel and Development, London

Fuller, A (1996) Modern Apprenticeship, process and learning: some emerging issues, *Journal of Vocational Education and Training*, **48** (3), pp 229–48

Green, A (1998) Core Skills, Key Skills and general culture: in search of a common foundation for vocational education, *Evaluation and Research in Education*, **12** (1), pp 23–43

Huddleston, P (2000) Work placements for young people, in *Training in the Workplace,* ed H Rainbird, Macmillan, London

IFF Research Ltd (2000) *Learning and Training at Work 1999,* DfEE Research Report RR202, DfEE, Nottingham

Institute of Personnel and Development (2000) *Success through Learning: The argument for strengthening workplace learning*, IPD, London

Keep, E (1987) Britain's attempts to create a national vocational education and training system: a review of progress, *Warwick Papers in Industrial Relations* No 16, University of Warwick, Industrial Relations Research Unit, Coventry

Keep, E (1999) Employers' attitudes towards training, *STF Research Paper* 15, DfEE, Sudbury

Keep, E (2000a) *Upskilling Scotland*, Centre for Scottish Public Policy, Edinburgh

Keep, E (2000b) *Creating a Knowledge Driven Economy – Challenges and opportunities,* SKOPE Policy Paper No 2, University of Warwick, SKOPE, Coventry

Keep, E and Mayhew, K (1998) Was Ratner right? Product market and competitive strategies and their links with skills and knowledge, *Employment Policy Institute Economic Report*, **12** (3)

Kodz, J, Djan Tackley, N, Pollard, E, Dench, S, Tyers, C and Dewson, S (2000) Modern Apprenticeship and National Traineeships: skills utilisation and progression, *DfEE Research Report* RR204, DfEE, Nottingham

Maguire, S (2000) The evolving youth labour market: a study of continuity and change. University of Warwick, Coventry (unpublished PhD thesis)

Manpower Services Commission (1981) *A New Training Initiative – An agenda for action,* MSC, London

Mansfield, B (2000) *Past Imperfect?,* PRIME Research and Development Ltd (mimeo), Harrogate

Oates, T (2000) New research paradigms for the new millennium, *College Research*, **3** (3), pp 20–22

Payne, J (2001) Reconstructing apprenticeship for the 21st century: lessons from the UK and Norway. Paper presented at the IIR Conference, Oslo, June

Rainbird, H (ed) (2000) *Training in the Workplace*, Macmillan, London

Ryan, P (2000) The institutional requirements of apprenticeship: evidence from smaller EU countries, *International Journal of Training and Development*, **4** (1), pp 42–65

Sims, D, Golden, S, Blenkinsop, S and Lewis, G (2000) *Barriers to Take-up of Modern Apprenticeships and National Traineeships by SMEs and Specific Sectors,* DfEE Research Report RR205, DfEE, Nottingham

Skills Task Force (1998) *Towards a National Skills Agenda – First report of the National Skills Task Force,* DfEE, Sudbury

Skills Task Force (2000) *Skills for All: Proposals for a national skills agenda,* DfEE, Sudbury

Training Standards Council (2000a) *Reaching New Standards. Annual report of the chief inspector, 1999–2000,* TSC, Coventry

Training Standards Council (2000b) *Modern Apprenticeships,* TSC, Coventry

Unwin, L and Fuller, A (2000) National Report on Apprenticeships – Great Britain, Centre for Labour Market Studies (mimeo), Leicester

Winterbotham, M, Adams, L and Lorentzen-White, D (2000) *Modern Apprenticeships: Exploring the reasons for non-completion in five sectors,* DfEE Research Report RR217, DfEE, Nottingham

Chapter 12

No rights, just responsibilities: individual demand for continuing training[1]

Helen Rainbird

Introduction

The concept of individual demand for continuing training needs to be defined carefully in the UK context. Unlike other European countries such as France, initial training takes place either in companies or by young workers undertaking courses at a college of further education. They therefore appear as employees rather than as full-time students in the education system. This makes comparison of statistics on continuing training problematic at European level. For the purposes of this chapter, continuing training refers only to the training of adults in employment and not the initial training of young people even though this may be funded by the employer.

It is also difficult to draw the boundaries between continuing vocational training and adult continuing education more generally. The Department for Education and Employment (now the Department for Education and Skills) reports that a further education college or a university is the most common location for off-the-job training received by employees (DfEE, 1996) yet both are sources of general education as well as vocational training. Although adult continuing education could be considered as 'second chance' general education, systems of credit accumulation organized through the Open College Network (OCN) and the universities' Credit Accumulation and Transfer Scheme (CATS) mean that these courses can serve as access courses to study in further education colleges and universities. In a context in which many jobs are increasingly emphasizing the need for customer service skills and report writing, the boundary between vocational training and education for personal development has been blurred. This requires 'self-confidence, communication and negotiating skills, capacity for initiative and ability to weigh situations up and make judgements. These skills and attributes are often seen as an outcome of wider liberal education, with its emphasis on personal development' (Caldwell, 2000: 247). The question of what learners and trainers count as continuing vocational training is also an issue, in a context in which Human Resource professionals have a growing interest in the ways in which informal learning in the workplace can be supported (CIPD, 2000).

A further complication is that there is no legislative framework requiring employers to spend a proportion of their payroll on training, to report on their training expenditure and to provide a breakdown of the resources (financial and in terms of release from work) allocated to different occupational groups. This means that there are no administrative returns that can serve as a reliable source of information about either employers' or individuals' expenditure on training. Indeed, the DfEE's annual Education and Training Statistics provide no data on either employer or employee expenditure on training (DfEE, 2000a).[2] This absence of information is the case even in the public sector where it might be anticipated that the state's role as an employer would mean that such data might be collected.[3] The most recent official publication on training statistics for England (DfEE, 2000b), based on the results of the Learning and Training at Work 2000 (LTW 2000) survey, conducted from July to October 2000, does not provide data on employers' expenditure on training, nor on training undertaken at the employees' own initiative. In contrast, adult continuing education has long been constituted as a field of enquiry, and has its origins in the foundation of the Workers' Educational Association at the beginning of the 20th century. Research on adults has therefore focused on their continuing education, rather than their work-related continuing training.

Equally, employees have no statutory entitlement to paid release from work for training. Again, there are no administrative returns that would allow an analysis of the extent to which individuals take up this entitlement. Nevertheless, the 1998 Workplace Employee Relations Survey (WERS) asks questions about the days of training taken by employees, which is broken down by occupation and gives some indication of the distribution of paid release from work (Cully *et al*, 1999). The LTW 2000 survey has data on the average number of days of training per employee, but does not break this down by occupational category. Since 1999 young people aged 16 to 17 have had an entitlement to paid release for education and training, but no central information is held on the numbers of young people who have used their entitlement, nor the estimated costs to the state and to private employers.[4] Therefore in Britain we have limited information about the patterns of training leave and no information about the extent to which these patterns represent training undertaken at the employees' own initiative.

Finally, in the UK the system of collective bargaining is highly decentralized, with many negotiations taking place at company level. Qualifications are not formally codified in pay structures, though they play an important role in recruitment practices and in the operation of internal labour markets. There is no concept of job mobility (cf the French 'promotion sociale') through the employment relationship. The attainment of a qualification does not automatically lead to a change in salary grade (though it might do under the terms of some collective agreements).

Nevertheless, as far as policy discourse is concerned, the role of individual demand for continuing training is central. Rather than continuing vocational training (CVT), it is the concept of lifelong learning that has generated considerable policy debate in recent years, although this can be viewed as both broader than CVT and a part of it (Brown and Keep, 1999: 71). This has occurred in a context of concern about economic competitiveness and skills development and the need for individuals to take responsibility for their own 'employability'. Although the Labour government broadly supports the voluntarist approach of the preceding Conservative governments (1979–97), there have been a number of significant developments in policy since Labour came to power in 1997. A range of initiatives has been taken on lifelong learning, widening participation in education and in addressing adult basic skills. A National Skills Task Force was set up and has produced a series of reports and recommendations (see NSTF, 2000). A major overhaul of the system of funding post-compulsory education and training (including school sixth forms but not higher education) is taking place in England and Wales from April 2001. The new Learning and Skills Councils will bring together the funding systems for further education (formerly administered by the Further Education Funding Council) and vocational training (formerly administered by the Training and Enterprise Councils).

The rest of this chapter is divided into four sections. The first seeks to interpret the concept of individual demand for CVT in the UK. It reviews, in the UK context, the equivalents to French concepts such as 'promotion sociale' (job mobility), 'gestion de carrière' (functional enlargement of tasks through training), 'reconversion volontaire' and 'reconversion forcée' (voluntary and compulsory preventative training programmes). It will make links to the policy debate on education and training for employability.

The second section reviews recent policy developments in vocational education and training (VET) and their impact on individual demand. This focuses in particular on the reform of the funding structures of VET, initiatives such as Individual Learning Accounts (ILAs) and the University for Industry (UfI) and their potential impact in the workplace. It also examines the growing role for trade unions in providing collective frameworks for participation in CVT and lifelong learning. Emerging from this have been demands for a statutory right to paid educational leave and for rights to consultation on the employers' training plan. The devolution of political powers to national assemblies in Scotland, Wales and Northern Ireland is reinforcing the development of distinctive national VET systems, with new dynamics.[5]

The third section reviews four studies of adult learners in relation to work. The conclusion examines the extent to which these findings can contribute to our understanding of individual workers' ability to engage in CVT.

The concept of individual demand for CVT

It is worth identifying some characteristics of the national policy context that make the concept of individual motivation and demand for training of great significance for understanding policy developments. Brown and Keep (1999), in their review of VET research in the UK, indicate a number of factors that have contributed to the DfEE's interest in funding research on individual motivation to undertake training. These include:

- The economic imperative of VET policy.
- The assumption that individuals must prepare themselves for an end to 'jobs for life'.
- The idea that participation in paid work is the major means of tackling social deprivation.
- That there is a limited role for legislation in underpinning employers' training activity.
- There is a limited role for the involvement of the social partners in training policy (although there have been some developments here).
- An emphasis on the individual taking responsibility for paying for their own skills development.
- A reliance on market mechanisms in training provision. (Brown and Keep, 1999: 13–15)

One consequence of this is that the DfEE has funded a number of reports on individuals' motivation to learn, their decision making processes and commitment, for example the reports by Crowder and Pupynin (1993); Firth and Goffey (1996); Hand *et al* (1994); Maguire *et al* (1993, 1996) and Tremlett *et al* (1995a, 1995b).

As far as CVT is concerned, Conservative and Labour governments alike have stressed that this is the responsibility of the employer, on the one hand, and the individual employee, on the other. The White Paper 'Employment for the 1990s' argued that 'developing training through life is not primarily a government responsibility' (Employment Department, 1988: 49). The White Paper 'People, Jobs and Opportunities' argued that 'individuals must be persuaded that training pays and that they should take more responsibility for their own development' (Employment Department, 1992: 24). This focus on individuals' responsibility for investing in their own education and training can be found in papers and reports produced by a wide range of interest organizations such as the Confederation of British Industry, the Association of Graduate Recruiters and the Royal Society of Arts 'Campaign for Learning'. Coffield has criticized this individual emphasis for failing to recognize that learning is a social and contextual activity. He argues that to focus on the rational choices of individuals detracts attention from national policy on education and training (Coffield, 1997: 83–5). Indeed, rather than focusing on employees' motivation, many writers have identified the failure of companies to invest in the training and development of their employees because of the need to provide short-term returns on investment and product market strategies based on price competition (eg Keep and Mayhew, 1999).

The Conservatives introduced a number of measures to encourage individuals to engage in their own training and development. For example, Career Development Loans were introduced, alongside tax allowances for self-funded training. Nevertheless, little was done to enshrine individual rights to training and to training leave. The Conservative government's response to the European Union's FORCE programme was to reject the individual's right of access to training on the basis of its opposition to 'all Community measures which could add to employment costs, impose unnecessary and bureaucratic regulation and therefore undermine jobs and living standards' (House of Lords, 1990: 13).

In contrast, from 1997 the Labour government has recognized its responsibility for lifelong learning, alongside that of employers and individuals. This is evident in the appointment of a Minister for Lifelong Learning, although high levels of turnover – three ministers have occupied this position in four years[6] – suggest that this may not be a very prestigious position within the government. A National Advisory Group for Continuing Education and Lifelong Learning (NAGCELL) (Fryer, 1997) was set up, which led to the publication of the Green Paper, 'The Learning Age' (DfEE, 1998). This identified three principal stakeholders in lifelong learning – the government, employers, employees and their representative trade unions – who might be expected to make different financial contributions to work-based learning. The government's role is perceived as 'lifting barriers to access and improving the quality of support available to businesses and individuals' (DfEE, 1998: 33). But what does this involve in the absence of an entitlement to paid educational leave and the formal representation of employees' interests in training institutions and in relation to their employers' training plans? Since workers have no rights to training and development enshrined in law, individual involvement in CVT takes the form of the employees' own responsibility for continually updating their own training and development.

It is also worth emphasizing that the replacement of the discourse of 'training' by 'lifelong learning' has been perceived as a challenge to established providers of education and training, marking a shift in focus 'from institutional structures to people's participation and learning. Conventional front end notions of education and training have been discursively displaced – even if actual practices have a long way to go to catch up' (Edwards et al, 1998: 8). The same authors argue that despite this challenge to established stakeholders, the voices of learners themselves are missing from the current discourse. They point to the emphasis on individual self-reliance to cope with change and the potential that individuals who do not participate in the 'learning society' could be pathologized as 'excluding themselves' (1998: 9). Keep (1997) argues that while there are good reasons for policy makers to place greater emphasis on individuals' responsibility for learning, there are structural and societal barriers confronting many adult learners.

It is therefore very difficult to identify equivalents in the British context to a number of terms that are found in French debates about CVT undertaken at the initiative of the individual. There is no equivalent concept to 'promotion sociale' (literally 'social promotion', but best translated as 'job mobility'), which is accessed through the employment relationship, although some recent initiatives taken by trade unions may contribute to the creation of progression routes in work – see below. This reflects the nature of job mobility within internal labour markets in the UK, which is restricted to the higher segments. McKnight's analysis of earnings inequality over a 20-year period (1977–97) demonstrates that the factors which have driven increasing pay dispersion have also restricted the ability of the low paid and low skilled workers to obtain better jobs. She argues that growth in the employment structure has been at the lower and upper ends of the employment hierarchy, limiting the extent to which individuals can move from lower to middle-ranking occupations. Since employees in the lowest occupational segments have least access to employer-provided training, she argues that access to lifelong learning has a key role in reducing lifetime earnings inequality (McKnight, 2000: 33).

The concept of 'gestion de carrière' would best be defined as the enlargement of functional activities (cf CNAM Info, 49, 1999). As a career development strategy, in the UK this may be achieved through informal job enrichment strategies, through secondments within one's own workplace or by undertaking courses. It is not a category for classifying CVT. There is a concept of 'career development' but this is normally applied only to managers and professionals. Development reviewing is a management tool that has been introduced in many organizations so that the training and development needs of employees are considered on a systematic basis. Even so, this is often restricted to the higher professional groups, and workers in routine and manual occupations may be excluded.

In the UK there is a concept of retraining but not really 'reconversion' training in the French sense. This is because companies rarely engage in preventative training programmes when workers are under threat of redundancy. Although we do not have a distinction between programmes that are voluntary and those that are obligatory, in practice they are becoming obligatory. This marks developments in the allocation of welfare benefits, which are becoming increasingly conditional on the acceptance of low paid work or training as part of the development of a 'workfare' regime (Peck, 1996). The courses provided usually combine experience on an employer's premises with formal training in a college or another training provider.

In the UK, the question of individual demand for CVT does not have a rationale that is clearly related to a series of institutional structures and legal entitlements. Therefore data on the funding and up-take of entitlements, and progression in work following the attainment of a qualification, are not readily available.

Policy developments under the Labour government (1997 to the present) and individual demand for CVT

In the previous section the evolving policy discourse concerning individual responsibility for lifelong learning was analysed. In this section the focus is on a number of measures introduced by the Labour government to promote training and development, on the one hand, and lifelong learning, on the other. As argued above, there are continuities with the Conservatives in the support for a voluntarist approach, rather than direct state intervention. Nevertheless, there appears to be a shift towards state as opposed to employer provision of training, and a rhetoric of inclusiveness and social partnership along with some funding to support community and trade union initiatives.

The reform of the funding system of post-compulsory education and training is the backdrop to the government's policies on skills development and merits a brief discussion here. In April 2001 the TECs in England and Wales were abolished, as well as the Further Education Funding Council. These have been replaced in England by a new national Learning and Skills Council (LSC) and a network of 47 local Learning and Skills Councils. In 1997–8 taxpayers' money funded 3.5 million students to study at colleges of further education, and work-based training funded 500,000 individuals (Felstead and Unwin, 2001: 91–2). The objective of creating a single system was to provide a coherent framework for funding, to avoid duplication and to provide a basis for planning education and training provision. The reform also aimed to overcome some of the shortcomings of the two funding systems, which had had different rationales and had created perverse incentives to training providers which met neither learners' nor local labour market needs (see Felstead and Unwin, 2001, for details). The Kennedy Report (1997) argues that funds were maintained for adult continuing education *despite* rather than because of these funding regimes. The new local LSCs will be responsible for workforce development in their localities and the LSC will also have this role, with responsibilities divided between a youth and an adult learning committee. The LSC has a statutory responsibility to promote adult learning. At the same time, sectoral level training organizations, the National Training Organisations, will have responsibility for developing sectoral workforce development plans although they control no resources.

The concept of individual responsibility for lifelong learning is strong in official policy documents such as the Labour government's Green Paper, 'The Learning Age', although emphasis is also given to the role of employers, trade unions and government (DfEE, 1998). The approach adopted by the Labour government has been facilitative rather than legislative: it gives encouragement through a number of financial and delivery mechanisms to lifelong learning rather than through statutory entitlements and formal institutional structures. It has also identified widening participation in further and higher education as an objective (Kennedy, 1997) and the need to address adult basic skills problems (Moser, 1998).

Two main developments are aimed specifically at supporting lifelong learning undertaken on the initiative of the individual. These are Individual Learning Accounts (ILAs) and the University for Industry (UfI). The ILA (suspended in late 2001) is worth £150 and the individual must contribute £25 of his or her own money in order to receive one. In addition, holders can attract discounts on the cost of course provision. By the end of 2000, it was estimated that 400,000 accounts had been opened (Wicks, 2001: 18).

Although attempts have been made to prioritize target groups (for example, people with low skills or qualifications, women returners to the labour market) there is concern that they may simply be used to subsidize existing learners and forms of provision (Caldwell, 2000). The Ufl is a system of online course provision. Alongside this, the government has set up 700 opening learning centres, called LearnDirect centres, in the most deprived communities so that people without access to IT facilities can use them. The training packages cover basic skills through to technology and business management skills. The objective is to create a flexible system of learning delivery in workplaces and communities that is accessible in principle to all. The concept of entitlement here concerns access to funding, rather than to paid leave from work.

A number of commentators have noted that these measures do little to address the structural difficulties that many workers face and that institutional structures are needed if these difficulties are to be overcome (Coffield, 1997, 2001; Keep, 1997; Rainbird, 2000). These patterns are well documented. As far as learning outside work is concerned, a survey for the National Institute of Adult and Continuing Education (NIACE) in 1996 indicated that 60 per cent of adults had not engaged in any formal or informal learning activity in the previous three years. The highest participation rates were among the younger adult cohorts and the higher socio-economic groups, and lowest among older adults and those who were unemployed or in the skilled manual or unskilled occupational categories (McGivney, 1997: 129–30). The distribution of resources for learning at work is also skewed towards those who have already benefited from an extended period of formal education. The 1998 Workplace Employee Relations Survey shows that employees' access to training is partly dependent on where they work. Training opportunities are positively associated with working in a large workplace; one which recognizes trade unions; one which is in the public rather than the private sector; and one which has achieved the Investors in People award. Nevertheless, the greatest differences in access to training provision are across occupational groups. Less than half of craft workers, operative and assembly workers and those in routine, unskilled jobs had received any training in the previous year. Part-time workers received less training than their counterparts in full-time jobs in all occupations. There was 'a clear bias' in favour of younger workers as against older workers (Cully *et al,* 1999: 149).

One way in which these structural problems can be overcome is through trade union involvement in creating collective frameworks that can support their members' access to lifelong learning in the workplace. The capacity of the collective to empower the individual is especially important for non-traditional learners who would not otherwise take the initiative themselves.

A number of trade unions have taken initiatives to set up collective ILAs (TUC, 2000). They are also involved in UfI hubs; for example, the TUC is involved in some regional hubs and the public sector union Unison has a sectoral one for online training provision in health and social care.

Some of these developments have been supported by the DfEE's Union Learning Fund, which was set up in 1998 to stimulate trade union innovation on training (for an evaluation, see Cutter, 2000). Initiatives taken on lifelong learning have been seen by many trade unions as a tool for organizational renewal and development. Trade unions have been developing new roles within their organizational structures, for example learning representatives, advocates for learning, and training shop stewards in advice and guidance. Largely as a result of this activity, David Blunkett, the then Secretary of State for Education and Employment, announced the government's intention to give trade union learning representatives a legal right to have paid release from work on the grounds that they will be 'foot soldiers' for raising skills and 'workplace experts on skills issues' (*The Guardian,* 28 August 2000). The DfEE's consultative paper on statutory learning representatives was issued in May 2001.

The TUC/TEC Bargaining for Skills projects have been developing a model for working with employers in supporting training for company need and training for employee need (the latter through the creation of workplace learning centres with IT resources for training). Unison has been developing partnerships with employers in the public sector to provide opportunities for low paid workers to have a second chance at education (through the 'Return to Learn' programme). Using this as a building block, Unison is developing work-based routes into professional qualifications in nursing, social work and teaching (see Rainbird *et al,* forthcoming, for a discussion). As the largest trade union dealing with the major public sector employers, Unison has been in a unique position to negotiate significant agreements on learning opportunities for low paid members. For example, in 2000 an agreement was reached with the NHS in England to create an entitlement for all workers in non-professional grades to have access to training and development involving five days paid educational leave (Unison, forthcoming).

Trade unions are now perceived as having a role to play in workplace learning, in particular in creating and supporting learning opportunities for groups of workers whose needs are often ignored by employers. As yet, this has not taken the form of a formal institutionalized role, enshrined in law, but rather a facilitative approach. In other words, funding has been made available since 1998 for trade union innovation through the DfEE's Union Learning Fund but, as yet, there are no institutional mechanisms for sustaining it. Nevertheless, the recognition of the role of the trade union learning representative may mark the beginning of the formalization of this role. The local LSCs' responsibilities for workforce development planning mean that they require information on organizations' training plans and needs. In addition, the union movement's current campaign for a right to paid educational leave is contributing pressure for a more formalized series of workers' entitlements.

Research evidence on continuing education and training: issues to be addressed

It will be clear from the preceding discussion that it is extremely difficult to use the distinction of vocational training provided on the employer's initiative and on the individual's initiative in the British context. Although individual responsibility for training and development is a leitmotif in the discourse of policy makers, we have no obvious sources of data that indicate the extent to which individuals undertake CVT on their own initiative and whether it leads to occupational progression. Nevertheless, there is clear evidence both in official policy documents and in specific initiatives of the idea that individuals *should* be taking responsibility for their own CVT. This is evident, above all, in ILAs and the UfI, which assume that individuals are able to take advantage of the financial and learning resources that the government makes available.

This raises other questions about what is meant by the concept of individual initiative in the British context. It could have a variety of meanings: for example, training paid for by the individuals concerned; training undertaken at the individuals' initiative but paid for by the employer; or training undertaken by individuals in their own time (paid for by themselves or by their employer).

As far as individuals paying for their own training, we have limited information on this. Payne (1991) points out that in the early 1990s levels of self-funding were extremely low and carried a high degree of personal risk. Furthermore, she argued:

> there are indications that self-funding is to some extent the resort of people who can not get training in any other way. . . It is possible that by shifting a greater proportion of training costs to private individuals, inequalities in access to training will be widened. (1991: 22)

It has not been possible to locate a more recent study of the self-funding of CVT, so the following discussion focuses on what we know about adult participation in education, progression and the other aspects of individual initiative.

Bynner's research on adult participation and progression in education: the significance of modularization and credit recognition

The National Child Development Study (NCDS) follows a sample of 16,000 people born in single weeks in 1958 and 1970 from birth to adulthood. Follow-up surveys were conducted at the ages of 7, 11, 16, 23 and 33, with data available on 11,400 adults participating at age 33. It contains data on their employment, education, family, health and citizenship, including a complete record of their work histories since leaving school. Family background, parental aspirations and attainment in school are key determinants of future participation. In relation to work-related training, Bynner (2001: 59) summarizes the main findings in the following terms:

> Our evidence points to early adult employment as enhancing participation and progression (through the work-based training encountered); though earlier on in the period after leaving school, full-time employment inhibits them. Notably, apprenticeship was largely phased out at the end of the eighties in favour of youth training, because of its identification with timeserving. Yet this form of work-based training appeared to be one of the main progression routes for early school-leavers in the NCDS cohort. . . On the other hand, being unemployed or being at home looking after a family appeared to work against participation and progression across the whole period studied.

A small minority of the sample had returned to education despite leaving school at the earliest opportunity. One of the reasons for the low numbers is the enormous time commitment needed for unqualified adults to engage in long courses. He argues:

> Even with supportive employers men and women find it difficult to give up work to do them; and even when unemployed, appear often to have little incentive to commit themselves to long-term study, especially if they are hoping an appealing job is around the corner. For women with small children, the long and often inconvenient hours involved and absence of adequate childcare facilities, can rule out participation, or make it very difficult, encouraging dropout. (Bynner, 2001: 51)

He points out that even the Open University's system of open education, which operates a modular scheme, which should facilitate participation, still requires a huge commitment of time and effort to obtain credits – equivalent to six or 12 months' full-time study. In contrast, the use of credits in further education and adult education, under the Open College system, allows education provision and the recognition of attainment to be more closely matched to potential students' needs. He argues that although there are 'deeply rooted cultural expectations and long-standing inequalities in Britain', the most effective approaches to increasing participation must start from the learner and the ways in which learning can be made attractive (Bynner, 2001: 60).

McIntosh and Steedman's research on learning in the workplace: the significance of job improvement and career progression

This comparative European study focused on workers with the lowest level of initial education and training as measured by the highest qualification achieved, or the lowest literacy levels, measured by the International Adult Literacy Survey. McIntosh and Steedman's analysis shows that those with the lowest literacy scores are more likely to refuse to participate in employer-provided training than those with higher scores. In the UK employers were more likely to provide training for workers who had higher literacy levels, and workers with lower levels were concentrated in the least skilled jobs where literacy requirements were low. In this context, daily work tasks did not require workers to develop higher levels of literacy skills; confidence in literacy skills was low; and job mobility was perceived to be restricted by inadequate literacy. These workers perceived further training and education as involving psychological costs – a high risk of failure and difficulties associated with their lack of ease in formal learning situations. They conclude that stronger incentives are needed, 'particularly job improvement and promotion on completion, but also attractive training methods (primarily not "school-type" learning) as well as training grants for those whose employers will not fund learning' (McIntosh and Steedman, 2001: 99).

Dowswell, Hewison and Millar's research on access and equity

This research focused on the effects on the home and family life of 89 nurses, midwives and other NHS staff of undertaking continuing education courses. The courses involved a range of provision, including a Masters level course for radiographers, an open learning upgrading course for enrolled nurses, part-time degree courses in midwifery and health studies, and a full-time specialist diploma in nursing.

NHS employees are under increasing pressure to improve their qualifications. Whereas in the past they used to take these courses on a day-release basis, now they are often expected to take them in their own time to save on the costs of replacement staffing. The research found that the courses made heavy demands on these workers' free time: 48 per cent of those interviewed thought their participation in continuing professional development put a strain on their home and family lives and 10 per cent thought it was causing a serious detrimental effect. Workers with children found it harder to manage their time with their families and partners than those without, and there were financial costs in the form of loss of overtime payments.

Dowswell *et al* (1999) conclude that for those in employment, having time to engage in continuing professional development is extremely important. Although open learning methods are sometimes presented as an effective way of combining work and learning, they believe that the popularity of this mode of delivery may reflect the limited options available to many workers rather than a positive choice. This is especially significant in the 'long hours' culture in the UK. Moreover, managers were exerting pressure on workers to get additional qualifications, and suitability for promotion may be assessed in terms of their willingness to undertake training.[7]

Rainbird, Munro, Holly and Leisten's research on workplace learning amongst low paid workers in the public sector

This research was based on case studies of three local authorities and three NHS trusts, involving 330 face-to-face interviews with workers on the four lowest job grades and their managers, trainers and supervisors. In two of the case study organizations, a postal survey was also conducted, which produced 323 responses.[8]

In the survey, the single most important goal of learning reported by respondents was to improve their general education (49.7 per cent), followed by computer and IT awareness (10.8 per cent). Among the remainder there was a range of learning objectives, including increasing self-esteem and speaking foreign languages. Others were more ambitious: two respondents wanted to achieve A-levels, seven sought degrees and one a postgraduate qualification. However, this must be set against the 18 per cent of respondents who did not reply to the question and the 7 per cent who reported no desired learning achievements. Few of the over-60s responded to this question and an interest in IT was greatest among the over-40s age group who would not have encountered it in their own school-based education.

In the survey a question was asked about barriers to learning, including those of time, money and lack of encouragement. Sixty per cent of the sample responded to the questions. Of these, just over 30 per cent reported no barriers to learning, but 17 per cent reported one, another 17 per cent reported two and 34 per cent reported all three barriers to learning. A number commented on these multiple barriers in their responses to open-ended questions. Some of these concerned release from work for training, and the difficulties of combining work, learning and family responsibilities; others concerned insufficient support and information from management, or a lack of self-confidence. For example:

> I want to take a BTEC qualification or an NVQ but can't get time off. The only way would be to give up work which as a single parent supporting three children is impossible.

> I don't seem to have enough time for work and study. There isn't enough encouragement to train from management.

> When I wanted to return to work (after children) I found I would have to give up my small job and income to train for nothing. I didn't have the opportunity to learn and earn. I feel I'm too old to go into a career.

> We are told nothing about courses so have no chance to enhance our learning.

> Training given at work is always on the 'cheap' and done only to benefit the employer.

> Because I left school without qualifications, it is assumed that you have no training and no wish to learn anything.

> The trust doesn't always recognize the achievements of staff who have taken courses.

> They therefore lose very good staff who look for better rewards financially and job satisfaction.

> As a catering assistant there isn't a great deal of time or money for me to take courses for my benefit. I feel alone with the problem and a bit discouraged. Management needs to inform all staff of training opportunities not just those on main sites. (Rainbird *et al*, 1999: 25)

Through the interviews it was apparent that many younger workers are overqualified for the jobs that they do. It is these groups of workers who are self-confident as learners and there was evidence that some of them were paying for training on their own initiative outside work. Their objective was not to progress in their current employment: indeed many were well aware of the limited job progression opportunities in a public sector that is contracting rather than expanding. However, paying for training and even leaving work for a full-time course are risks that can only be taken by younger workers who have no family responsibilities. Once they have family responsibilities they become dependent on training provided by the employer and it is here that access to paid educational leave becomes central to their ability to participate and progress. Managers' willingness to facilitate this is extremely significant, but it is also constrained by insufficient staffing levels and the ability to provide cover for staff absence.

The research also highlighted the fact that although the majority of workers in these jobs have annual development reviews with their managers, the courses identified are usually restricted to 'the needs of the job'. This means that if jobs are narrowly defined in the first place and there are no opportunities for promotion, training and development will be restricted too. Therefore job design as well as absence of job progression routes can constrain access to employer-provided training.

Finally, this research demonstrated that some learning opportunities were initiated by managers, others jointly through the development review process, or through a partnership between the union (Unison) and the employer. But there was considerable evidence that employees themselves had taken the initiative, in relation to employer-provided training, in relation to courses taken outside work in their own time, and by seeking informal learning opportunities through expanding the range of tasks they performed (Rainbird *et al*, 1999: 71).

Conclusion

It is difficult to apply the distinction made in France between CVT provided on the initiative of the employer and on the initiative of the employee. The statistics available do not provide an indication of the extent to which individuals invest in their own training and development. Individual institutions such as further education colleges and universities may collect these data but they are not published in official statistical sources. The reason for this probably lies in the fact that the question has not been posed in the UK in terms of a right of the worker not the citizen ('un droit du travailleur et non du citoyen', cf Correia *et al,* 2001). Rather, the issue has been perceived in relation to the tradition of adult continuing education, which has recently been re-branded as 'lifelong learning' and remoulded to have economic as well as social objectives.

Despite this, there is considerable interest among policy makers in the concept of individuals taking responsibility for their own lifelong learning and professional development. The subtext of this discourse is that they should take responsibility for paying for it and for undertaking it in their own time. This sits uneasily with the Labour government's concerns with improving employers' investment in training, widening participation and improving adult basic skills. The voluntary and facilitative measures taken to date seem unlikely to challenge the scale of structural problems that need to be addressed. Despite this, the discourse of lifelong learning has found resonances in the trade union movement, where it has been perceived as a means of working with employers to provide training and development as a service to members as well as a tool for building trade union organization.

How does all this link to the questions of student wastage on courses of CVT undertaken at the worker's own initiative, which was the initial starting point for this analysis? From a UK perspective, it seems that some of the questions relating to individual initiative and progression are similar, despite our different starting points. Bynner's work focuses on adults and the fact that time is an important dimension to their ability to study. He points to the need for flexible delivery and the need for systems of credit recognition and accumulation. In contrast, the work of Dowswell, Hewison and Millar demonstrates that it is not just having courses available in smaller modules and in online form that is the central issue. They emphasize the high levels of stress that workers, particularly those with families, experience when they are required to undertake continuing professional development in their own time. Paid release from work is a prerequisite for engaging in CVT, whether it is on the employers' or on the individuals' initiative.

McIntosh and Steedman's work suggests that financial rewards and job progression are significant as an incentive to workers, particularly those with low levels of literacy or whose jobs make little demands on their literacy skills. Their work points to the need to overcome the psychological costs of engaging in learning and, in particular, dealing with the potential for failure.

The research by Rainbird *et al* suggests that there is a range of structural factors that contribute to workers' inability to engage in CVT. Some of these relate to job design and job progression opportunities; some to the absence of management encouragement; some to a lack of confidence in learning; others to family circumstances. Even though there is evidence of workers taking the initiative in pursuing learning opportunities at work, the possibilities of paying for it and taking the risk of leaving full-time work are restricted to younger workers who are already self-confident about their learning skills. For the majority of workers, paid release from work is central. These findings support Payne's view that self-funding carries considerable risk and is an option for the few. A system based on technocratic solutions, token funding and individuals taking responsibility for their own learning will benefit some, mainly already successful learners. But for an inclusive strategy, entitlements and supportive institutional structures are needed to underpin individual initiative on CVT and lifelong learning.

Notes

1. An earlier version of this chapter was written for a workshop 'La formation des adults suivie aux leur propre initiative' organized by the Conseil National des

Arts et Métiers, held in Paris, 2 April 2001. This has been published in *Les Cahiers de LASMAS*, 'Formation tout au long de la vie: logiques institutionelles et usages individuels de la formation' (2001). I am grateful to the editors for permission to reproduce the material here.

The workshop was concerned with continuing training undertaken by adult workers on their own initiative. The concept of individual initiative in France refers to the category of training that exists under the provisions of the law of 1971 on CVT, which requires companies to allocate a proportion of their payroll to CVT. It makes a distinction between the organization's training plan and training undertaken on the individual workers' initiative. In France there is a right to paid educational leave ('congé individuel de formation'), which is a right linked to employment rather than to citizenship. The Conseil National is concerned at the large numbers of CVT students who are failing to complete their studies and sought a comparison with practices in other European countries to understand the concept of individual demand for CVT.

2. The sources used are the following: education expenditure; further education statistics; higher education statistics; labour force survey; public examinations; school leavers' destinations; schools statistics; TEC-delivered government supported training; vocational qualifications.

3. A parliamentary question was put to the Secretary of State for the Environment, Transport and Regions in 2000 on the funding and allocation of resources to the training of local government staff, broken down by occupational grade, type of employment and gender for the previous five years (reference 109604). The response was: 'The Department does not hold information of this type.' At the same time, a similar question was put to the Secretary of State for Health (reference 109605). The response was: 'Information is not held centrally on the total amount spent on the training of National Health Service staff by gender or occupational grade.'

    In the NHS there are three service-specific education and training levies which have operated since 1996–7. The allocations and expenditure for each of these are known, but information on the amount spent on the training of other staff groups outside the scope of the levies on continuing professional training by NHS trusts and health authorities is not held centrally.

4. The DfEE's own evaluation suggested that the right had stimulated activity to promote training to young people and had had a positive effect on recruitment to modern apprenticeships, but the Department was unable to quantify its effect. (Reply to a parliamentary question to the Secretary of State for Education and Employment in 2001, reference 149611.)

5. This was the subject of the Working to Learn workshop on 'Home international comparisons of work-based programmes' held at the University of Edinburgh, 3 November 2000.

6. Kim Howells, George Mudie and Malcolm Wicks.

7. The Open University is concerned at a decline in the completion of degree courses, which it is believed is due to employers' increasing unwillingness to allow employees time for paid educational leave. (Personal communication, A Tait.)

8. 2010 questionnaires were sent out, so this represents a 14.6 per cent response rate. For details of the research methodology and preliminary findings, see Rainbird *et al,* 1999.

References

Brown, A and Keep, E (1999) *Review of Vocational Education and Training Research in the United Kingdom,* Cost Action A11, European Commission, Office for Official Publications of the European Communities, Luxembourg

Bynner, J (2001) Adult participation and progression in education, in *What Progress Are We Making With Lifelong Learning? The evidence from research,* ed F Coffield, Department of Education, University of Newcastle

Caldwell, P (2000) Adult learning and the workplace, in *Training in the Workplace. Critical perspectives on learning at work,* ed H Rainbird, Macmillan, Basingstoke

CIPD (2000) *Workplace Learning. Discussion document.* Chartered Institute of Personnel and Development, London

Coffield, F (1997) Introduction and overview: attempts to reclaim the concept of the learning society, *Journal of Education Policy,* **12** (6), pp 449—55

Coffield, F (2001) Realising the potential of lifelong learning, in *What Progress are We Making on Lifelong Learning? The evidence from research,* ed F Coffield, Department of Education, University of Newcastle, Newcastle upon Tyne

Correia, M, Berton, F and Pottier, F (2001) 'Formation tout au long de la vie. Logiques institutionelles et usages individuelles de la formation.' Note de presentation de la journée CNAM – LASMAS, 2 April

Crowder, M and Pupynin, K (1993) *The Motivation to Train,* Employment Department Research Series 9, HMSO, Norwich

Cully, M, Woodland, S, O'Reilly, A and Dix, G (1999). *Britain at Work as Depicted by the 1998 Employee Relations Survey,* Routledge, London

Cutter, J (2000) *A Second Evaluation of the Union Learning Fund,* DfEE Research Report RR208, DfEE, Nottingham

DfEE (1996) *Training Statistics, 1996,* HMSO, Norwich

DfEE (1998) *The Learning Age. A renaissance for a new Britain,* HMSO, Norwich

DfEE (2000a) *Statistics of Education. Education and training statistics for the UK,* HMSO, Norwich

DfEE (2000b) *National Statistics. First release,* Department for Education and Employment, London, http://www.dfee.gov.uk/statistics/DB/SFR/

Dowswell, T, Hewison, J and Millar, B (1999) The costs of learning: the policy implications of changes in continuing education for NHS staff, in *Speaking Truth to Power: Research and policy on lifelong learning,* ed F Coffield, Policy Press, Bristol

Education Department (1991) *People, Jobs and Opportunities,* HMSO, Norwich

Edwards, R, Raggatt, P, Harrison, R, McCulloch, A and Calder, J (1998) *Recent Thinking on Lifelong Learning – A review of the literature,* DfEE, Sudbury

Employment Department (1988) *Employment for the 1990s,* HMSO, Norwich

Employment Department (1992) *People, Jobs and Opportunities,* Cm 1810, HMSO, Norwich

Felstead, A and Unwin, L (2001) Funding post compulsory education and training: a retrospective analysis of the TEC and FEFC systems and their impact on skills, *Journal of Education and Work*, **14** (1), pp 91–111

Firth, D and Goffey, L (1996) *Individual Commitment: Tracking learners' decision making*, DfEE Research Studies, 6, Stationery Office, Norwich

Fryer, R H (1997) *Learning for the Twenty-first Century*, First report of the National Advisory Group for Continuing Education and Lifelong Learning, Northern College, Barnsley

Hand, A, Gambles, J and Cooper, E (1994) *Individual Commitment to Learning: Individuals' decision making about lifetime learning*, Employment Department Research Series, 42, HMSO, Norwich

House of Lords Select Committee on the European Communities (1990) *Vocational Training and Re-training*, HMSO, Norwich

Keep, E (1997) 'There's no such thing as society'. . . some problems with an individual approach to creating a learning society, *Journal of Educational Policy*, **12** (6), pp 457–71

Keep, E and Mayhew, K (1999) The assessment: knowledge, skills and competitiveness, *Oxford Review of Economic Policy*, **15** (1), pp 1–15

Kennedy, H (1997) *Learning Works: How to widen participation*, Further Education Funding Council, Coventry

McGivney, V (1997) Adult participation in learning: can we change the pattern?, in *A National Strategy for Lifelong Learning*, ed F Coffield, Department of Education, University of Newcastle

McIntosh, S and Steedman, H (2001) Learning in the workplace: some international comparisons, in *What Progress Are We Making With Lifelong Learning? The evidence from research*, ed F Coffield, Department of Education, University of Newcastle

McKnight, A (2000) *Trends in Earnings Inequality and Earnings Mobility, 1977–1997: The impact of mobility on long-term inequality*, Employment Relations Research Series, 8, Department of Trade and Industry, London

Maguire, M, Hasluck, C and Green, A (1996) *Identifying Target Groups for Individual Commitment Policies*, Department of Employment Research Series, 20, HMSO, Norwich

Maguire, M, Maguire, S and Felstead, A (1993) *Factors Influencing Individual Commitment to Lifetime Learning*, Department of Employment Research Series, 20, HMSO, Norwich

Moser, C (1998) *Improving Literacy and Numeracy. A fresh start. The report of the working group chaired by Sir Claus Moser*, DfEE, Sudbury

NSTF (2000) *Skills for All: Proposals for a national skills agenda. Final report of the National Skills Task Force*, DfEE, Sudbury

Payne, J (1991) *Women, Taining and the Skills Shortage. The case for public investment*, Policy Studies Institute, London

Peck, J (1996) *Workplace. The social regulation of labour markets*, Guildford Press, New York

Rainbird, H (2000) Skilling the unskilled: access to workplace learning and the lifelong learning agenda, *Journal of Education and Work*, **13** (2), pp 183–97

Rainbird, H, Munro, A, Holly, L and Leisten, R (1999) *The Future of Work in the Public Sector: Learning and workplace inequality*, ESRC Future of Work Programme Discussion Paper No. 4, University of Leeds

Rainbird, H, Sutherland, J, Edwards, P K, Holly, L and Munro, A (forthcoming) *Employee Voice and its Influence over Training Provision*, research report commissioned by the Department of Trade and Industry

Tremlett, N, Park, A and Dundon-Smith, D (1995a) *Individual Commitment to Learning. Further findings from the individuals' survey,* Employment Department Research Series, 54, HMSO, Norwich

Tremlett, N, Thomas, A and Taylor, S (1995) *Individual Commitment to Learning – Providers' attitudes*, Employment Department Research Series, 42, HMSO, Norwich

TUC (2000) *Collective Learning Funds. A trade union guide,* Trades Union Congress, London

Unison (forthcoming) *The New Learning Agenda. Unison's approach to lifelong learning*. Unison, London

Wicks, M (2001) The learning society: the challenging agenda, in *What Progress Are We Making on Lifelong Learning? The evidence from research*, ed F Coffield, Department of Education, University of Newcastle

Chapter 13

Six challenges for the future

Working to Learn Group: Ewart Keep, Helen Rainbird, Karen Evans, Lorna Unwin, Phil Hodkinson and Peter Senker

The tendency for skills and workplace development policies to operate in isolation from, rather than being grounded within, wider debates about competitive strategies, labour market regulation, collective bargaining, people management systems, work organization and job design, produces policy that is often poorly connected with the complexity and harshness of reality. There are some excellent examples of innovative and well-supported approaches to workplace learning in both the public and private sectors but organizations are subject to many pressures.

At the end of the day, training is a derived need and (at best) a third order issue, dependent upon other strategic decisions within organizations, such as first order decisions about product market strategy, and second order decisions about people management systems and policies (Coleman and Keep, 2001). Unless and until workplace learning debates are connected with these drivers and the kinds of employer behaviour and attitudes that result, they will continue to produce worthy platitudes and schemes and initiatives that are founded upon the shifting sands of optimism. Sooner or later, and it would be preferable if it were sooner, we need to arrive at a better, more holistic approach to skills issues. As the Cabinet Office Performance and Innovation Unit in its review of workforce development issues has said: 'Workforce development needs to be addressed in the wider context of government and business strategies towards product strategy, innovation, market positioning, IT, HR policies and so on' (Cabinet Office PIU, 2001: 74).

To conclude, we identify six major challenges that researchers, practitioners and policy makers have to confront if workplace learning is to have a credible future and a part to play in the further democratic development of societies based on commitments to learning, equality and social justice.

The first challenge is to make a realistic assessment of the progress that is being made towards the achievement of a 'learning society'.[1] Researchers cannot accept at face value the discourses of managers and policy makers concerning the 'learning society', the 'learning organization', 'knowledge management' and the 'knowledge-based economy'. We need a sound understanding of the way in which work is changing, its implications for employers' demands for skills and knowledge, and their consequences for formal and informal learning at work. In the UK we are fortunate in having two major surveys: the Workplace Employee Relations Survey and the Skills Survey, which provide a sound empirical base on which to make an assessment. These surveys are further supported at regional level with data collected by the learning and skills councils. The ESRC's programme of the Future of Work is another valuable source. It should be this evidence, rather than ideological constructs, that forms the basis of our analysis. We need to understand that the institutional factors which shape employer demand for skills are fundamental to our understanding of where the problems in the UK lie (cf Keep and Mayhew, 1999).

This involves having a much better understanding of the relationship between corporate policy and practice on training and development in organizations. We need to understand the ways in which structural constraints can impact on formal and informal learning opportunities at work. In addition, some of the assumptions about different groups of workers' needs for training and development need to be questioned. For example, why is it that disproportionate resources are put into the training of managers and professionals, who are already well-qualified and confident as learners? Moreover, why is it that release from work and cover to attend courses are seen to be less of a problem for the highly paid than they are for the low paid? The answers to some of these questions lie in the relationship between management development and corporate strategy, and the autonomy and flexibility that managers can exercise over their workloads. But we must also question the extent to which training and development are also seen as a reward and a statement of status, and that access to it reinforces the hier-archical order of the workplace.

If we are to assess the contribution of workplace learning to the achieve-ment of a learning society, information on a number of key indicators is required. These might include whether organizations have a plan for training and development; the extent to which training is embedded in organizational processes; and the distribution of learning opportunities among different occupational groups within the organization. In particular, this means focusing on the distribution of resources for learning to workers on the lowest pay grades, as well as those who have traditionally received the largest share of employers' investment. Without such information, it is difficult to monitor progress towards the achievement of a learning society. Moreover, it is difficult to see how institutions that have been charged with the task of planning workforce development at local, sectoral and national level can engage in this task in a meaningful way without such information.[2]

The second challenge is to examine critically the discourse about the nature of work modernization and its effect on employers' demand for skills and more participative forms of management. Research findings (Rainbird, 2000) suggest that routine manual and clerical work is developing in a number of different ways: there is an increasing demand for skills in some areas, but in others the pattern is one of de-skilling, work intensification and the continued existence of routine work. As a result, we cannot assume that increasing demand for skill is inevitable, particularly in the jobs on the lowest grades of wage structures.[3] We must therefore assume that, for the foreseeable future, there will continue to be a range of jobs that provide few opportunities for career progression and little intrinsic opportunity for informal learning. Coffield's definition of the learning society (1997) refers to workers having 'a job (or series of jobs) worthy of a human being while continuing to participate in education and training throughout their lives'. In order to achieve this, the question of progression in work must be linked to access to broader development opportunities, rather than those that are defined by the nature of the job. If we believe that such development opportunities should underpin the type of economy and society we want to see in the future, then this suggests a more active role for the state in creating a supportive institutional framework.

The third challenge is to recognize explicitly that employers and employees have different interests in relation to training and development and both contribute to economic success, to the changing demands of employment and to an inclusive society. Employees' interests in relation to learning are not well represented in the workplace. Nevertheless, the presence of a trade union in providing a collective voice for employees on training and development can have a positive impact and result in the inclusion of groups who are normally excluded.

One often overlooked dimension in relation to this challenge is that work forms only a part of a person's life and identity, and workers' interests in and needs for learning are related to these wider dimensions of their lives. Greater attention should be paid to the ways in which their previous lives enable and constrain their dispositions to current learning and work, and to the problems of learning for the future, which may well be outside the firm where they are currently employed.

We also believe that there is a gap in existing research around workplace learning in relation to this issue. Much of the best current insights, broadly in a Vygotskyan tradition, focus on the situated and social dimensions of learning. This sort of thinking could be usefully expanded to focus more explicitly upon the interaction between the communities of practice or activity systems of the workplace, and the individual learning careers of the workers who are constituent parts of those communities or systems.

The fourth challenge is to recognize the many different forms of workplace learning. There is a range of ways in which managers and employees themselves can create learning opportunities, sometimes jointly, sometimes through the development review process, or through a partnership between a trade union and the employer. If the workplace is to realize its potential as a site of learning and as a site for accessing learning, then we need to recognize the full range of these activities and to find mechanisms for supporting and encouraging them.

Employers and policy makers also need to understand that traditional models of workplace learning need to be adapted to contemporary conditions. For example, traditional models of apprenticeship and formation or initial training more generally are based on the belief that young people enter the workplace as 'novices' who then embark on a journey towards becoming an 'expert'. Just as workplaces are changing, so too are young people. They stay for longer periods in full-time education, they have experience of new technologies from an early age, and they tend to have more confidence vis-à-vis interpersonal skills than their more mature work colleagues. As a result, young people bring skills and knowledge into the workplace that they can share with others, and they may learn to do jobs more quickly than was the case in the past. Such developments challenge the linear model of the 'novice to expert' journey and pose major implications for the way in which young people are inducted into the workplace, the purpose and design of their training programmes, and their relationships with older workers.

In the UK, the only constant in the VET 'system' as it relates to the workplace is constant reform. The field is littered with organizations that have either been changed or abolished:

- Manpower Services Commission (MSC)
- Training Agency (TA)
- Training Commission (TC)
- Local Employer Networks (LENs)
- National Council for Vocational Qualifications (NCVQ)
- The Group of 10
- Skills Training Agency (STA)

- Training and Enterprise Councils (TECs)
- National Advisory Committee on the Education and Training Targets (NACETT)
- Training Standards Council (TSC)
- National Training Organizations (NTOs)
- National Training Organization National Council

It seems worth asking whether this ceaseless reinvention of the institutional landscape is useful, or whether it might not be viewed as a form of displacement activity. Coupled with an almost equal instability in the format of government-supported schemes for workplace training (particularly at the level of initial training) this ceaseless shifting of structure renders the 'system' incomprehensible to many key user groups – young people, their parents, employers, etc.

There are also questions to be asked, at least in the English context, about the way in which strategic responsibility for workplace learning is being discharged. There are several government departments and a host of quangos and interest groups, all of which have a stake in the issues, but between whom the division of responsibility remains exceedingly unclear. The following are some of the key players:

- The Treasury
- Performance and Innovation Unit (Cabinet Office)
- No 10 Policy Unit
- Government offices
- Department of Trade and Industry
- Department for Education and Skills
- Department for Work and Pensions
- Department for Transport, Local Government and the Regions
- Small Business Service
- Connexions (careers service)
- Learning and Skills Council
- Local Learning and Skills Councils (47)
- Local Learning Partnerships
- Regional Development Agencies
- Local government, including Local Education Authorities
- Voluntary bodies
- Sector Skills Councils and Sector Skills Development Agency
- Other employer bodies (eg Confederation of British Industry)
- Higher Education Funding Council
- Professional bodies

- Investors in People UK
- Trade unions
- University for Industry
- Qualifications and Curriculum Authority
- Basic Skills Agency
- Council for Excellence in Management and Leadership
- Equal Opportunities Commission, Commission for Racial Equality, etc

This plethora of institutions, operating under competing regimes of perform-ance indicators, targets and objectives, and with their own territory to defend, renders progress problematic, the more so in the absence of an over-arching body or strategic framework for workplace development.

It is also the case that institutional change and complexity help to obscure the need to arrive at a better understanding of the necessity for tradeoffs between competing needs and interests. For example, the Learning and Skills Council, in taking charge of funding and planning government-supported initial VET (in schools, colleges and the workplace) is charged with coordin-ating and reconciling the needs of national, regional, local, sectoral and occupational labour markets. The local Learning and Skills Councils will also have to balance the sometimes conflicting needs of individual learners, employers and wider society. More open recognition that there are potential conflicts of interest might lead to better ways of tackling these problems.

The management of the learning system is also open to question in terms of its tendency to be structured around low trust, command-and-control methods of governance that disempower individual employers and learners. This approach leads to an over-concentration on outputs and targets (usually whole qualifications achieved), and too little attention to, and investment in, the learning process.

In terms of policy, the linkages between workplace learning and economic outcomes are all too often assumed to be simple, positive and unilinear despite the fact that the evidence to support this view remains extremely elusive. This is of particular importance in a nation state like the UK, which possesses extremely deregulated labour markets, and where there exist numerous routes to competitive advantage, many of which have little if anything to do with upskilling the majority of the workforce (Keep and Mayhew, 1987). The comparisons between UK diversity and German regulation have developed new dimensions since the reunification of Germany. The creation of new labour market conditions in Eastern Germany shed fresh light on the dynamics of workplace learning and economic outcomes in primary and secondary labour markets, and also underline the complexity of the relation-ships and their political ramifications (Evans *et al*, 2000). Understanding and engaging with these linkages at the level of UK policy and international comparison is our fifth challenge.

The final challenge relates to our wider society. We argue that citizenship rights should not become a quid pro quo, a social contract in which rights are tied to employment status. However, it can be argued that social rights should be re-examined in the light of increased demands for people to be 'flexible' and 'adaptable' in relation to the labour market, with the high insecurity that entails. When people become more flexible to employers' needs, this can often mean reduced scope for flexibility in other aspects of their lives. Seeing citizenship as a process has implications for rights as well as responsibilities. Expanded social rights can include, for example, the right to choose more family-friendly patterns of living and working.[4] A greater concentration on 'brokerage' for people caught in the insecurities of the labour market could also go some way to redressing the emphasis on the 'deficits' and 'skills lacks' which research results show to be so demotivating for those in difficult life situations (Behrens and Evans, 2002). Expanding the conception of social rights in this manner could go some way to stabilizing the high insecurity society and countering some of its most damaging features, while providing a strengthened base for a citizen culture.

Notes

1. Some of these points were originally made in Rainbird, 2000.
2. A similar point was made by Fairley and Paterson in their response to the Scottish Executive's 'Skills for Scotland' strategy paper (*Herald,* 14 September 1999).
3. In its response to the European Commission's green paper 'Partnership for a New Organization of Work', the Industrial Relations Research Unit points out: 'Competitive success based on quality and upskilling is only one of a number of strategies available to organizations. Others include seeking protected or monopoly markets; growth through take-over and joint venture; shifting operations overseas; cost-cutting and new forms of Fordism' (IRRU, 1997: 7).
4. These points are developed further in the essay 'Relationships between work and life' by Karen Evans in Crick (2001).

References

Behrens, M and Evans, K (2002) In control of their lives?, *Comparative Education Journal*, in press

Cabinet Office Performance and Innovation Unit (2001) Workforce development project – analysis paper, http://www.cabinet-office.gov.uk/innovation/2001/workforce/report/index.html

Coffield, F (1997) Introduction and overview: attempts to reclaim the concept of the learning society, in *Journal of Education Policy*, 12 **6**, pp 449–55

Coleman, S and Keep, E (2001) Background literature review for PIU Project on Workforce Development, University of Warwick, Coventry, SKOPE (mimeo) (or Cabinet Office PIU Web site)

Crick, B (2001) Citizens: towards a citizen culture, *Political Quarterly*, Blackwell, Oxford

Evans, K, Behrens, M, and Kaluza, J (2000) *Learning and Work in the Risk Society. Lessons for the labour markets of Europe from Eastern Germany,* Palgrave, London

IRRU (1997) Comments on the European Commission's Green Paper, 'Partnership for a New Organization of Work', mimeo, Industrial Relations Research Unit, Coventry

Keep, E and Mayhew, K (1997) Was Ratner right? Product market and competitive strategies and their links to skills and knowledge, *EPI Economic Report*, **12** (3), pp 1–14

Keep, E and Mayhew, K (1999) The assessment: knowledge, skills and competitiveness, *Oxford Review of Economic Policy*, **15** (1), pp 1–15

Rainbird, H (2000) The contribution of workplace learning to a learning society, in *The Learning Society and the Knowledge Economy*, eds W Richardson and L Unwin, NACETT sponsored lecture series, Learning and Skills Council, Coventry

Appendix: Economic and Social Research Council Teaching and Learning Research Programme

Research network: improving incentives to learning in the workplace

Prof. Helen Rainbird (University College Northampton)
Prof. Karen Evans (Institute of Education, University of London)
Prof. Phil Hodkinson (University of Leeds)
Prof. Lorna Unwin (University of Leicester)

Start date: 1 April 2000 (3 years)

Summary

The network aims to contribute to improved practice in teaching and learning in the workplace among a wide range of practitioners – including trainers, human resource professionals and trade unionists – through a better understanding of the operation of incentives to learning. It will build research capacity in the field of workplace learning and will contribute to improved outcomes to learning.

The workplace is an important site of learning and access to learning opportunities, yet its primary purpose is the production of goods and services. Therefore, in order to understand the incentives and barriers to learning at work, learning must be located in the broader context of the employment relationship, looking at developments in work organization which can support or undermine effective learning strategies.

Through five interrelated research projects, the network will work with practitioners to develop an interdisciplinary understanding of the processes and context of workplace learning.

- **Project 1** Regulatory structures and access to learning: case studies in social care and cleaning services;
- **Project 2** Recognition of tacit skills and knowledge in work re-entry;
- **Project 3** The workplace as a site for learning: opportunities and barriers in small and medium sized enterprises;
- **Project 4** An exploration of the nature of apprenticeship;
- **Project 5** The school as a site for work-based learning.

Two major themes run through the projects: 1) the role of the broader regulatory framework of the employment relationship in supporting a learning environment (including the influences of wages and conditions, contractual arrangements, the presence of the voice of the employee and the establishment of entitlements to learning); and 2) the concept of apprenticeship as a model of learning. Apprenticeship, understood as membership of a community of practice, recognizes the significance of informal learning linked to job design, work organization and workgroup dynamics, as well as the role of managers, supervisors and experienced practitioners, in creating formal and informal learning opportunities.

A better understanding of learning practice at, for and through the workplace will enable the concept of apprenticeship as a model of workplace teaching and learning to be developed.

Index